10,000

ways to say

i love
you

The Biggest Collection of Romantic
Ideas Ever Gathered in One Place

From "the voice of romantic love"
Gregory J.P. Godek

Casablanca Press
A Division of Sourcebooks, Inc.
Naperville, Illinois

• *1001 Ways To Be Romantic*® is a federally
registered trademark of Gregory J.P. Godek.
• Cover rose by Maria Thomas at Pendragon Ink,
(508) 234-6843

Published by Casablanca Press
A Division of Sourcebooks
P.O. Box 372
Naperville, Illinois   60566

ISBN: 1-57071-434-7

Information line, book orders, seminar dates, and
availability: (630) 961-3900 or fax: (630) 961-2168

Printed and bound in the United States of America

10   9   8   7   6   5   4   3   2   1

Dedication

Tracey Ellen Godek (#276)
Thomas Valentine Godek (#901)

Acknowledgments

Tracey Ellen Godek
Jean Ann Mancuso-Godek
Barbara Jane Godek
Bonnie Whitman
Mara Scribner
Craig Schreiber
Mary Marcell
Celine Dion
Wolfgang Amadeus Mozart

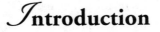

Introduction

No one in the history of the world has ever attempted to gather a list of 10,000 ways to express love. I've learned that 10,000 is a really, *really* big number. At one idea per day, this book will last you 27.4 years!

The questions I get asked most often about my books are "How?" "How long?" and "Why?"

"How? *How* do you gather 10,000 ways to say I love you? I can't even think of ten!" The most important factor is what I call having a "romantic mindset." It's a way of looking at the world and filtering information—and that filter is *love*. Another important factor is my sophisticated filing system for keeping track of the scraps of paper and napkins that I use to capture ideas as they leap from my brain—plus a high-powered portable computer.

"How long? How *long* does it take you to write your books?" This book took only three months to write. But it's taken forty-three years to research.

"Why? *Why* would you write *10,000 Ways to Say I Love You*? Do we really *need* 10,000 ways? Aren't you getting a wee bit obsessed?" Of *course* I'm obsessed. Teachers and artists are *always* obsessed by their topics. And yes, we really *do* need 10,000 ways. Every idea doesn't "fit" for every person. And as to "why": Because people (*thousands* of people) continually ask me for ideas, suggestions, and tips. This book is the ultimate practical resource for couples. It contains the basics of romance, the essence of expressing love, creative twists on classic ideas, concepts you probably never thought of, and resources gathered from one thousand sources.

More answers to the question "Why 10,000?" Because it's a *big* number. Because people are *fascinated* by numbers. And, by combining the concept of *love* with the concept of *numbers*, you start to get a feeling for how *big* love is, how big love *can be*. Actually, love is *infinite*. And as far as I'm concerned, 10,000 ways to say I love you is just the *beginning*.

~Gregory J.P. Godek

1. Honor your partner's individuality
2. Sign your letters: "Forever and a day"
3. Attend a lousy movie, sit in the balcony, and make out in the dark
4. Promise to be her Prince Charming
5. Promise to be his one-and-only
6. Osculate
7. Strive to be an A+ couple
8. Place a heart-shaped sticker on your wristwatch to remind you to call
9. Shoot your TV
10. Get a bumper sticker that reflects his view of life
11. Romantic resource: 1-800-FLOWERS
12. Become an artist of your relationship
13. Write custom word balloons on his favorite newspaper comic strip
14. Change one bad habit
15. Give her a gold bracelet made of X's and O's
16. Blindfold him and take him to a new restaurant
17. Take a gondola ride in Venice
18. Keep mistletoe hung in your home *year-round!*

19. Go "above and beyond" for your partner

---

20. On Monday: Be debonair
21. On Tuesday: Be enchanting
22. On Wednesday: Be sexy
23. On Thursday: Be funny
24. On Friday: Be playful
25. On Saturday: Be romantic
26. On Sunday: Be zany

---

27. On your lover's birthday, send his/her mother a "Thank You" card
28. For harried parents: Hire a babysitter on *retainer*
29. Hide a pair of earrings in a box of chocolates
30. Trust your intuition
31. Try this: Go one solid week without saying anything negative
32. Shower together by candlelight
33. Warm her bath towel in the dryer for her
34. Upside down stamps on envelopes mean "I love you"
35. Kiss her hand—the *proper* way (lower

your lips to her hand)

36. Celebrate the anniversary of when you first met

37. Never, never, *never* wallpaper together

38. Carry a wedding photo in your wallet

39. Program her computer's start-up screen to flash a love message from you

40. Use the little strips of paper from Hershey's Kisses as coupons redeemable for one kiss each

41. Get a sleeping bag built-for-two

42. View romance as "Adult Play"

---

43. For newlyweds only: Talk about your hopes and dreams for your future together

44. Write them down and store the document in a safe deposit box

45. Open it on your twenty-fifth anniversary

---

46. "On this earth, though far and near, without love, there's only fear." ~ Pearl S. Buck

47. Share a Whitman's Sampler

48. Write to Dear Abby. Share the inspiring story of your relationship
49. Mail a little box of candy conversation hearts

50–57
8 Songs to Help You Express Your Feelings: *Love & Tenderness*

1. "Always on My Mind," Willie Nelson
2. "The First Time Ever I Saw Your Face," Roberta Flack
3. "I Honestly Love You," Olivia Newton John
4. "In My World," The Moody Blues
5. "Through the Years," Kenny Rogers
6. "Longer Than," Dan Fogelberg
7. "Evergreen (Love Theme from *A Star Is Born*)," Barbra Streisand
8. "Still," Commodores

---

58. Get an astrological "Couples Chart" created by master astrologer Eric Linter: (617) 524-5275
59. Plan a "Mystery Date" for sometime next month

60. Cool travel resource: *Dream Sleeps: Castle & Palace Hotels of Europe*, by Pamela Barrus
61. Plan sexy surprises
62. Eat in St. Louis' most romantic restaurant: Tony's
63. Tell your mate that you—love, adore, admire, cherish, desire, want, need, prize, esteem, idolize, revere, treasure—him/her

---

64–72
9 Ways to Love a Taurus
(21 April–21 May)

1. Taurus is an *earth* sign: Cater to his/her grounded, practical nature
2. Gift tip: Quality over quantity
3. Get the finest chocolates for your Taurus
4. Elegant items make great gifts
5. Limoges boxes, quality prints
6. Roses, apple blossoms
7. Gourmet and rich foods
8. The rustic and unhurried scenery of Ireland
9. Wrap gifts in pastels for your Taurus

73. Get a vanity license plate with both of your initials on it
74. "If you judge people, you have no time to love them." ~ Mother Teresa
75. Get an *ergonomically correct* chair if he/she spends lots of time at a desk
76. Revive Victorian-era manners
77. Spend a week sightseeing in Katmandu
78. Romantic Play Alert: Shakespeare's *Romeo and Juliet*
79. Use your logical abilities *and* your creative abilities to express love
80. Cuddle in front of a campfire
81. February 29, "Leap Year Day": Take a private romantic holiday every four years
82. Romantic resource: *Intuition*, by R.B. Fuller
83. Devote yourself to your partner's happiness

Favorite Love Songs from 1920
84. "I Never Knew I Could Love Anyone Like You"
85. "I'll Be with You in Apple

Blossom Time"

86. "When My Baby Smiles at Me"

---

87. "A life lived in love will never be dull." ~ Leo Buscaglia

88. Do something out-of-the-ordinary this weekend

89. Surprise your partner with two tickets to a local play

90. Boredom comes from bad attitude, *not* from familiarity

---

91. Get a charm bracelet with a charm to commemorate each of your children

92. Surprise him/her at the office—wearing an overcoat with nothing on underneath!

93. "I loved him for himself alone." ~ Sheridan

94. If you're an expressive, loud person, try *whispering* your love to your partner

95. Leave written clues that lead her to a restaurant where you're waiting for her

96. Wash windows together, with you on the outside, your partner on the inside, facing each other

97. "Confidence is the sexiest thing a woman can have." ~ Aimee Mullins

98. Hide a little gift for her so she'll find it during a walk together

99. Save restaurant reviews to use when creating dates

100. Remember your anniversary

101. Be her groom

102. "I like not only to be loved, but to be told I am loved." ~ George Eliot

103. Romantic Math: Red roses *equal* love

104. Tell your lover something you've never told *anyone* before

105. Hide a love note among a bunch of flowers

106. A note: "I know we're soulmates because . . ."

107. "In literature as in love, we are astonished at what is chosen by others." ~ Andre Maurois

---

108. Send postcards

109. Send greeting cards

110. Send an envelope with lingerie
111. Send a love letter via express mail
112. Send a love note in code

---

113. Say this: "Boy, I'm glad I met you!"
114. Get a charm bracelet with a charm to commemorate each year you've been together
115. A romantic resource: *Bed & Breakfasts and Country Inns*, from the American Bed & Breakfast Association
116. Be his devoted Lady-In-Waiting
117. Gals: Don't buy him cheap tools
118. Peruse *The Book of Massage*, by Lucinda Lidell
119. "Patience is passion tamed." ~ Lyman Abbott
120. Give phone-kisses
121. For busy couples: Schedule time for romance
122. Clip ads that give you romantic ideas
123. "Imagination is more important than knowledge." ~ Albert Einstein
124. Attend a PAIRS seminar (Practical Application of Intimate Relationship Skills): Call (888) 724-7748

125. "Live as you would have wished to live when you are dying."
~ Charles F. Gellert

126. Make love your Number One Priority

127. Talk with your mate about how both of you can balance your lives better

128. Live every day with passion

129. Give her your jacket when she's chilly

130. Work overtime, and save-up for a romantic vacation

131. "Nothing is impossible to a willing heart." ~ Heywood

132. Spend a week in New York City

133. Create a library of romantic music (at least one hundred CDs)

134. Visit romantic international cities: London, Paris, and Rome

135. Touch more

136. Eat erotic chocolates and pastries

137. Massage Coupon: Includes a copy of *The Massage Book*, by George Downing; the coupon-giver will practice one chapter per week on the coupon-holder

138–144
7 Questions for Women
(That Men Desperately Want to
Know the Answers To)

Communication *works* (Once you're a couple, being coy usually backfires)

1. Have you ever faked an orgasm?
2. Do you consider yourself a feminist?
3. What is your most *feminine* trait?
4. What is your most *masculine* trait?
5. How do feel about your masculine traits? Do you *use* or *suppress* them?
6. What is the *best* thing about being female?
7. What is the *worst* thing about being female?

---

145. Continue to woo your mate throughout your relationship
146. Guys: Hold her dinner chair
147. "One does not fall 'in' or 'out' of love. One grows in love."
    ~ Leo Buscaglia
148. Spend one solid hour shopping for greeting cards

149. Give lovey-dovey greeting cards
150. Discuss how you each define "love"
151. Tease your partner in a subtly sexy way while out in public
152. Freeze a bracelet charm inside an ice cube
153. Send love notes via email every day for a year
154. Practice your cuddling skills while watching TV
155. "Perfection is neither possible nor necessary." ~ Maria Regnier Krimmel
156. Swing together on playground swings
157. Replace the lightbulbs in your bedroom with candles
158. Attend the Tournament of Roses Parade in Pasadena, California
159. Hide a love note in his gym bag
160. Hide a string of pearls in an oyster
161. Create a Gift Closet: Stockpile gifts ahead-of-time!
162. "Love does not insist on its own way; it is not irritable or resentful." ~ I Corinthians 13:5
163. Read aloud to each other in bed:

A Book for Couples, by Hugh &
Gayle Prather

164. Buy him a new red car; present the key in a velvet jewelry box
165. Attend a Marriage Encounter weekend: Call (800) 795-5683
166. "Loved people are loving people."
    ~ Katharine Hepburn
167. Go camping together
168. Get season tickets to a local professional theater
169. A note: "Thank you for being the mother of our children."
170. Believe in your partner
171. Blow bubbles on a breezy afternoon
172. Make love to the light of a single candle
173. Get tickets for an event; keep it a secret until the day arrives
174. Cook dinner together
175. Read your partner's mind
176. Spend two weeks sightseeing in Hong Kong
177. Buy your dream home together
178. Go away for a week in Venice

179. "Life is not what you did. It's what you are doing." ~ Jim Burns
180. Romantic Opera Alert: Mozart's *Le Nozze Di Figaro*
181. Spend two weeks in Tahiti
182. Mark your partner's calendar with your birthday and anniversary

---

183–194
12 Commitments That Will Improve Your Relationship

1. Commit yourself to your relationship
2. Commit to spending 10% more time together
3. Commit yourself to being less judgmental
4. Commit yourselves to living up to your wedding vows
5. Commit yourselves to having more fun together
6. Commit yourself to practicing your religious beliefs on your partner
7. Commit yourself to seeing your partner's negative behaviors as *calls for love*
8. Commit to communicating your

feelings fully

9. Commit yourself to your partner's happiness
10. Commit yourself to *feeling* your feelings of love
11. Commit yourself to *acting* on your feelings of love
12. Commit yourself to listening to the voice of love inside you

---

195. Enjoy a ski vacation in Switzerland
196. Spend $50 in a Hallmark store
197. A note: "When I think about you in the middle of my day . . ."
198. Trip the light fantastic
199. Surf www.1001waystoberomantic.com
200. Guys: Help her on with her coat
201. Bake homemade muffins together
202. Use gummy-letter candies to spell out love messages
203. A note: "I'm kind of uncomfortable saying this out loud, but I want you to know how I feel about you . . ."
204. Roll up the rug and dance together at home

205. Place a small bouquet of violets on the kitchen table

206. A Movie Date Coupon: The coupon-holder chooses the flick. The coupon-giver treats. (Includes popcorn, soda, and Milk Duds)

207. Use a passage from Kahlil Gibran's *The Prophet* to inspire your love

208. "Keep in mind this daily notion: There are no ordinary moments." ~ Dan Millman

209. Explore some used bookstores together

210. Tattoo his/her name on your left shoulder

211. Buy her an outfit while she's trying it on; let her wear it out of the store

212. Hide a greeting card under your partner's pillow

213. Blindfold him and take him away for a romantic weekend

214. Decorate with a Christmas tree ornament that symbolizes your partner's hobby or passion

215. Walk along the Great Wall of China
216. Do-It-Yourself Romantic Afternoon:
2 bicycles, 5 hours, 1 bottle of wine
217. For tea lovers: Keep her tea stash
well stocked

---

218. Divorce. Divorce yourself from the
many distractions that keep you from
living your love
219. Read *Inner Simplicity*, by Elaine St.
James
220. Simplify your life—and you'll find
that love is a top priority

---

221. Give her your house key on a silver
chain with a note: "You own the key
to my heart."
222. Hang a romantic print by painter
Pierre Auguste Renoir
223. Arrange to have him meet his sports
idol
224. "Passionate love is a quenchless
thirst." ~ Kahlil Gibran
225. Arrange a *surprise* day off work for
your partner

226. Read *A Kick in the Seat of the Pants— Using Your Explorer, Artist, Judge & Warrior to Be More Creative,* by Roger von Oech
227. Believe in the healing power of love
228. "Intellect strips, affection clothes." ~ Ralph Waldo Emerson
229. Work on your communication skills
230. Learn more about your partner by listening to his/her family
231. You don't have to be your lover's *best* friend—but you must be *a* friend
232. A note: "When I think of you I smile because . . ."
233. Surprise your partner at work with a single red rose
234. Build your self-esteem—you'll be more loving if you love *yourself*
235. Give him a red rose boutonniere to wear during your next date

---

236. Cultivate humility
237. Practice forgiveness
238. Learn compromise
239. Foster understanding

240. Encourage humor

241. Slip a little love note into his wallet,
      in-between the dollar bills

242. "Kiss: A contraction of the mouth
      due to an enlargement of the heart."
      ~ Anonymous

243. When attending a wedding, whisper
      the vows to one another

244. Save a box of candy conversation
      hearts—and give them in *July*

245. Literally *race* to complete your
      chores—spend time with one another

246. Splurge on a beach vacation in
      Jamaica

247. Slip your photo into his/her wallet

248. Serve breakfast in bed—using your
      finest china and crystal

249. Drip chocolate syrup on selected
      body parts before lovemaking

250. Keep some greeting cards in a drawer
      at work—mail one every month

251. Bum around Europe together

252. Be waiting for him in the bathtub
      when he returns from work

253. Double-date with other fun couples
254. Eat in Toronto's most romantic restaurant: Scaramouche
255. For tea lovers: Practice the Japanese Tea Ceremony

256–260
5 Yoga Retreats
Recommended for Couples

Get away from it all—Get in touch with yourself—Get in touch with your partner

1. Kripalu Center for Yoga, in Lenox, Massachusetts: (800) 741-7353
2. Expanding Light, in Nevada City, California: (800) 346-5350
3. Sivananda Ashram Retreat, on Paradise Island, Bahamas: (242) 363-2909
4. Sivananda Ashram Yoga Camp, in Valmorin, Canada: (819) 322-3226
5. Satchidananda Ashram, in Yogaville, Virginia: (800) 858-9642

---

261. Spend a week exploring Cairo
262. On cold mornings get up first and

turn up the heat

263. Read the Sunday funnies aloud (use appropriate voices)

264. Give him a written bill after dinner: "Salad: One kiss. Entree: Eight kisses. Dessert: Three kisses. (Tipping is *strongly* encouraged)"

265. Explore some local antique shops together

266. Read *Massage and Loving*, by Anne Hooper

267. Save articles on new sexual techniques

---

268. Remember: Romance is about the *little things*

269. Little things that bring a smile to her face

270. Little things that remind him of you

271. Little things that bring a tear to his/her eye

272. Little things that have special meaning to just the two of you

273. Little things done on a consistent basis

274. Share stories from high school
275. Use body paints!
276. Be his bride
277. Believe in magic
278. Let a poem by Elizabeth Barrett Browning express your feelings
279. The "King for a Day" Coupon: The male coupon-holder is entitled to be treated like royalty for a twenty-four-hour period
280. Stock-up on romantic gifts during the Valentine season
281. Wander a local bookstore together
282. Clip newspaper headlines that include your partner's name

---

283–292
10 Quirky Questions to Help Couples Get Inside Each Other's Heads (and Hearts)

1. What three nouns best describe you?
2. What three adjectives best describe you?
3. If you could save time in a bottle, what would you do with it?
4. What do you want to be remembered for?

5. What are your prized possessions?
6. What did you want to be when you grew up?
7. Would you rather be rich or famous?
8. What's the most fun you've ever had with your clothes on?
9. What's the most fun you've ever had with your clothes off?
10. If you were going to write a self-help book, what would you title it?

---

293. Leave a blatantly sexual message on the answering machine
294. In your calendar, write a reminder to yourself *one week in advance* of your anniversary
295. Trace your family genealogies together
296. Remove the TV from your bedroom
297. Put a romantic CD in a Walkman; attach a note: "Play me"
298. Use the Bible as a guide to living your love
299. Apologize after an argument
300. Be your lover's biggest cheerleader

301. To inspire your romantic creativity, read *A Whack on the Side of the Head: How You Can Be More Creative*, by Roger von Oech

302. Do-It-Yourself Romantic Date: 2 movie tickets, 1 Tub-O'-Popcorn, 2 Cokes

303. "People want riches. They need fulfillment." ~ Bob Conklin

304. Visit a local art gallery together

305. Complete his/her collection of CDs by a favorite singer

306. Shower together (It's sexy—*and* you'll save water!)

307. Love Enhancer: Tenderness

308. Bring home his favorite kind of ice cream

309. Reduce your TV watching to a maximum of one hour a day

310. Promise that you'll never go on *Jerry Springer* or *Ricki Lake*—no matter *how bad* things get!

311. Create a Keepsake Album from the memorabilia of your life together

312. Read one book per month on

improving your relationship

313. Treat her to a facial
314. Engagement idea: Place the diamond ring in a glass of champagne
315. For *Titanic* movie fans: Recognize April 15 (*they'll* know why)
316. Online resource for sporting events and concerts: www.inetdirect.net/tnt
317. Surprise her with a silhouette portrait
318. Do-It-Yourself Romantic Picnic: 1 loaf of bread, 1 hunk of cheese, 1 bottle of wine
319. Encourage your partner's dreams
320. End each day together with a kiss
321. Romance Coupon: "Good for a manicure at a local salon."
322. "One always loves the person who understands you." ~ Anaïs Nin
323. Right after Christmas, stock up on wrapping paper and bows—on sale!
324. Concept: "Date night"
325. Take a day hike together
326. Read *Travel & Leisure* magazine: Plan a major vacation
327. Cherish the present

328. When you're both out, have a friend deliver a gourmet dinner to your home

329. Spend this month's golf money on romance

330. Rent a recreational vehicle for a comfy cross-country vacation

331. Insert a funny comic in his box of cereal

332. Inspiration for long-time lovers: "The older the violin, the sweeter the music." ~ Anonymous

333. Give him a great big bear hug

334. "People who are sensible about love are incapable of it." ~ Douglas Yates

335. Give him a hickey

336. Let a Billy Joel song express your feelings for you

---

337. Make your bedroom your private, romantic hideaway

338. Control the mood of this intimate environment

339. Get rid of that desk, TV, and exercise equipment

340. Surprise her with flowers on the nightstand
341. Add candles and massage oil

---

342. Gift resource for very quirky stuff: The Neiman Marcus "Christmas Book" catalog: (800) 634-6267
343. After driving his car, return the radio to his favorite station
344. Live your lives as romantic role models for anyone who knows you
345. Question: Do you want to be *happy*, or do you want to be *right*?
346. Place a rose under the car windshield wiper
347. Live in the moment
348. A note: "Here's something I haven't said to you in a long, long time . . ."
349. A good thing to know: *How to Make Friends with Your Feelings*, by Jay Uhler
350. When your partner earns an advanced degree, greet him/her at home by playing "Pomp and Circumstance"

3551–364
14 Miscellaneous Skills
Lovers Need to Know

1. How to cook your lover's favorite meal

2. How to be affectionate while being sexual

3. How to share your feelings without dumping them on your partner

4. How to do the laundry without destroying your partner's clothing

5. How to be supportive without being controlling

6. How to listen *actively* instead of *passively*

7. How to give a *really skillful* massage

8. How to be independent without being distant

9. How to be dependent without being co-dependent

10. How to talk about your feelings without using "psycho-babble"

11. How to make love in that "special way" that your partner loves so much

12. How to grow *together* instead of

growing *apart*

13. How to keep your relationship your number one priority amid life's many demands
14. How to choose gifts that your partner will *love*

---

365. Get a favorite comic strip blown-up to poster size
366. Collect "Love Is . . ." comics
367. Get familiar with local musicians, and attend their concerts
368. Get a local artist to draw caricatures of you on some eggs; put them in the refrigerator; wait for your partner to notice
369. Proof that "Real Men" *are* romantic: Clint Eastwood starred in the romantic film *The Bridges of Madison County*
370. Millionaires need love, too: Diamonds and furs and yachts (Oh, my!)
371. Gently brush her cheek with your lips

372. Sweep her off her feet
373. "All love is sweet, given or returned."
   ~ Percy Bysshe Shelley
374. Do something *wacky* every full moon

Favorite Love Songs from 1921

375. "Ain't We Got Fun"
376. "Make Believe"

---

377. When he's away, buy him an *awesome* easy chair
378. Vacation for a month in Australia
379. "Nobody had ever measured, even poets, how much the heart can hold."
   ~ Zelda Fitzgerald
380. For Married Folks: Think like a single person: Seduce your spouse
381. Nibble his ear
382. Send a musical greeting card
383. Gals: Update your concept of Valentine's Day (Many guys are uncomfortable with all the pink and frills)
384. Believe in miracles

385.   Stop expecting your partner to
       be perfect
386.   Stop expecting yourself to be perfect
387.   Stop expecting your relationship to
       be perfect

388.   Create a time capsule to be opened
       on your 50th anniversary
389.   Play hooky from work—and spend
       the day together
390.   Watch whales on a cruise in
       New England
391.   Decorate your desk with a heart-
       shaped crystal paperweight
392.   Give him a lottery ticket. Attach a
       note: "You're one in a million."
393.   Spend this month's beer money
       on romance (which is a better
       investment?)
394.   Keep a file of magazine articles that
       inspire romantic ideas
395.   Spend a week hiking the Alps
396.   Do a "time budget" to see where
       your time *really* goes. Schedule more
       time for romance

397. Send suggestive notes via email
398. Take a hot air balloon ride; check the Web: www.bfa.ycg.org/
399. Recite Shakespearean sonnets
400. Check local hotels for "Escape Weekend" packages
401. Concept: "Courtship after marriage"
402. While using his car, take it through the car wash
403. Offer to host your in-laws for the holidays
404. Be his "Vargas Girl": Commission an air-brush portrait of yourself for him
405. Write your New Year's resolutions together
406. Create a large and loving family together
407. A date: Dinner and dancing—*at home*
408. Attend an auction together: Buy *something* for each other
409. Be the Best Mother in the World to his children
410. A note: "I first fell in love with you when . . ."
411. Get matching tattoos

412. Create a videotape of favorite love scenes from his/her favorite movies
413. Subtly flirt with your partner while out at a party
414. "If you would be loved, love and be lovable." ~ Benjamin Franklin
415. Practice "Old World" manners
416. Join a "Show-of-the-Month Club"
417. Bedrooms with fireplaces (♥♥♥♥♥ Household Romance Rating)
418. Spend a month touring Europe
419. On a frosty winter morning, scrape the ice off her car windshield
420. Clip newspaper headlines that are funny or suggestive
421. Enemy of Love: Stress
422. Musical lovenote: "Play the CD *Meet the Beatles*. My message to you is song No. 6"
423. Create your own greeting cards on your computer
424. Get your southpaw sweetie *Lefthander Magazine*: Box 8249, Topeka, Kansas 66608
425. Do one of your partner's chores

426. Wear "Sex Appeal" cologne—Show him that you feel he has *plenty already*!

427. Delegate more at work; get home at a reasonable hour

428. Plan one surprise for next week

429. Become entrepreneurial partners as well as life partners: Go into business together

430. Get him a Mickey Mouse watch

431. Resource for parents: *Trouble-Free Travel with Children*, by Vicki Lansky

432. Put the needs of your relationship ahead of your personal desires

433. Fly to London; have dinner in the West End; fly home

434. Place a love note in the newspaper personal ads

435. Rent a classic car from the year of his/her birth

436. Eat dinner at the best restaurant within one hundred miles

437. Dress in your finest party clothes and dance at home like Fred Astaire and Ginger Rogers

438. Take your film buff to the Cannes

Film Festival

439. Watch a crackling fire together
440. Take candles into McDonald's with you: Dine in style!
441. Get season tickets to an amateur theater
442. Save all of your overtime pay for romance
443. Bake homemade cookies together
444. Surprise your partner at the office with his/her favorite candy
445. Learn to read your lover's body language
446. Be creative: Think-up two small surprises and one big one
447. A romantic dinner at a quaint restaurant in SoHo
448. Use the song "Shall We Dance" to invite your partner out for a night of dancing
449. Celebrate the first Spring day over 70°
450. Add a "Romance" category to your budget
451. Plan a three-day weekend together

452. Be a gentleman
453. Be a good, old-fashioned Lover Boy
454. While slow dancing at a party, whisper something tender to her

---

455. Watch planes land at the airport
456. Watch the stars appear
457. Watch shooting stars
458. Watch fireflies on a hot summer night
459. Watch the snow fall on a winter day
460. Watch the leaves turn colors on an autumn afternoon
461. Watch a garden grow on an early spring morning
462. Watch your manners

---

463. When she's away, paint that room she's been bugging you about
464. Create a file of magazine articles on how to improve your relationship
465. Make an appointment for your partner's annual physical exam
466. Try out together for parts in an amateur theater production

467. Let a Beatles song speak for you
468. Use a thesaurus to help you describe how you're—crazy about/mad for/nuts about/smitten with/stuck on/sweet on/wild about—your mate

---

469–490
22 Kinds of Romantic Surprises

1. Once-in-a-lifetime surprises
2. Unfolding surprises
3. Bait-and-switch surprises
4. Shocking surprises
5. Mystery-event surprises
6. Total surprises
7. Big surprises
8. Little surprises
9. Expected-but-not-right-now surprises
10. Expensive surprises
11. Surprise tickets
12. Group surprises
13. Surprise vacations
14. Public surprises
15. Private surprises
16. Surprises involving a collaborator
17. Midnight surprises

18. Surprises at work
19. Sexy surprises
20. Funny surprises
21. Meaningful surprises
22. Out-of-character surprises

---

491. Romantic Music Library: The CD *Time*, by Lionel Richie
492. Learn more about her favorite hobby
493. Whistle at her from across the room
494. Get backstage passes for your partner to meet her favorite singer
495. Plan for a romantic retirement: Put extra money into your 401(k) plan
496. Do something *super* on June 1 (Superman's birthday)

Favorite Love Songs from 1922

497. "Dreamy Melody," by Art Landry
498. "Hot Lips," by Cotton Pickers
499. "I Love Her, She Loves Me"
500. "L'Amour—Toujours—L'Amour"

---

501. Clip newspaper articles of romantic ideas

502. Learn to bake two new gourmet desserts

503. Celebrate New Year's Eve in Times Square

504. Romantic Math: Perfume *equals* romance

505. Share your work bonus with your partner

506. Share stories from junior high school

507. Get married on Valentine's Day

---

508. Gift & Date Idea: Get the song "I Will Always Love You," by Whitney Houston—

509. And rent the movie *The Bodyguard*, featuring the song

---

510. Carry a photo of your lover in your wallet

511. When attending a wedding, whisper, "If I had it to do over, I'd marry you again."

512. Love your partner *unconditionally*

513. Become an artist of your relationship

514. Learn to cook three gourmet dishes

515. Get new CDs to replace all his old albums
516. Add to her collection of horse figurines
517. "In expressing love we belong among the undeveloped countries."
    ~ Saul Bellow
518. Paint the town red
519. Make up your mind to add more *surprises* to your romantic repertoire
520. Backpack through Europe for a summer
521. Read *The Enneagram in Love & Work*, by Helen Palmer
522. Go on a trekking vacation in Nepal
523. Make a "Just Married" sign and drive around with it taped to your car
524. Hide a teeny, tiny gift somewhere on your body; make him find it
525. Fill his toolbox with lingerie—make him "work" to get his tools back

---

526. Once-a-week for a year: Jot down two reasons you love your partner
527. Once-a-week for a year: Jot down

one great thing he/she did

528. Once-a-week for a year: Jot down one inspirational thought

529. At the end of the year: Print all this out on a big scroll and present it to him/her

530. Repeat next year

---

531. Read the Travel Section of the Sunday newspaper every week: Dream together

532. Find a local "romantic hideaway"— like a quiet corner at a public garden

533. Take a cruise through the fjords in Scandinavia

534. Visit a local museum together

535. Tour the Louvre

536. Classical music lovers celebrate January 27—Mozart's birthday

537. Fold a love note in a fluffy bath towel

538. Toss out letters from previous loves

539. "Kindness is the insignia of a loving heart." ~ Anonymous

540. Love Enhancer: Faith

541. Go on an Autumn hayride

542. "Love doesn't make the world go round—but it *does* make the ride worthwhile!" ~ Anonymous
543. Have realistic expectations of love; frankly, love alone *isn't* enough
544. Plan weekend get-aways
545. After getting married, have new stationery printed up with both your names on it
546. "Make out" like when you were a teenager
547. Raise money for a favorite cause together
548. Volunteer to chaperone a high school dance together—to observe and rediscover what infatuation *really* is!
549. Trekkers celebrate James T. Kirk's birthday: March 21, 2228 A.D.
550. Use one of her pet names for your computer password
551. Surprise your partner at work with a "trinket gift"
552. Run your hands under warm water before coming to bed
553. Send a love note via FedEx—because

your love just can't wait!

554. Replace the Cheerios with candy conversation hearts

555. Put his/her things back where you found them

556. Shop at end-of-season sales

557. Love Enhancer: Focus of attention

558. Spend *several days* touring the Smithsonian museums: www.si.edu/newstart.htm

---

559. Single gals: Accept him as he is—don't try to change him

560. Single guys: Be who you are—don't be on such "good behavior" that you're no longer acting like *you*

---

561. Celebrate Sweetest Day, the third Saturday in October

562. Program your multiple-disc CD player for eight hours of non-stop romantic music

563. Wear matching "friendship rings"

564. Emotions will keep you going when logic tells you to quit

565. Plan one surprise for next month
566. Collect mementos from every place you visit together
567. Create a personalized "Beer-of-the-Month Club" for him
568. Remember the past together
569. Resource: *The Complete Guide to Bed & Breakfasts, Inns and Guesthouses*, by Pamela Lanier

---

570–576
7 Ways to a Man's Heart

1. Thai Cooking School at the Oriental, in Bangkok, Thailand: (800) 526-6566
2. L'Ecole des Chefs, in Paris, France: (610) 469-2500
3. Jane Butel's Cooking School, in Albuquerque, New Mexico: (800) 472-8229
4. Giuliano Bugialli's Cooking in Florence, Italy: (212) 813-9552
5. A La Bonne Cocotte, in Nyons, France: (212) 675-7736
6. The Apple Farm, in the Napa Valley,

California: (707) 895-2461
7. Cuisine International, for classes in
Italy, France and Brazil:
(214) 373-1161

---

577. Go on an extravagant date
578. Remember the simple pleasures
579. Work on having more fun
580. Giftwrap even the *smallest* little gifts
581. Tear down the walls that separate the
two of you
582. Watch reruns of *The Love Boat*
583. Get a personal (and secret) toll-free
number for just the two of you to use
when calling each other
584. Be *extra* attentive after your partner
has had a tough day
585. Substitute his/her Christmas stocking
with a real silk stocking
586. For birthday cards, use design
elements from his/her birth year
587. Let a Shakespearean quote speak
for you
588. Ask his/her parents for stories about
your partner's childhood

589. Become a student of love
590. Gals: Never, never, *never* talk about your past boyfriends in front of him
591. Hire a string quartet to play your wedding music at an anniversary party
592. Take a nap on the couch together
593. While slow dancing at a party, whisper something sexy to him
594. "Say what you feel when you feel it." ~ S. James
595. Make love in slow motion
596. Devote yourself to your partner's growth
597. Sit on his lap
598. Create a time capsule to be opened by your great, great grandchildren
599. Wink at her from across a crowded room
600. Love Enhancer: Funloving attitude
601. Plan anniversary surprises
602. Remind her that you really *do* adore her
603. Attach a gift to the dog's collar, and have him deliver it to her

604.　Practice public displays of affection

605–611
7 Ways to Woo Workaholics Away from Work

1.　Promise your partner the best sex of his/her life—
2.　Follow through on your promise!
3.　(If you can't beat 'em, join 'em!): Create a business *together*
4.　Make a "Mission Impossible" audio tape that leads him/her to a mystery date with you
5.　Book a hotel room—within *walking distance* of his office—and invite him over for an afternoon "meeting"
6.　Meet him for lunch; dress *very* sexy; then coyly ask him if he'd like *another* lunch date next week
7.　Have a courier deliver a steamy love letter to her office in the afternoon

---

612.　Plan big surprises
613.　Sign your letters: "Forever and a day"
614.　Write a love letter in the margins of her romance novel

615. Spend your next commission check on your lover
616. Pick-up a gift on a whim
617. Romantic Play Alert: Shakespeare's *A Midsummer Night's Dream*
618. Spend a day at The Art Institute of Chicago
619. Give your partner a kiss, smooch, peck, smack
620. Guys: While out together, stand whenever she enters or leaves the room
621. Eat in Montreal's most romantic restaurant: LeEau a la Bouche
622. Plan birthday surprises
623. "It takes a smart husband to have the last word and not use it."
    ~ Anonymous

---

624. "But to see her was to love her, Love but her, and love her for ever."
    ~ Robert Burns
625. Yes, there *is* such a thing as "Love at first sight." It can be instant, deep, and long-lasting

626. If this is your experience, glory in it!

627. But remember: "Love at first sight" isn't the *only* way to find true love

628. Many people are best friends first, then gradually fall in love

629. If *that's* your path, celebrate your *friendship* as well as your love

---

630. Surprise her with a funny caricature made of the two of you

631. Place a birthday greeting in the newspaper personal ads

632. How to arouse an intellectual: *The Erotic in Literature: A Historical Survey of Pornography as Delightful as It Is Indiscreet*, by David Loth

633. "Marriage is our last, best chance to grow up." ~ Joseph Barth

634. Don't sell his old "junk" at a garage sale before checking with him

635. Learn to play "your song" on the piano or guitar

636. Frame a favorite wedding photo

637. Write a love letter on the chalkboard in your kitchen

638.   Remove the ice cream in a single slab; place a love note in a plastic bag in the bottom of the carton; replace the ice cream

639.   Celebrate his/her birthday every day for a *month*

640.   "Mutual love, the crown of bliss."
        ~ John Milton

641.   Wear green on St. Patrick's Day—even if you're not Irish

642.   Acknowledge and validate your partner's feelings

643.   A romantic ritual: Pause and kiss at your front door

Favorite Love Songs from 1923

644.   "Linger Awhile"

645.   "Twelve O'Clock at Night"

---

646.   "If you only look at what is, you might never attain what could be."
        ~ Anonymous

647.   Give her a romantic print by painter Claude Monet

648.   Create a videotape of favorite scenes

from his/her favorite movies
649. Weed her garden for her
650. Adopt a child, and be the most loving parents in the world
651. Instead of giving a standard Valentine card, give a copy of "My Funny Valentine" from *Babes in Arms*

652–658
7 Questions for Men (That Women Desperately Want to Know the Answers To)

Very often, the topics that are the most difficult to talk about are the very topics that will bring the two of you much closer

1. Ideally, how often would you like to have sex?
2. Do you feel that you understand women?
3. Do you feel it's *possible* to understand women?
4. What is the *best* thing about being male?
5. What is the *worst* thing about being male?

6. What one thing about women are you most jealous of?

7. Do you feel misunderstood by women?

---

659. Keep your "pet names" *private*!

660. Give the best chocolate in the world: The gift of Varda Chocolates: (800) HI-VARDA

661. Make a 20-foot HAPPY BIRTHDAY banner

662. Eat dinner at the restaurant with the most romantic atmosphere

663. Be slightly sexy and somewhat sensuous

664. Sign your cards and letters with X's and O's

665. For *proof* that love improves your health, read *Love & Survival: The Scientific Basis for the Healing Power of Intimacy*, by Dr. Dean Ornish

666. Discover cozy little inns

667. Do something so out of the ordinary that you surprise even *yourself*

668. Learn to imitate his favorite actress

669. Send sexy greeting cards
670. Romantic Music Alert: *Oh, What a Night: The Steve Allen Songbook*, by George Bugatti
671. Donate to her favorite charity
672. Play romantic music by Claude Debussy
673. Share a bubble bath
674. Send funny greeting cards
675. Be wild and wacky
676. Fulfill a fantasy: Let him fly a real fighter plane; check the Web: www.skywarriors.com/
677. Practice focusing 100% of your attention when listening to him/her

---

678–692
15 Things to Never, Never, *Never* Do While Making Love

1. Never answer the phone
2. Never call her by a former lover's name
3. Never glance at your watch
4. Never interrupt yourselves for a whining pet

5. Encourage openmindedness, but never push too far
6. Never leave too little time
7. Never say anything negative about your partner's body
8. Never criticize his/her technique (but do discuss it *later*)
9. Never get into arousal without dealing with birth control *first*
10. Never criticize your lover in any way
11. Never lose your sense of humor
12. Never videotape your lovemaking without his/her permission
13. Never talk about mundane, un-sexy topics in bed
14. Never fake orgasm
15. Never leave the bedroom door unlocked if kids are in the house

---

693. Romance Coupon: "Good for a pedicure at a local salon."
694. Spend two weeks in Rio de Janeiro
695. Revisit the site of your first date
696. Wrap your anniversary gifts in *wedding* paper

697. Give him something to carry that will remind him of you...
698. A kerchief or scarf
699. A short verse to carry in his wallet
700. A pair of panties
701. A greeting card *drenched* in your favorite perfume
702. A lock of your hair
703. A current photo
704. A photo of you as a child

---

705. Definition: "Jeepin'": Having sex in the back seat of a car
706. Learn to make origami animals for your nature-loving partner
707. Have big pillows and cozy blankets near the fireplace
708. Find a hobby the two of you can share
709. Visit Los Angeles' most romantic restaurant: Patina
710. Create a "Romantic Idea Jar": 1,001 numbered slips of paper; choose a number, then refer to the book *1001 Ways To Be Romantic*

711. Guys: Dress as her version of Prince
     Charming...
712. Whether it's in a tuxedo
713. Or a tank-top T-shirt and hardhat
714. Or jeans and a flannel shirt
715. Or silk boxer shorts

---

716. The un-asked-for gesture is most
     appreciated
717. The surprise gift is most cherished

---

718. Celebrate New Year's Eve in bed
     together
719. Get a vanity license plate with his/her
     name on it
720. Watch cartoons together to celebrate
     Donald Duck's birthday, June 9
721. Gather significant quotes from
     his/her favorite movie characters
722. Spend time in bed-and-breakfasts
723. Be irrepressible and just a touch
     irresponsible

---

724. Go through her Victoria's Secret
     catalog and rate the items 1 thru 10

725. Have his/her portrait painted from a photograph

726. Make a list of "Relationship Firsts," and celebrate your *many* anniversaries

727. When your partner has a big deadline, help by doing his/her chores

728. Eat popcorn and soda at the movies

729. Live your values

730. Love is timeless—and to prove it, cover-up all the clocks in your house for the weekend

731. In your calendar, write a reminder to yourself *one week in advance* of his/her birthday

732. Wrap an expensive piece of jewelry in a Big Mac container

---

733. Have your Valentine card postmaked from a romantic city...

734. Valentine, Texas 79854

735. Valentine, Nebraska 69201

736. Loveland, Colorado 80537

737. Loveland, Ohio 45140

738. Loving, New Mexico 88256

739. Bridal Veil, Oregon 97010

740. Kissimmee, Florida 32741

---

741. Take turns taking family photos so you'll *both* be in them!

742. Be more romantic than any other couple you know

743. Get a vanity license plate with your anniversary date on it

744. Believe in yourself

Favorite Love Songs from 1924

745. "Deep in My Heart, Dear"

746. "I'll See You in My Dreams"

747. "Lady, Be Good"

748. "Somebody Loves Me"

749. "There's Yes Yes in Your Eyes"

---

750. Treat her to a "make-over" at a spa

751. Create a personalized "Sweet-Treat-of-the-Month Club"

752. "Human beings have the *ability* of logic, but we are not *ruled* by logic; we are ruled by emotion."
~ Gregory J.P. Godek

753. Hang mistletoe over your bed

754.   Focus on your partner's *wants*, not just on his/her *needs*

755.   Review your assumptions

756.   Install a lock on your bedroom door

757–775
19 Bits of Ancient Wisdom for Modern Lovers

1.   "One word frees us all of the weight and pain of life. That word is Love." ~ Sophocles

2.   "Skill makes love unending." ~ Ovid

3.   "Let us not love with words or tongue but with actions and in truth." ~ 1 John 3:18

4.   "Many waters cannot quench love, neither can floods drown it." ~ Song of Solomon 8:7

5.   "Take away leisure and Cupid's bow is broken." ~ Ovid

6.   "The anger of lovers renews the strength of love." ~ Publilius Syrus

7.   "Love is a grave mental disease." ~ Plato

8.   "No act of kindness, no matter how small, is ever wasted." ~ Aesop

9. "The madness of love is the greatest of heaven's blessings." ~ Plato

10. "To be able to say how much you love is to love but little." ~ Petrarch

11. "The happiness of your life depends on the quality of your thoughts."
~ Marcus Antonius

12. "To be loved, be lovable." ~ Ovid

13. "The more a man knows, the more he forgives." ~ Confucius

14. "To be wronged is nothing unless you continue to remember it."
~ Confucius

15. "Union gives strength." ~ Aesop

16. "When male and female combine, all things achieve harmony."
~ Tao Te Ching

17. "From their eyelids as they glanced dripped love." ~ Hesiod

18. "He is not a lover who does not love forever." ~ Euripides

19. "My love for you is mixed throughout my body."
~ Ancient Egyptian Love Song

776. Millionaires need love, too: Take her shopping on Rodeo Drive
777. Elope (Ladder and all)
778. Take an old bottle of unused medicine capsules; empty the medicine; insert *teeny-tiny* love notes; write him a "Prescription for Love"
779. Go beyond the expected
780. "Love, and a cough, cannot be hid." ~ George Herbert
781. Be strong when your partner is not
782. Write funny messages in the margins of his magazines
783. Love Enhancer: Stay in touch with your feelings
784. Make a love letter dictated on an audio cassette tape
785. Celebrate "Husband Appreciation Day" (a made-up holiday; *you* choose when!)
786. Locate a copy of "your song" recorded in French or Italian
787. Remember that conversation involves *two-way* communication
788. Be impetuous and impractical

789. Buy two relationship bestsellers per year: Read and discuss them
790. Spend two weeks in Fiji

791–794
4 Relationship Concepts Based on Your Sense of Taste

Just as the incredible variety of food, tastes, and meals are all based on just four primary tastes—sweet, sour, salty, bitter—a well-rounded relationship is composed of these four elements:

Sweet: The tender, meaningful, deep aspects of life—those we cherish and treasure

Sour: The challenging, educational aspects of life—those which help us to grow and learn patience and flexibility

Salty: The zesty, sexy, passionate aspects of life—those high points and memorable times

Bitter: The hard, painful, frustrating aspects of life—those which force us to change, mature and often reach our true potential

795. Give a vintage bottle of wine from the year of his/her birth

796. Create a "*perfect* vacation" (your *partner's* definition of perfect)

797. Guys: Don't buy cheap flowers (they wilt quickly)

798. Tell your lover that you're—enchanted by/captivated by/enamored of/fond of—him/her

799. Challenge the cultural stereotypes of men and women

800. Keep a wedding photo on your desk at work

801. Ask your friends to list their favorite romantic restaurants

802. *Practice* kissing

803. Carry a copy of your wedding license in your wallet

804. Some help for your love letters: "I'm feeling—loving, affectionate, amorous, ardent, erotic, fond, lovesick, hot—for you."

805. Frequent drive-in movies

806. Tell him what you really appreciate about him

807. Give her the window seat when flying together

---

808. Learn your partner's "hot buttons"—
809. And vow to never hit them
810. Learn your partner's pet peeves—
811. And avoid them
812. Learn your partner's "blind spots"—
813. And help him/her cope
814. Learn your partner's "soft spots"—
815. And indulge them
816. Learn what turns your partner off—
817. And avoid those behaviors
818. Learn what turns your partner *on*—
819. And practice, practice, practice!

---

820. Write a love letter, and present it to him/her *one sentence at a time*—over two months!
821. Enemy of Love: Overly practical attitudes
822. While out together, whisper to him/her, "You're the *best*."
823. Provide the popcorn while watching a movie at home

824. Create monthly files to keep track of romantic things you're going to do

825. Visit the Red Mountain Spa, in Ivins, Utah: (800) 407-3002

826. Ask your friends to share their secrets for keeping love alive

827. Plan surprise birthday parties

828. Express your love every day, every day, every day, every day

829. Guys: Open the car door for her

830. Love Enhancer: Kindness

831. Buy him penny candy

832. Do one thing to simplify your life

833. Cater to her every whim for a week

834. FYI: Guys really *do* have feelings—it's just that they're often "on hold"

835. Musical lovenote: "Play the CD *Rock 'N' Roll No.2*, by Elvis Presley. My message to you is song No. 7"

836. Gals: Please, oh *please*, don't give him boring gifts

---

837. Remember: A man's ego is fragile

838. (But then again, so is a woman's)

839. Greet her at the door with confetti
840. Love Enhancer: Simplicity
841. "There is no difficulty that enough love will not conquer." ~ Emmet Fox
842. Hire a harpist to play during Sunday brunch at home
843. Put a tiny love note *inside* a balloon
844. Eat dinner at the restaurant with the best view
845. Read *Romantic Mischief: The Playful Side of Love*, by Gregory J.P. Godek
846. Stock up on firewood for those cold winter nights
847. Gaze into each other's eyes

---

848. English: "I'm in love with you"
849. French (spoken to a guy): "Je suis amoureus"
850. French (spoken to a gal): "Je suis amoureuse de toi"
851. Italian (spoken to a guy): "Mi sono innamorato"
852. Italian (spoken to a gal): "Mi sono innamorata di de"
853. German: "Ich bin in dich verliebt"

854. Spanish (spoken to a guy): "Estoy enamorado"

855. Spanish (spoken to a gal): "Estoy enamorada de ti"

856. Portugese (spoken to a guy): "Estou apaixonado"

857. Portugese (spoken to a gal): "Estou apaixonada por você"

---

858. Get a fancy brass bed

859. Wrap a gift in the colorful Sunday comics

860. Create a "*perfect* date" (your partner's definition of perfect)

861. A+ Rating, Romantic Music Artist: David Sanborn

862. Visit Lovers' Lane in your town

863. Let a poem by Susan Polis Schutz express your feelings of love

864. A+ Romance Rating: Le Bristol Hotel, in Paris, France

865. Love Enhancer: Clarity of your life's priorities

866. Spend $250 on red roses

867–892
26 Romantic Countries to Visit

Gather info on places you'd like to plan a romantic vacation

1. Austria: (310) 477-2038;
   www.anto.com
2. Belgium: (212) 758-8130;
   www.visitbelgium.com
3. England: (212) 986-2266;
   www.usagateway.visitbritain.com
4. Cyprus: (212) 683-5280;
   www.cyprustourism.org
5. Czech Republic: (212) 288-0830;
   www.czech.cz
6. Denmark: (212) 885-9700;
   www.visitdenmark.com
7. Finland: (800) 346-4636; 212-885-9700;
   www.travelfile.com/get/finninfo
8. France: (310) 271-6665;
   www.francetourism.com
9. Germany: (800) 637-1171; email:
   gntolaz@aol.com
10. Greece: (213) 626-6696
11. Hungary: (212) 355-0240;

www.hungary.com/tourinform
12. Iceland: (212) 885-9700;
www.artic.is
13. Ireland: (800) 223-6470;
www.ireland.travel.ie
14. Italy: (310) 820-0098
15. Luxembourg: (212) 935-8888; email:
luxnto@aol.com
16. Malta: (212) 695-9520;
www.tourism.org.mt
17. Monaco: (800) 753-9696;
www.monaco.mc/usa/
18. Netherlands: (888) 464-6552;
www.goholland.com
19. Norway: (212) 885-9700;
www.norway.org
20. Poland: (212) 338-9412;
www.polandtour.org
21. Portugal: (800) 767-8842;
www.portugal.org
22. Russia: (800) 847-1800
23. Spain: (800) 992-3976;
(213) 658-7188; www.okspain.org
24. Sweden: (212) 885-9700;
www.gosweden.org

25. Switzerland: (310) 460-8900;
    www.switzerlandtourism.com
26. Turkey: (212) 687-2194

---

893. Go star gazing at a planetarium
894. Decorate the house for the holidays together
895. Announce your wedding anniversary in the newspaper personal ads
896. Learn a dance routine on ice skates
897. A busy mom coupon: "I'll cook the kids' dinner."
898. Create an Easter basket full of chocolate treats
899. Parent's coupon: "It's my turn to stay home with the next sick kid."
900. Leave a romantic message on the answering machine
901. Make a baby!
902. Design a family logo that expresses who you are
903. Turn a wedding photo into a Christmas tree ornament
904. "Even one hundred years isn't enough time to express all the love in the

human heart." ~ Gregory J.P. Godek

905. Turn to him/her in public and whisper, "I'm glad I married you."

906. Romantic Math: Champagne *equals* celebration

907. "Thou art to me a delicious torment." ~ Ralph Waldo Emerson

---

908. Flirt with each other at a party, as if you both were single

909. For beginners: Flirt just a *little*; wink; compliment each other

910. For intermediate students: Act out a complete "pick-up" fantasy (without any of the other guests being aware of what you're doing)

911. For advanced students: Continue the fantasy as you return home

912. For extra credit: At the party, sneak into an empty room and make mad, passionate love!

---

913. Keep your passports up-to-date for spontaneous foreign travel opportunities

914. Plan a surprise get-away weekend
915. Give a mug with his/her name on it
916. Laugh together
917. Explore your feelings of anger
918. Give one rose for every child
919. Make his/her favorite gourmet dessert
920. Look through your wedding album together

---

921. "Familiar acts are beautiful through love." ~ Percy Bysshe Shelley
922. Take a familiar act and give it a little, creative, loving twist
923. Tie a ribbon around a cup of bedtime tea
924. Eat dinner by candlelight—*tonight*
925. Upon waking in the morning, say something loving
926. Make dinnertime a time for re-connecting
927. Plan some kind of big surprise for next year
928. Buy her a new sporty car; wrap it in a giant red bow

929. Do something so incredible that it would get you into the Romance Hall of Fame

930. Give her a lottery ticket. Attach a note: "Take a chance on me."

931. Serve breakfast tomorrow using your fine china and silverware

932. Join the Association for Couples in Marriage Enrichment; call (336) 724-1526

933. Make a custom romantic lapel button ("I ♥ Tracey")

934. If you're traveling during a holiday, send a romantic I.O.U.

935. Get him a rare baseball card of his favorite player

936. Visit any one of the four Guggenheim Museums

---

937. Go out dancing

938. Go out of your way for one another

939. Go out on a limb—share your deepest feelings

940. Go out on a limb—build a treehouse for her

941. Go out!

_____

942. "Life is either a daring adventure—
or it is nothing." ~ Helen Keller

943. Make your daily life a daring
adventure

944. Make your next vacation a daring
adventure

_____

945. Love Enhancer: Sense of adventure

946. On long car trips, read aloud to each
other

947. Bring her a cup of tea in bed every
night—without her asking for it

948. Call to see if you can pick-up
anything on the way home from
work

949. Create a complete library of favorite
romantic movies on video

950. Send a dozen roses: 11 red roses and
1 white one. The note: "In every
bunch there's one who stands out—
and you are that one."

951. Make a twenty-foot HAPPY
ANNIVERSARY banner

952. Design a Web site that features your family histories

953. Place an audio tape of romantic music in his/her car stereo—and cue it to start when the car is started

954. Take a train ride

---

955. (800) MARRIAGE: *Marriage Magazine*

956. (800) SANDALS (Couples-only Caribbean vacations)

957. (800) JIGSAWS (Intricate puzzles from Bits & Pieces)

958. (800) FARE-OFF ("Travel Smart" newsletter)

959. (800) FULL-LEAF (Spice-of-the-Month)

960. (800) AH-KAUAI (Kauai, Hawaii)

961. (800) 3-BANNER (Custom giant banners)

962. (800) 9-GODIVA (For serious chocoholics)

963. (800) LUV-YOGA (Retreat center in La Jolla, California)

964. Busy parent coupon: "Five 'taxi trips': Hauling the kids to soccer practice."

965. Guys: Don't mess with her junk drawer

966. Leave a small bouquet of daisies on her night stand

967. "The 11th commandment: Thou shalt be happy." ~ Anonymous

968. Serenade her

969. Talk together for ten minutes in bed before rising in the morning

970. Give the Lladro figurine titled "Happy Anniversary"

971–978
8 Questions About Eroticism
That Every Couple Should Discuss

A+ Couples understand that no matter how intuitive they are, they still must talk about erotic and sexual issues

1. What words do you want to hear during lovemaking?

2. What are the two most sensitive areas on your body?

3. What's the difference between "sexy"

and "erotic"?

4. How do you define the fine line between "sexy" and "sleazy"?
5. How would you like your partner to *dress* during lovemaking?
6. Which of your five senses is the most sensitive?
7. What are your favorite erotic films?
8. Do you feel comfortable asking your partner for specific kinds of sexual stimulation?

---

979. Create a personalized "Wine-of-the-Month Club" for her
980. Classical music lovers celebrate February 23: Handel's birthday
981. Play "your song" on the stereo
982. Honor your partner's parents
983. Float a love note in a bottle in the bathtub
984. Give subtly suggestive greeting cards
985. Create a shared vision of your future together
986. Greet him at the front door wearing a big red ribbon—and nothing else!

987. Work on being *friends*—as well as
     lovers
988. Bring home dinner from a gourmet
     take-out café
989. "One forgives to the degree that one
     loves." ~ La Rochefoucauld

990–997
8 Questions to Ask Yourself About Yourself
Understanding *yourself* is required if you want
an A+ Relationship.
(It wouldn't hurt if you *partner* understood
these things about you, too!)

1. How do you balance work and play?
2. Can you make an honest assessment
   of your weaknesses?
3. Are you utilizing your strengths?
4. How do you rank these priorities in
   your life? Work, love, family,
   community, spirituality, community,
   money, friends, kids
5. How do you face *change* in your life?
6. In a nutshell, what is your
   philosophy of life?
7. What motivates you to do your best?

8. What do you feel is your life's central emotional challenge?

_____

998. Sail the South Seas

999. Get a scent ring and a variety of fragrances

1000. Together, write a letter to your children on every one of their birthdays

1001. Recreate her bridal bouquet

1002. Return home with travel brochures and plane tickets sticking out of your pocket. Wait for your partner to notice

1003. A "Lighthearted Weekend" Coupon: You will be treated to a weekend of fun, frivolity, silliness, goofiness, and ease

1004. Read *The Good Marriage: How & Why Love Lasts*, by Judith S. Wallerstein

1005. Mindset: Every marriage is a private club for two

1006. Enemy of Love: Lack of self knowledge

1007. Carry her up to bed

1008. Eat dinner at home—*in the nude!*
1009. Run a bath; leave a note leading her there; leave the house

---

1010. Dress her in the morning
1011. And undress her in the evening

1012. Remember: Relationships have cycles
1013. This will help you keep your eye on the future—
1014. While you act lovingly *today*

1015. "Love is a little haven of refuge from the world." ~ Bertrand Russell
1016. "Love is the fairest flower that blooms in God's garden." ~ Anonymous
1017. "Love is, above all, the gift of oneself." ~ Jean Anouilh
1018. How do you define love? How does your partner?
1019. Revisit this question every year on your anniversary
1020. Keep a journal of your thoughts about the nature of love

1021. Collect quotes and verses on love

1022. Anticipate his needs
1023. A+ Rating, Romantic Music Artist: Larry Carlton
1024. During your wedding ceremony, wink at her
1025. Give him a tie that illustrates his favorite sport
1026. Have a picnic at midnight

1027. Argue when you need to
1028. Remember: The *purpose* of arguing with your lover is not to *win*—
1029. (Because even when you *win* you *lose*)
1030. —Its purpose is to blow off steam, then re-connect
1031. "Learn to laugh at your troubles and you'll never run out of things to laugh at." ~ Lyn Karol

---

1032. Be faithful to your partner
1033. In both word—
1034. And deed

1035. Discuss how you define "sexy"

1036. "You can give without loving, but you cannot love without giving."
~ Amy Charmichael

1037. Love Coupon: This coupon entitles the holder to one candlelight dinner (with the issuer of the coupon) at the most romantic restaurant in town!

1038. Wear matching outfits while on vacation

1039. Use food coloring to create multi-colored popcorn

1040. Meet for coffee after work every Friday

1041. Revisit the place where you proposed
1042. Take along a bottle of champagne
1043. Propose again
1044. Reminisce!

1045. Give each other a "trinket gift" for every day you're apart

1046. Choose to focus on your partner's good points—compliment them

1047. Resolve to call her more often

1048. Resource: *What Can I Say? How to*

Write Verse for All Occasions,
by Sadie Harris

1049. Install dimmer switches on every light in your house

1050. Guys: No sexist attitudes

1051. Slow dance to the light of one candle

1052. Forget "The Golden Rule" ("Do unto others as you would have them do unto you")—

1053. Practice instead "The Platinum Rule," which states: "Do unto others *as they would have you do unto them*"—it promotes more empathy

1054. Get the great book *The Platinum Rule*, by Tony Alessandra

---

1055. Take a ride on the Napa Valley Wine Train

1056. Explore your feelings of fear—overcoming fear leads to love

1057. Call him at work and say, "Hello, handsome. Are you free tonight?"

1058. Fill your partner's briefcase with flowers

1059–1067
9 Ways to Love a Gemini
(22 May–21 June)

1. Gemini is an *air* sign: Cater to his/her light, funloving nature
2. Gift tip: Pairs, sometimes opposites
3. (Sometimes, one simply isn't enough)
4. Matching items, like a bracelet and matching necklace
5. Keep in mind Gemini's dual nature
6. Lily-of-the-Valley; lavender
7. Light and subtle foods
8. The excitement and glamour of New York City
9. Wrap gifts in yellow for your Gemini

1068. Write a short, romantic and sexy story. Mail it to your mate
1069. Cuddle together under a blanket at a football game
1070. Go to a local spa every Friday to unwind together
1071. Take your art lover to the Andy Warhol Museum in Pittsburgh
1072. Give your partner his/her favorite

movie on video

1073. Give your partner more reassurance
1074. Reinforce her good qualities
1075. Compliment his talents and abilities

1076. Be aware that men and women tend to have different styles of communicating
1077. Men tend to view communicating as hierarchical interactions
1078. Women tend to experience communicating as network (connecting) interactions
1079. (But remember that these are *tendencies*—not unassailable truths)

1080. Be *extra* loving after he/she has had a hard week
1081. "The art of love…is largely the art of persistence." ~ Dr. Albert Ellis
1082. Share your feelings of tenderness
1083. Get a VW "Love Bug"
1084. Give yourself more *time* for your relationship

1085. Be her bridge partner
1086. Millionaires need love, too: Give one
another Rolex watches

1087–1101
15 Sensuality Enhancers

1. Bring more *sensuality* into your lover's
life, and you'll *both* reap many
benefits
2. Run your fingers gently through your
lover's hair
3. Focus on one of the five senses at a
time
4. For one week, create a romantic
mood at home through soft lighting
5. For one week, have great music
playing in the background all the
time at home
6. For one week, keep three bouquets of
fragrant flowers in the house
7. For one week, focus on touching a
different part of your partner's body
each day
8. For one week, prepare an extra-
special *taste treat* for your lover

9. Include more sensuality into your lovemaking
10. Slow down, make time, relax
11. Over the next five weeks, get five small gifts that focus on each of the five senses
12. Focus on the present moment; appreciate the "now"
13. Buy ten *scented* candles
14. Give him a great shoulder massage as he watches TV tonight
15. Buy a basketful of *scented* bath oils and products

1102. Re-enact your first date
1103. Go Christmas caroling together
1104. Change the baby's diaper (when it's not your turn)
1105. Place a special audio tape in a Walkman when you present it
1106. Lend a hand—without being asked
1107. Three times during the day, stop whatever you're doing, think about your mate, and smile to yourself

1108–1114
7 Favorite Spots to Take a Fishing Fanatic

1. Housatonic River, Cornwall Bridge, Connecticut
2. Connecticut River, Pittsburgh, New Hampshire
3. Androscoggin River, Lewiston, Maine
4. Little Kennebago River, Rangerley, Maine
5. Falling Springs Creek, Chambersburg, Pennsylvania
6. Madison River, Ennis, Montana
7. Rock Creek, Missoula, Montana

1115. Leave a greeting card on his car seat when he's about to run errands
1116. "Love, like death, changes everything." ~ Kahlil Gibran
1117. Create a 10% increase in the amount of fun you have together
1118. The "Flower Power" Coupon: Redeemable for one dozen long-stemmed red roses
1119. Aphrodisiac Alert: *The Foods of Love*, by Max de Roche

1120. Write the date on your hidden love notes—they might not be found for a long time!

Favorite Love Songs from 1925

1121. "Five Foot Two," Art Landry
1122. "If You Were the Only Girl"
1123. "Yes Sir, That's My Baby," Gene Austin

1124. Have no hidden agendas
1125. Make love in as many countries as possible
1126. The "Blitz of Balloons" Coupon: Good for: 1) A ride in a big hot air balloon, or 2) One hundred helium-filled balloons!
1127. Love Enhancer: Creative attitude

1128. The gift: A bottle of "Passion" cologne
1129. The activity: A night of passion
1130. The background music: "Passion," by Rod Stewart

1131. Gals: Loosen your inhibitions—and choreograph a *real* striptease for him
1132. The classic music: "The Stripper," by David Rose & His Orchestra
1133. Or "You Can Leave Your Hat On," by Joe Cocker
1134. For inspiration: See Kim Basinger's strip scene in the movie *9 1/2 Weeks*

1135. Place a heart-shaped sticker on your wristwatch to remind you to call
1136. Give *fragrant* flowers: Freesia, Rubrum Lilies, Lilacs
1137. Eat dinner at the "best-kept secret" restaurant
1138. Get your picture taken together where you poke your heads through cardboard cut-outs of famous people
1139. Celebrate three-day weekends
1140. Mark your partner's birthday in your calendar
1141. Buy her an elegant evening gown
1142. Get a favorite toy from his/her childhood

1143. Slip little love notes into several CD cases

1144. Make some of the notes relate to the title of the album—

1145. *Come Upstairs* by Carly Simon

1146. *This Is Love* by Johnny Mathis

1147. *Lazy Afternoon* by Barbra Streisand

1148. *All The Way* by Frank Sinatra

1149. *Nobody's Perfect* by Deep Purple

1150. *Erotica* by Madonna

1151. *Everybody Loves a Nut* by Johnny Cash

1152. *Help!* by The Beatles

1153. *Goin' Out of My Head* by The Lettermen

1154. *The Language of Love* by Jerry Vale

1155. *Never* forget your anniversary

1156. The "Fun-and-Games" Coupon: Your choice of games: Monopoly, Risk, Yahtzee, chess, bridge, or Parcheesi

1157. Watch old movies on TV together

1158. When he/she's sick, be the *perfect* caretaker

1159. Stay at the fanciest hotel in Stockholm: Hasselby Slott

1160. Fill his/her entire answering machine tape with romantic messages

1161. Write him/her a check for a million kisses

1162. "Love bears all things, believes all things, hopes all things, endures all things." ~ I Corinthians 13:7

1163. Enemy of Love: Lack of patience

1164. Give tulips. Attach a note: "I've got two-lips waiting for you!"

1165. Prepare for a vacation in the beautiful Bahamas: http://TheBahamas.com/

1166. Give your partner a special good luck charm

1167. Thank him with a hot bath for doing the yard work

1168. (When he's finished, see if you can think of *another* way to thank him)

1169. Find a favorite young artist you both like

1170. Follow and support his/her career

1171. Purchase original pieces of artwork

1172–1197
Romantic Advice from A to Z

Always kiss each other upon departing
Be there for each other—always
Create an environment of love
Do it—now
Escape from the kids
Fight fair
Give of your time
Handle with care
Inspire your partner with your love
Judge not
Keep your good memories alive
Listen to each other
Make love with your partner's needs foremost
Never go to bed mad
Offer to handle an unpleasant chore
Praise your partner
Quality time isn't just for kids
Respect his/her feelings
Say what you feel when you feel it
Tell her you love her every day. Every day
Understand your differences
Valentine's Day is every day
Walk together; talk together

X-rated stuff is *OK* between consenting,
    loving couples
You can never say "I love you" too often
Zero-in on his little passions

1198. Make a Valentine's Day resolution
    rededicating yourself to your partner
1199. Install a hot tub in your back yard
1200. Flowers that match her name: Rose,
    Ivy, Daisy, Lily, Iris
1201. For your anniversary: A lottery ticket
    and a note: "I hit the jackpot when I
    married you."
1202. Hire a masseuse to give your partner
    a professional massage at home
1203. For tea lovers: Buy a medley of teas
1204. Splurge on a $50 shopping spree at
    The Disney Store
1205. Customize his/her horoscope in the
    morning paper
1206. Carry love stamps in your wallet at
    all times
1207. Send your mate silly/cheap souvenirs
    from your trips

1208–1217
10 Outrageous Places to Make Love

1. Make love in a hammock (if you can)
2. Make love in an elevator (if you dare)
3. Make love in the bathtub (if you fit)
4. Make love in the shower (if you can balance)
5. Make love on a Ferris wheel (if you're not afraid of heights)
6. Make love in an airplane restroom (if you're both flexible)
7. Make love in a library (if you're very quiet)
8. Make love on the hood of your car (if you're fast)
9. Make love at a party (if you're discreet)
10. Make love in a pool (if you're really good swimmers)

1218. Share your dreams for the future
1219. The Elegant "Sunday Morning Breakfast-In-Bed" Coupon: The coupon-giver will treat you to a gourmet breakfast on any Sunday

1220.   Never, never, *never* throw out
        something that belongs to him/her
1221.   Go "above and beyond the call of
        duty" in expressing your love

1222–1228
7 Love Songs That Put
Women on a Pedestal

1. "Island of Life," Jon Anderson (with
   Kitaro)
2. "Lady," Kenny Rogers
3. "Oh, Pretty Woman," Roy Orbison
4. "She's a Lady," Tom Jones
5. "She's Always a Woman," Billy Joel
6. "Three Times a Lady,"
   The Commodores
7. "When a Man Loves a Woman,"
   Percy Sledge

1229.   Switch sides of the bed for a night
1230.   Switch housekeeping roles for a day
1231.   Switch off the lights: Use candles

1232.   Pay attention to your romantic
        daydreams

1233. Take action the moment a romantic whim hits you!

1234. Buy an acoustic music CD simply because of its romantic cover art

1235. Buy a book with a romantic-sounding title

1236. Eat in the most romantic restaurant in Vienna: Steirereck

1237. Get new wedding bands for your 25th anniversary

1238. On cold mornings warm up her car

1239. Get an alarm clock that awakens you to any music CD you insert—and awaken to romantic selections

1240. Sing "your song" together whenever it comes on the radio in your car

1241. Use a thesaurus to help you describe your—love, beau, beloved, darling, truelove, dearest, flame, inamorata, paramour, swain, sweet, valentine

1242. The "Favor-On-Demand" Coupon: You want a favor? Just ask the coupon-giver: He or she is obligated to do as you ask

1243. Embark on a safari in Kenya

1244.   String a necklace around a stuffed
        animal's neck—and wait for her to
        notice

1245.   Watch the sun rise
1246.   Watch the sun set
1247.   Watch your mouth: Don't say things
        you'll regret

1248–1254
7 Best Love Songs by Lionel Richie

1.   "Endless Love" (with Diana Ross)
2.   "Truly"
3.   "You Are"
4.   "Say You, Say Me"
5.   "Stuck on You"
6.   "My Love"
7.   "Love Will Conquer All"

1255.   Remember: Romance doesn't have to
        cost a fortune
1256.   It's the size of the *thought*—*not* the
        size of the price tag—that counts

1257.   For husbands only: Describe yourself

as "uxorious"

1258. Make love at the stroke of midnight on New Year's Eve

1259. Make your partner your No. 1 priority

1260. Call your partner when you're running late

1261. Buy matching team jackets

1262. Following a stressful week, consciously spend the weekend *reconnecting*

1263. Once a month, retire to bed together at 8:00 P.M.

1264. Millionaires need love, too: Hop the Concorde for dinner in Paris

1265. Plan your vacations around major chocolate-producing locations

1266. Have a romantic Italian dinner in Boston's North End

1267. Bring flowers home for no specific reason

1268-1295
28 Relationship Do's and Don'ts

1. Do the *opposite* everyone *else*

2. Don't gloat when you're right
3. Don't sulk when you don't get your way
4. Don't worry—be happy
5. Don't try to pack too much into the weekend
6. Don't over-schedule your vacations
7. Don't make the same mistake twice
8. Don't undermine your partner's authority with your kids
9. Don't reveal the ending of a movie!
10. Don't spend your "Prime Time" watching *TV*
11. Don't drink and drive—not ever
12. Don't stop
13. Don't be a "cover-stealer" in bed
14. Don't interrupt when he/she's talking
15. Don't wait—express your love *right now*
16. Don't even *try* to leave the house during a blizzard; snuggle together for a romantic day off
17. Do: Learn the gentle art of loving compromise
18. Don't: Negotiate—as if your

relationship were a business deal

19. Don't hold grudges
20. Don't take one another for granted
21. Don't go a single day without saying "I love you"
22. Don't let your mind wander during conversations!
23. Don't wait for your partner to read your mind
24. Don't wait until the last minute to make Valentine's Day dinner reservations!
25. Do call *in advance* to get a babysitter for Valentine's Day evening!
26. Don't just sign "Love" on your Valentine's Day card; be *eloquent*
27. Do reserve a room at a bed-and-breakfast *three months* in advance
28. Don't be so judgmental

1296. Fill your lover's car with balloons
1297. Go somewhere you've always *dreamed* of visiting
1298. Get pre-decorated boxes for instant, hassle-free giftwrapping

1299. Give sunflowers—along with Stevie Wonder's song "You Are the Sunshine of My Life"

1300. Refurbish an antique table together and add it to your collection!

1301. Go sledding in the snow

1302. Rent skis for the two of you

1303. A "One Week of Breakfast-In-Bed" Coupon: Seven straight days of luxury!

1304. For your car nut: Make a cake to look like a radial tire

1305. Be romantic on a whim

1306. Give your *partner* a gift on *your* birthday. Surprise!

1307. English: "I'm crazy about you"

1308. French (spoken to a guy): "Je suis fou"

1309. French (spoken to a gal): "Je suis folle de toi"

1310. Italian (spoken to a guy): "Sono pazzo"

1311. Italian (spoken to a gal): "Sono pazza di te"

1312. German: "Ich bin verrückt nach dir"
1313. Spanish (spoken to a guy):
"Estoy loco"
1314. Spanish (spoken to a gal):
"Estoy loca por ti"
1315. Portugese (spoken to a guy):
"Eu sou louco"
1316. Portugese (spoken to a gal):
"Eu sou louca por você"

1317. Create a "photo wall" for displaying
your best memories
1318. Romantic Resource: Scan a bridal
magazine for travel and gift ideas
1319. Newlyweds: Carry her over the
threshold

1320. Place small wagers on various fun
events
1321. Bet on the winner of the Miss
America Pageant or the World Series
1322. Bet odd amounts, like $5.27
1323. Bet for *services*, like backrubs or
making dinner

1324. Linger over coffee at home together
1325. Linger over coffee at a local café
1326. Linger over dinner, and simply enjoy each other's company
1327. Linger after making love
1328. Linger in bed together in the morning

1329. Daily affirmation: "I am a lovable—and loving—person"
1330. Hide a love note in a book on a bookstore shelf—and give clues to its location
1331. Visit elegant inns around the country: Check out *Recommended Romantic Inns*
1332. Add to her collection of tchotchkes
1333. Enemy of Love: Guilt
1334. Brush against him "accidentally" while out in public
1335. Furniture for lovers: A love seat
1336. Hire a string quartet to provide musical accompaniment for a picnic
1337. For every day you've been together give him/her a penny

1338–1356
19 Time-Saving Tips for Lovers

1. Every minute you save can be devoted to your relationship
2. Delegate more responsibilities at work—and get home earlier
3. Run all your errands *in one place*—don't run all over town
4. Read a book on time management: *The 8-Day Week*, by John Ward Pearson
5. Use paper plates, so you don't have to bother washing dishes
6. Double your recipes so you can get two days' meals of cooking done at once
7. Don't leave chores half-done: They prey on your mind
8. Speed up when you have to do mindless chores
9. Slow down to appreciate your time when you're *together*
10. Have designated duffel bags and backpacks for various activities
11. Buy in bulk!

12. Get rid of all your extra credit cards
13. Hold weekly "family meetings" to coordinate schedules
14. Learn the art of speed cleaning: You can learn to clean the average house in under two hours
15. Create a travel check-list so you can zip through packing
16. Assign chores to your children—
17. And keep *increasing* their responsibilities (and allowances) every year
18. Shop by catalog whenever possible
19. Do your holiday shopping *way* in advance

1357. Propose in front of the Grand Hotel, Mackinac Island, Michigan
1358. Write a little love note on your mate's dinner napkin
1359. Have a dozen red roses delivered to your restaurant table
1360. Wear matching winter scarves
1361. Musical lovenote: "Play the CD *Songs in the Key of Life, Volume 2*, by Stevie

Wonder. Listen to song No. 6"

1362. Volunteer to walk the dog on a cold winter night

1363. "Love is always expressed by making a sacrifice."
~ Swami Chinmayaananda

1364. Tip for writing love letters: Don't worry about being poetic or eloquent. What matters is the thought, the effort, and the emotion

1365. Read *1001 **More** Ways To Be Romantic*, by Gregory J.P. Godek

1366. Love Coupon: Good for one afternoon of window shopping with the coupon giver. Transportation and lunch included. Wishing and dreaming are encouraged.
No purchase necessary

1367–1377
11 *Little* Touches That Can Make a *Big* Difference

1. Wrap all presents in her favorite color

2. A single rose on her pillow
3. For an anniversary note or certificate, use fonts that were popular that year
4. The *perfect* perfume or cologne
5. Spray a favorite perfume or cologne on a love letter
6. Bathe together—*by candlelight*
7. TGIF: Unwind together with wine and cheese
8. Kiss the nape of her neck
9. *Matching* bra and panty sets
10. Guys: Hold open doors for her
11. Satin sheets on the bed

1378. Seduce your partner tonight
1379. Be loving *even when you don't feel like it*
1380. A good read: *This Is My Beloved,* by Walter Benton
1381. Get him that car he's been dreaming of his whole life
1382. Go for a walk in the woods
1383. Make love with the only goal being to prolong arousal as long as possible
1384. Be romantic only on days that end in the letter "Y"

1385. The "Romantic I.O.U." Coupon:
You are entitled to one evening of
romance—on an evening *next month*
chosen by you

1386. The Classic "Bubblebath-For-One"
Coupon: You'll be pampered with
scented bubblebath and refreshments

1387. Sign your love letters: "Your adoring
subject"

1388. Romantic Resource: *New Think: The
Use of Lateral Thinking*, by E. DeBono

1389. Drop hints about an upcoming
mystery date

1390. Love Enhancer: Patience

1391. For engaged gals: Make a photocopy
of your hand and new engagement
ring. Mail it to him with a note: "I've
got a piece of the rock"

1392. Visit theme parks across the
country...

1393. Disneyland in Anaheim, California

1394. Sea World of California in San Diego

1395. Six Flags Great Adventure in Jackson,
New Jersey

1396. Knott's Berry Farm in Buena Park, California
1397. Sea World of Florida in Orlando, Florida
1398. Paramount's Kings Island in Kings Island, Ohio
1399. Magic Kingdom at Walt Disney World in Lake Buena Vista, Florida
1400. Santa Cruz Beach Boardwalk in Santa Cruz, California
1401. Busch Gardens in Tampa, Florida
1402. Epcot Center in Lake Buena Vista, Florida
1403. Cedar Point in Sandusky, Ohio

1404. Take turns
1405. Take her out to dinner
1406. Take him out to the ballgame
1407. (Buy him some peanuts and Cracker Jack)

1408. Give her some Fireballs candies with a note: "I'm hot for you!"
1409. Love Coupon: Entitling you to a night of watching shooting stars together

1410. Make homemade Christmas
ornaments

1411–1420

**10 Most Important Relationship
Issues Ranked in Order—by Readers
of *Marriage Magazine***

1. Intimacy
2. Communication
3. Spirituality
4. Sexuality and sensuality
5. Dealing with adversity
6. Leisure/humor/play
7. Self-empowerment
8. Family
9. Romance
10. Rituals and celebrations

♥ How would *you and your partner* rank
these issues?
♥ How would you *grade yourselves* in
each area?
♥ Would you add any issues to this list?
♥ How are you going to improve in
each area?

1421. Create your own series of custom greeting cards that use lyrics from songs

1422. Throw a party specifically to *honor* your partner

1423. Eat dinner at the best Cajun restaurant around

1424. Emulate those rare couples who have an A+ Relationship

1425. Drink from two champagne flutes with your initials engraved on them

1426. Gather romantic ideas from your friends

1427. Hide a stuffed animal in his gym bag

1428. Does your partner have a "namesake" town?

1429. Plan a surprise trip there

1430. Get postcards and brochures from the town

1431. Have a love letter postmarked from the town

1432–1832
401 "Namesake" Towns Across America
Ada: Kansas, Minnesota, Ohio, Oklahoma

Adrian: Georgia, Michigan, Minnesota,
        Missouri, Oregon, Texas, West
        Virginia
Albert: Kansas
Alberta: Virginia
Alexander: Kansas, North Dakota, Texas
Alexandria: Indiana, Kentucky, Louisiana,
        Minnesota, Missouri, New
        Hampshire, Nebraska, Ohio, South
        Dakota, Tennessee, Virginia
Alfred: Maine, New York, North Dakota
Alice: Texas
Alicia: Arkansas
Allen: Kansas, Kentucky, Nebraska, South
        Dakota, Texas
Allison: Colorado, Iowa
Alvin: Illinois, Texas
Amanda: Ohio
Amber: Oklahoma
Amelia: Louisiana, Nebraska, Ohio
Angelica: New York
Angie: Louisiana
Anita: Iowa, Pennsylvania
Anna: Illinois, Texas
Annabella: Utah

Anna Maria: Florida
Annette: Alabama
Anson: Maine, Texas
Anthony: Florida, Kansas, New Mexico,
    Rhode Island
Anton: Colorado, Texas
Archie: Missouri
Arden: California, Nevada
Arial: South Carolina
Arnold: California, Kansas, Maryland,
    Missouri, Nebraska, Pennsylvania
Arthur: Illinois, Nebraska, North Dakota
Arvin: California
Ashley: Illinois, Indiana, North Dakota, Ohio
Aubrey: Arkansas, Texas
Austin: Kentucky, Minnesota, Nevada,
    Pennsylvania, Texas
Ava: Illinois, Missouri, New York
Avery: California, Idaho, Texas
Barry: Illinois, Texas
Beatrice: Alabama, Nebraska
Benjamin: Texas
Bennett: Colorado, North Carolina,
    Wisconsin
Benson: Arizona, Minnesota, North

Carolina, Vermont
Bernard: Maine
Bernice: Louisiana
Bernie: Missouri
Bertha: Minnesota
Bethany: Illinois, Missouri, Ohio, Oklahoma
Beverly: Kansas, Massachusetts, New Jersey,
Ohio, Texas, Washington
Bill: Wyoming
Blaine: Kentucky, Maine, Minnesota,
Washington
Blair: Nebraska, Oklahoma, Wisconsin
Boyce: Louisiana
Boyd: Minnesota, Montana, Texas
Bradford: Arkansas, Illinois, Maine, New
Hampshire, Ohio, Pennsylvania,
Rhode Island, Tennessee, Vermont
Bradley: Arkansas, California, Illinois, Maine,
South Dakota, West Virginia
Brent: Alabama
Bronson: Florida, Kansas, Michigan, Texas
Bronte: Texas
Bruce: Mississippi, South Dakota, Wisconsin
Bruno: Michigan
Bryan: Ohio, Texas

Bryant: Arkansas, Florida, South Dakota,
     Wisconsin
Buford: Colorado, Georgia, Wyoming
Burke: Idaho, New York, South Dakota,
     Virginia
Burton: Michigan, Nebraska, Ohio, Texas,
     Washington
Byron: California, Georgia, Illinois, Maine,
     Minnesota, Oklahoma, Wyoming
Cameron: Arizona, Louisiana, Missouri,
     Montana, North Carolina, South
     Carolina, Texas, West Virginia,
     Wisconsin
Carlton: Kansas, Minnesota, Oregon, Texas,
     Washington
Carlyle: Illinois, Montana
Carmen: Indiana, Oklahoma
Carroll: Iowa, Maine, Nebraska
Carter: Kentucky, Montana, Oklahoma,
     South Dakota, Wisconsin, Wyoming
Cary: Maine, Mississippi, North Carolina
Casey: Illinois, Iowa
Catharine: Alabama
Cecil: Georgia, Oregon, Pennsylvania,
     Wisconsin

Cecilia: Kentucky
Celeste: Texas
Celina: Ohio, Tennessee, Texas
Chandler: Arizona, Indiana, Minnesota,
        Oklahoma, Texas
Charlotte: Michigan, North Carolina,
        Tennessee, Texas, Vermont
Chelsea: Alabama, Massachusetts, Michigan,
        Oklahoma, Vermont
Christian: Alaska
Christiana: Tennessee
Christina: Montana
Christine: North Dakota, Texas
Christopher: Illinois
Clairemont: Texas
Clancy: Montana
Clara: Mississippi
Clare: Michigan
Clarence: Iowa, Missouri, New York
Clarissa: Minnesota
Clark: Colorado, South Dakota
Claude: Texas
Cliff: New Mexico
Clifford: Kentucky
Clint: Texas

Clyde: California, Kansas, New York, North
        Carolina, North Dakota, Ohio, Texas
Cody: Nebraska, Wyoming
Conrad: Iowa, Montana
Cornelius: North Carolina, Oregon
Courtenay: North Dakota
Craig: Alaska, Colorado, Kansas, Missouri,
        Montana, Nebraska
Crissey: Ohio
Crystal: Maine, Minnesota, North Dakota
Curtis: Arkansas
Cyril: Oklahoma
Cyrus: Minnesota
Dale: Illinois, Indiana, Oregon, Texas,
        Wisconsin
Dana: Indiana
Daniel: Maryland, Wyoming
Davy: West Virginia
Dawn: Texas
Dennis: Massachusetts, North Carolina
Devon: Kentucky, Montana, Pennsylvania
Dexter: Georgia, Iowa, Kansas, Kentucky,
        Maine, Michigan, Missouri, New
        Mexico, New York
Diana: Texas

Dixie: Alabama, Georgia, Idaho, Washington
Dolores: Colorado
Domingo: New Mexico
Donna: Texas
Donovan: Illinois
Douglas: Arizona, Georgia, Michigan, North
    Dakota, Oklahoma, Wyoming
Drake: North Dakota
Drew: Mississippi, Oregon
Dudley: Georgia, Massachusetts
Duke: Alabama, Oklahoma
Duncan: Arizona, Mississippi, Nebraska,
    Oklahoma
Dustin: Oklahoma
Dusty: New Mexico
Dwight: Illinois, Kansas, Nebraska
Earle: Arkansas
Edgar: Montana, Nebraska, Wisconsin
Edina: Minnesota, Missouri
Edith: Georgia
Edmond: Kansas, Oklahoma
Edna: Kansas, Texas
Elbert: Colorado, Texas
Eleanor: West Virginia
Elizabeth: Illinois, Louisiana, Minnesota,

Mississippi, New Jersey, West
Virginia
Elliott: South Carolina
Elmer: Missouri, New Jersey, Oklahoma
Elmira: New York
Elsie: Michigan, Nebraska
Elwood: Illinois, Indiana, Kansas, Nebraska
Ely: Minnesota, Nevada
Emily: Minnesota
Enid: Mississippi, Montana, Oklahoma
Erick: Oklahoma
Erin: Tennessee
Ester: Alaska
Ethan: South Dakota
Ethel: Mississippi, Washington, West Virginia
Eugene: Oregon
Eunice: Louisiana, New Mexico
Eva: Tennessee
Everett: Georgia, Massachusetts,
Pennsylvania, Washington
Faith: South Dakota
Felicity: Ohio
Ferdinand: Indiana
Floyd: Louisiana, New Mexico, Virginia
Francis: Oklahoma, Utah

Frannie: Wyoming
Frederic: Michigan, Wisconsin
Frederick: Colorado, Maryland, Oklahoma,
        South Dakota
Gail: Texas
Garrett: Indiana, Kentucky, Wyoming
Gary: Indiana, Minnesota, South Dakota,
        Texas
Gay: West Virginia
Geneva: Alabama, Georgia, Idaho, Illinois,
        Indiana, Minnesota, Nebraska, New
        York, Ohio
George: Iowa, Washington
Georgiana: Alabama
Gerald: Missouri
Gifford: Florida, Pennsylvania, Washington
Gilbert: Louisiana, Minnesota, Oregon, West
        Virginia
Girard: Georgia, Illinois, Kansas, Ohio,
        Pennsylvania, Texas
Gisela: Arizona
Gladys: Virginia
Gordon: Alaska, Georgia, Nebraska, Texas,
        Wisconsin
Grace: Idaho

Grady: Arkansas, New Mexico
Graham: North Carolina, Texas
Grant: Michigan, Montana, Nebraska,
    Oklahoma
Gregory: South Dakota, Texas
Griffith: Indiana
Grover: Colorado, Pennsylvania, Wyoming
Hale: Colorado, Michigan, Missouri
Hanna: Arkansas, Indiana, Oklahoma, Utah,
    Wyoming
Hannah: North Dakota
Harlan: Indiana, Iowa, Kansas, Kentucky,
    Oregon
Harris: Minnesota, Oklahoma
Harvey: Illinois, Louisiana, North Dakota
Hazel: Kentucky, South Dakota
Hector: Arkansas, Minnesota
Henrietta: New York, North Carolina, Texas
Henry: Illinois, Nebraska, South Dakota
Herman: Michigan, Minnesota, Nebraska
Hernando: Mississippi
Holly: Colorado, Michigan, Washington
Homer: Alaska, Georgia, Illinois, Louisiana,
    Michigan, Nebraska, New York
Hope: Alaska, Arkansas, Idaho, Indiana,

Kansas, New Mexico, North Dakota,
Rhode Island
Horace: Kansas, North Dakota
Horatio: Arkansas
Howard: Kansas, South Dakota
Hugo: Colorado, Minnesota, Oklahoma
Ida: Louisiana
Ignacio: California, Colorado
Ina: Illinois
Inez: Kentucky, Texas
Iona: Idaho, Minnesota, South Dakota
Ira: Texas
Irma: Wisconsin
Irving: Texas
Irwin: Texas, Pennsylvania
Isabel: Kansas, South Dakota
Isabela: Puerto Rico
Isabella: Minnesota
Ivan: Arkansas
Jay: Florida, Maine, New York, Oklahoma
Jean: Nevada, Tennessee
Jena: Florida
Jennie: Arkansas
Jerome: Arizona, Arkansas, Idaho,
Pennsylvania

Joanna: South Carolina
Joaquin: Texas
Johnson: Kansas, Nebraska, Vermont
Jordan: Alabama, Minnesota, Montana, New
      York
Joseph: Alaska, Oregon, Utah
Joshua: Texas
Joy: Illinois
Juanita: Washington
Judson: North Dakota
Julian: California
Kathryn: North Dakota
Katy: Texas
Kaycee: Wyoming
Kelly: Kentucky, Louisiana, Wyoming
Kendall: Florida, Kansas, New York,
      Wisconsin
Kenney: Illinois
Kent: Connecticut, Minnesota, Ohio,
      Oregon, Texas, Washington
Kevin: Montana
Kimberly: Idaho, Oregon, Wisconsin
Kirby: Arkansas, Texas, Wyoming
Kirk: Colorado
Kyle: South Dakota, Texas

Lacey: Washington
Lambert: Mississippi, Montana
Lane: South Carolina, South Dakota
Laurel: Delaware, Indiana, Maryland,
       Mississippi, Montana, Nebraska,
       Virginia
La Verne: California
Laverne: Oklahoma
Lavonia: Georgia
Lawrence: Indiana, Kansas, Massachusetts,
       Michigan, Mississippi, Nebraska,
       New York, Pennsylvania
Lee: Florida, Maine, Massachusetts, Nevada
Lena: Illinois, Louisiana, Mississippi,
       Wisconsin
Lenoir: North Carolina
Lenora: Kansas
Leo: Indiana
Leon: Iowa, Kansas, Oklahoma, West Virginia
Leonard: North Dakota, Texas
Leroy: Alabama
Leslie: Arkansas, Georgia, Idaho, Michigan
Lester: Washington
Lewis: Colorado, Indiana, Iowa, Kansas,
       New York

Libby: Montana
Lilly: Georgia, Kentucky, South Dakota,
      Wisconsin
Linda: California
Lindsay: California, Montana, Nebraska,
      Oklahoma
Livonia: Michigan, New York
Lloyd: Florida, Montana
Logan: Iowa, Kansas, Montana, New
      Mexico, Ohio, Utah, West Virginia
Loleta: California
Lolita: Texas
Loretta: Wisconsin
Lorraine: New York
Louann: Arkansas
Louisa: Kentucky, Virginia
Louise: Mississippi, Texas
Lucas: Iowa, Kansas, Michigan, Ohio, South
      Dakota
Lucerne: California, Missouri, Washington
Lucy: Tennessee
Lulu: Florida
Luther: Michigan, Montana, Oklahoma
Lydia: Minnesota, South Carolina
Lyle: Minnesota, Washington

Lyndon: Illinois, Kansas, Vermont
Lynn: Alabama, Indiana, Massachusetts
Mabel: Minnesota
Madeline: California
Marcella: Arkansas
Marcus: Iowa, South Dakota, Washington
Margaret: Texas
Margie: Minnesota
Marianna: Arkansas, Florida
Marissa: Illinois
Martha: Oklahoma
Martin: Kentucky, Michigan, North Dakota,
     South Dakota, Tennessee
Mason: Illinois, Michigan, Nevada, Ohio,
     Tennessee, Texas, Wisconsin
Mathias: West Virginia
Maud: Ohio, Oklahoma, Texas
Maurice: Louisiana
Maury: North Carolina
Max: Nebraska, North Carolina
Maxwell: California, Iowa, Nebraska, New
     Mexico
May: Idaho, Oklahoma, Texas
Melba: Ohio
Merlin: Oregon

Merrill: Iowa, Mississippi, Oregon,
       Wisconsin
Mildred: Montana, Pennsylvania
Milo: Iowa, Maine
Mitchell: Georgia, Illinois, Indiana,
       Nebraska, Oregon, South Dakota
Mona: Utah
Morgan: Georgia, Minnesota, Pennsylvania,
       Texas, Utah
Morley: Michigan, Missouri
Morton: Illinois, Minnesota, Mississippi,
       Texas, Wyoming
Murphy: Idaho, Missouri, North Carolina,
       Oregon
Murray: Iowa, Kentucky, Utah
Myrtle: Mississippi
Nancy: Kentucky
Neal: Kansas
Nelson: Arizona, Georgia, Nebraska, Nevada,
       Pennsylvania
Neville: Pennsylvania
Nicolaus: California
Noel: Missouri
Nora: Illinois, Virginia
Norma: South Dakota

Norman: Arkansas, Oklahoma
Olga: North Dakota, Washington
Olivia: Minnesota
Ollie: Kentucky
Opal: South Dakota, Wyoming
Pablo: Montana
Paulina: Oregon
Pearl: Mississippi, Texas
Philip: South Dakota
Pierce: Colorado, Idaho, Nebraska
Pierre: South Dakota
Prentice: Wisconsin
Prentiss: Maine, Mississippi
Preston: Georgia, Idaho, Iowa, Kansas,
          Minnesota, Missouri, Oklahoma
Quinn: South Dakota
Ralph: South Dakota
Ramona: California, Kansas, Oklahoma,
          South Dakota
Randall: Kansas, Minnesota
Ray: North Dakota
Rebecca: Georgia
Rector: Arkansas
Rhonda: Kentucky
Richey: Montana

Roberta: Georgia
Roscoe: Montana, New York, Nebraska,
        South Dakota, Texas
Rose: Nebraska
Rosita: Texas
Roslynn: New York, Pennsylvania, South
        Dakota, Washington
Ross: Nebraska
Ruby: Alaska, South Carolina
Rudy: Arkansas
Russell: Arkansas, Iowa, Kansas, Kentucky,
        Minnesota, New York, Pennsylvania
Ruth: Mississippi, Nevada
Ryan: Oklahoma
Sarah: Mississippi
Savanna: Illinois, Oklahoma
Savannah: Georgia, Missouri, Tennessee
Scott: Georgia, Louisiana, Mississippi,
        Pennsylvania
Selma: Alabama, California, North Carolina,
        Oregon, Texas
Shelley: Idaho
Sherman: Maine, Mississippi, New York,
        Texas
Shirley: Arkansas, Indiana, Massachusetts,

New York
Sidney: Iowa, Montana, Nebraska, New
York, Ohio, Texas
Stella: Nebraska
Stephan: North Dakota
Stephen: Minnesota
Stewart: Minnesota, Mississippi, Nevada, Ohio
Stuart: Florida, Iowa, Nebraska, Oklahoma,
Virginia
Sylvester: Georgia, Texas
Sylvia: Kansas
Terry: Mississippi, Montana
Theodore: Alabama
Theresa: New York
Thomas: Oklahoma, West Virginia
Tony: Wisconsin
Tracy: California, Minnesota
Tyrone: New Mexico, Oklahoma, Pennsylvania
Ulysses: Kansas, Nebraska, Pennsylvania
Van: Texas
Vaughn: Montana, New Mexico, Washington
Vera: Oklahoma, Texas
Victor: Colorado, Idaho, Iowa, Montana,
New York
Victoria: Illinois, Kansas, Texas, Virginia

Vincent: Alabama, Texas
Violet: Louisiana
Virgil: Kansas, South Dakota
Virginia: Alabama, Idaho, Illinois, Minnesota
Vivian: Louisiana, South Dakota
Wesley: Iowa, Maine
Wilbur: Oregon, Washington
Willard: Montana, New Mexico, Ohio, Utah
Willis: Texas, Virginia
Winston: New Mexico, Oregon
Wynne: Arkansas
Wynona: Oklahoma

1833. If he was in the military, have a
       21-gun salute wake him on his
       next big birthday

1834. Bring home one flower a day for a
       solid month

1835. To get in the mood for an upcoming
       vacation, rent movies that take place
       in that location

1836. *Double* the length of your average
       lovemaking session

1837. "Love is the most wonderful thing in
       the world." ~ Francoise Sagan

1838. Sing her a song

1839. The "Love Phone" Coupon: On a day of the coupon-holder's choice, the coupon-giver will call you once an hour all day long and give one reason why he or she loves you

1840. Share a steamy hot cocoa on a frosty winter evening

1841. Collect romantic and inspirational quotes

1842. Write them in a journal and give it to your partner as a gift

1843. Frame the quotes that best express your love

1844. Remember: Money can't buy you love—

1845. But it *can* rent you a little romance!

1846. Have a bed custom-designed for the two of you

1847. Create a "Valentine Ad" on a local cable TV station

1848. Take turns taking the romantic lead

1849. End the day in a special way: Give each other a massage

1850. Leave a love note on an Etch-A-Sketch

1851. The Soothing "Hot Tub for Two" Coupon: The coupon-giver will secure an hour in a Jacuzzi for the two of you. Aaahh!

1852. Share a sauna

1853. Exercise more—so you'll be a healthier lover

1854. Eat better—so you'll be around longer to enjoy one another

1855. Read more—so you'll have more to talk about

1856. Meditate regularly—to center yourself

1857. Take a class—to improve your self-esteem

1858. Slow down—and savor life more

1859. Write a short essay together, titled "What We've Learned About Marriage"

1860. Have it rendered in calligraphy and frame it

1861. Submit it to your local weekly newspaper for publication

1862. Submit it to *Marriage Magazine* (955 Lade Dr., St. Paul, MN 55120)

1863. Include it with every engagement gift and wedding gift you give to others

---

1864. The "Bicycle-Built-For-Two" Coupon: The coupon-giver will secure the bike, pack a picnic lunch, and plan a romantic afternoon

1865. Stay at the fanciest hotel in Amsterdam: The Pulitzer

1866. Copy the lyrics from a hymn that is especially meaningful to you

1867. Be sensitive

1868. Keep candles in your glove compartment at all times— just in case

1869. Place an elegantly giftwrapped item inconspicuously on the fireplace mantle, and see how long it takes him/her to notice it

1870. Act like newlyweds
1871. Act like you did on your first date
1872. Act like your favorite movie couple
1873. Take an acting class together; it will help you express emotions!

1874. Be charming
1875. Be thoughtful
1876. Be outrageous
1877. Be yourself

1878. Romance is the icing on the cake of your relationship
1879. So spread it on *thick*

1880. Enemy of Love: Too many responsibilities
1881. Compliment him on his cooking
1882. Plan to be spontaneous
1883. Say "I love you"—and really, really, really, really, *really* mean it!
1884. Give each other a "trinket gift" every day you're on vacation
1885. Buy $50 of greeting cards—so you'll always be prepared

1886–1904

19 Ways for Guys to *Stun* Their Gals with Romance

1. Take her out to dinner during the Superbowl. (Record it and watch it later!)
2. Get tickets to a *sold-out* show
3. Wear a tuxedo home from work and take her out for a night on the town
4. Create (what she considers to be) the "Perfect Romantic Date"
5. Send her on a $500 shopping spree at the Mall of America!
6. Arrange a surprise second honeymoon to her dream vacation spot
7. Upgrade the quality of the diamond in her engagement ring
8. Treat her to a Saturday evening of *sensual* (not *sexual*) delights
9. Read *You Just Don't Understand*, by Deborah Tannen, and discuss it with her
10. Tell her you want to learn how to help her experience multiple orgasms

11. Rent, and watch with her: *Casablanca* on Friday night, *Gone with the Wind* on Saturday night, and *Titanic* on Sunday night

12. Make love by catering to *her* sexual desires 100%—and putting *your* sexual desires on hold until tomorrow

13. Get tickets to be in the audience of her favorite daytime talk show

14. Write a love song for your lover

15. Sing her the love song you wrote

16. Have the song professionally recorded on cassette tape—

17. Write the lyrics and present them on a scroll—

18. Have the lyrics rendered in calligraphy—

19. Then have them framed

1905. Gals: Required reading: *Perfect Husbands (& Other Fairy Tales): Demystifying Marriage, Men, and Romance*, by Regina Barreca

1906. Learn to imitate her favorite actor

1907. Wear matching gold rings

1908. Serve homemade lemonade on a hot summer afternoon

1909. Read & learn: *Pairing*, by G. Bach and R. Deutsch

1910. Give one dozen red roses

1911. Save menus as mementos of your dates together

1912. Attend Shakespeare-in-the-Park in NYC's Central Park

1913. As a secret surprise: Set up a hammock in your back yard

---

1914. Compile your combined family history together

1915. Interview each other's grandparents and elderly relatives

1916. Write it down and create a keepsake for your children

1917. Reduce your TV watching by 50%...

1918. Spend half of that time improving *yourself* (reading or exercising)

1919. Spend the other half on improving your *relationship*

1920–1928
9 Ways for Business Executives to Earn Romantic Dividends

1. Use your *business* skills to improve your relationship
2. Use time management techniques so you'll have more time together
3. Use your customer service skills to "keep your 'customer' satisfied"
4. Use your sales skills—instead of lapsing into nagging or complaining
5. Be as considerate of your partner as you are of your best customer
6. Write an "Inter-Office Memo" complimenting him/her for something
7. How could you "give your partner a raise" to show your appreciation?
8. If you can keep your *staff* motivated, you can keep your *mate* motivated!
9. Work some "overtime" on your relationship

1929. The Official Valentine's Day Coupon: In addition to providing you with a heart-shaped box of chocolates and a dozen red roses, the coupon-issuer will treat you like the unique, special, wonderful person you are

1930. Read *On Kissing: Travels in an Intimate Landscape,* by Adrianne Blue

1931. Be the Best Father in the World to her children

1932. Say this: "Will you marry me?"

1933. "Loving is not just caring deeply, it's above all, understanding."
~ Francoise Sagan

1934. Go tobogganing together

1935. Make a custom audio tape of music that makes you feel *young*

1936. Give flowers that match his/her eyes

1937. Make a regular Saturday date: Listen to Garrison Keillor's *Prairie Home Companion* on National Public Radio

1938. Ride the Tunnel of Love at a carnival

1939. Create Valentine cookies

1940. The first ever "Second Valentine's Day of the Year" Coupon: Yes, this coupon allows you to celebrate a *second* Valentine's Day on a day of your choosing! Complete with roses, chocolates, cards, etc.

1941. Read *Creating Love: The Next Stage of Growth*, by John Bradshaw

---

1942. A Classic Dinner Date Coupon: At the most romantic restaurant in town. Coupon-giver's treat
1943. *Another* Dinner Date Coupon: At a local restaurant that you've never visited before
1944. And yet *another* Dinner Date Coupon: The coupon-holder chooses the date, the coupon-giver chooses the restaurant

---

1945. Favorite gifts for women: Jewelry
1946. Favorite gifts for women: Perfume
1947. Favorite gifts for women: Flowers

1948. Visit the Nestle chocolate factory in Broc, Switzerland. Call (41) 296-5151
1949. Buy her a kitten
1950. Trace "I love you" on a stick of butter

1951. While flying, call from the airphone just to say "I love you"

1952. Ask your grandparents to share their secrets for keeping love alive

1953. Spend weekend at a ski lodge, even if you don't like to ski!

1954. A "Carnival Coupon:" Good for a full afternoon of rides on the roller coaster, tilt-a-whirl, Ferris wheel, and merry-go-round

---

1955–1961
7 Best Love Songs by Elvis Presley

1. "I Need Your Love Tonight
2. "I Want You, I Need You, I Love You"
3. "I'm Yours"
4. "(Let Me Be Your) Teddy Bear"
5. "Love Me"
6. "My Wish Came True"
7. "The Wonder of You"

1962. "Don't change a mind; change a mood." ~ Aim Ginott

1963. Use music to change the mood

1964.   You could use soft lighting to change the mood

1965.   Try changing the mood by changing your *attitude*

1966.   How do you get a guy to be more romantic? *Not* by nagging or manipulating!

1967.   How do you get a gal to be more sexual? *Not* by arguing or cajoling

1968.   You can't change another's *mind*—but you *can* change the environment, the context, the mood of your relationship

---

1969.   When he/she's traveling alone, have an airline attendant deliver a gift to your mate mid-flight

1970.   Splurge on a $100 shopping spree at Frederick's of Hollywood

1971.   Reserve your weekends for each other

1972.   Visit the Romantic Love Hall of Fame. Call for information at 877-ROMANCE

1973.   Take your partner on your next

business trip and upgrade your hotel room to the Honeymoon Suite

1974. New parents coupon: "I'll get up in the middle of the night with the baby."

1975. A "Sweet Stuff" Coupon: Redeemable for *lots* of your favorite candy or chocolate

1976. Mail a wedding photo to your partner with a romantic note attached

1977. Share your religious beliefs

1978. "Make the most of yourself, for that is all there is of you."
~ Ralph Waldo Emerson

1979. Generate 33% more laughter in your life together

1980. Use the song "All of Me" as part of your marriage proposal

1981. Give flowers that begin with the first letter of your lover's name

1982. Write cartoon caption balloons for some funny photos

1983. Touch your partner—*with your eyes*

1984. Touch your partner—*with your words*
1985. Touch your partner—*with your actions*
1986. Touch your partner—*with gifts and presents*

1987. This year: Give twenty *small, inexpensive* gifts for Christmas
1988. Next year: Give just one *perfect, elegant, special* gift
1989. The following year: Give gifts that all reflect a *music* theme
1990. And the next year: Give gifts that all reflect a *sports* theme
1991. And the year after that: Give nothing but *books*
1992. And the year after that: Give gifts that all reflect a *travel* theme
1993. And the year after that: Give the "Gift of Time": Twenty-five hours of your time

---

1994. On your wedding day: Get a friend to buy fifty current magazines and newspapers
1995. Hide them away—then present them

to your partner on your 25th anniversary

1996. Do a *Cosmo* quiz together
1997. Hire a housecleaning service to free more time for yourselves
1998. The "Sex-Sex-Sex" Coupon: The coupon giver promises to fulfill one sexual fantasy of the coupon holder's choosing. Participants must be at least 18 years of age
1999. Meet for lunch every Wednesday
2000. Reduce your complaining by 50% and your criticizing by 62%

Favorite Love Songs from 1926
2001. "After I Say I'm Sorry"
2002. "If I Could Be with You One Hour To-Night"
2003. "Someone to Watch over Me"
2004. "You Made Me Love You"

2005. An "Adventure Date" Coupon: Your partner will take you somewhere neither of you have been. Not for the timid

2006. Enemy of Love: Over-reliance on logic

2007. The "Ultimate Pizza Date" Coupon: The coupon-holder chooses the pizza joint and the toppings. Coupon-giver's treat!

2008. Go for a walk on the beach

2009. Read famous people's love letters in *Love Letters*, edited by Antonia Fraser

2010. When staying with relatives, intentionally choose to sleep together in a single bed

---

2011. Have a pillow fight

2012. Have a pillow embroidered with your names

2013. Get some heart-shaped pillows

2014. Get monogrammed pillow covers

2015. Get a blow-up airplane neck pillow for your traveler

2016. Get a "maternity body pillow" when she's pregnant

2017. Save the ring bearer's satin pillow from your wedding

2018. Learn the subtle art of "pillowtalk"

2019–2024
6 Film Festivals to Attend
with Your Movie Buff

1. Chicago International Film Festival, October: (312) 644-FILM

2. Hawaii International Film Festival, December: (808) 944-7007

3. New York Film Festival, June: (212) 362-1911

4. Seattle International Film Festival, June: (206) 324-9996

5. Telluride Film Festival, August: (603) 643-1255

6. Wine Valley Film Festival, July: (707) 935-FILM

2025. Create quirky, custom "tickets" for your lover—

2026. Season tickets for "Friday Night Mattress Testing"

2027. A ticket for "Dinner for Two at Home (Formal attire required)"

2028. Always have tapes of romantic, acoustic music in the car

2029. A ticket to "A Personal Striptease"

2030. The "Queen for a Day" Coupon:
The female coupon-holder is entitled
to be treated like royalty for a
twenty-four hour period

2031. Give your partner a small national
flag from the country his ancestors
came from

2032. Plant a rose garden together

2033. A Cuddle Coupon: Good for two
hours of cuddling with the coupon-
issuer in front of a roaring fire or on
a porch swing

2034. The ultimate pizza cookbook: *Pizza*,
by James McNair

2035. Barely Nothings Catalog:
(800) 4-BARELY

2036. Dream Dresser Catalog:
(800) 963-7326

2037. Frederick's of Hollywood Catalog:
(800) 323-9525

2038. Maitresse Lingerie Catalog:
(800) 456-8464

2039. The Outlet: (800) 599-3283

2040. Playboy Catalog: (800) 423-9494

2041. Victoria's Secret Catalog:
(800) 888-8200

2042. Memorize "How Do I Love Thee
(Let Me Count the Ways)" by
Elizabeth Barrett Browning
2043. Love Enhancer: Empathy
2044. Bake an outrageous French pastry
2045. Stick up for your partner at all times
2046. Take an enlightening vacation at
The Esalen Institute, in Big Sur,
California: (408) 667-3000
2047. Musical lovenote: "Play the CD
Christopher Cross; my message to
you is song No. 1"
2048. A first anniversary card idea: "Happy
50th Anniversary—49 years in
advance!"

2049–2058
10 Ways to Turn a Simple Bubblebath
into a Memorable Romantic Event
1. Float rose petals in the bathtub
2. Add scented bath oils
3. Add floating candles

4. Add champagne
5. Add cheese and crackers
6. Add soft music
7. Add a book to read
8. Have romantic music playing in the background
9. Do all of the above in a *heart-shaped bathtub*—
10. At a honeymoon resort *in the Poconos*

2059. Pack a dozen of his favorite cookies in his suitcase
2060. For an Elvis fan: Get collector's original singles of all eighteen of his No. 1 hits
2061. A "Kids-Free Day!" Coupon: You two get to play all day—*and* all night—as the coupon-giver finds a caretaker for the kids for twenty-four hours
2062. Romantic Opera Alert: Mozart's *The Magic Flute*
2063. Compliment her on her looks
2064. Buy her cotton candy
2065. Get an autographed photo of his/her favorite athlete

2066. Drape a giant banner in front of your house to celebrate his/her return from a trip

2067. Stay married—through thick and thin

2068. When you're in the car together, tune-in to her favorite station

---

2069–2078

10 Ways to Drive Your Lover *Crazy*

1. Write love notes on all six sides of a Rubik's Cube, then scramble it!

2. Leave tantalizing messages in her voice mail

3. Engage in three hours of foreplay

4. Give him hints about what his birthday gift is

5. While he/she's out of town, have "phone sex" every day

6. Wrap a *tiny* gift in a box, inside a larger box, inside a larger box, etc.

7. Send a series of sexy notes signed from "A Secret Admirer"

8. Call him at work and describe in *excruciating detail* the sexy lingerie

you're wearing and what you want to
do to him

9. Place her wrapped birthday gift on
the mantle *a week early*, and drive her
crazy with anticipation

10. Circle a date in her calendar in red,
but don't tell her *why*

2079. Gals: Don't mess with his work bench

2080. Christmas stockings

2081. Bake him a pie

2082. Hang a romantic print by
Impressionist painter Paul Cézanne

2083. The "Indoor Picnic" Coupon: You
pick the date, and your partner
provides the basket full of goodies

2084. A "Carnival" Coupon: Good for a
day at the fair. Included: Unlimited
rides and all the cotton candy you
can eat

2085. Give one dozen pink roses

2086. Create a personalized "Music CD-of-
the-Month Club"

2087. Take your car nut to the car show

2088. Take your gardener to the flower show
2089. Take your space nut to Cape Canaveral
2090. Take your fashionable mate to some designer fashion shows
2091. Take your boating enthusiast to the boat show
2092. Take your Trekkie to a Star Trek convention
2093. Take your baseball fan to the World Series
2094. Take your history buff on a tour of European cathedrals
2095. Take your art lover to the Getty Museum in Los Angeles
2096. Take your race fan to some NASCAR races
2097. Take your ski bum to the Swiss Alps
2098. Take your chef to a gourmet cooking class
2099. Take your motorcyclist to a bike rally
2100. Take your history buff on a tour of Civil War battlefields
2101. Take your theater buff to a Broadway show

2102. Take your sun worshiper to Waikiki
2103. Take your sci-fi fan to the Palomar Observatory
2104. Take your "star gazer" to Hollywood's Avenue of the Stars
2105. Take your tennis fan to Wimbledon

2106. The Wine Lover's Coupon: Redeemable for a favorite bottle of wine. Coupon-holder's choice; coupon giver's treat!
2107. Understand your feelings of jealousy
2108. The "Field of Dreams" Coupon: Redeemable for a relaxing afternoon in a quiet meadow. Picnic and romantic companionship included
2109. Dine atop a revolving restaurant
2110. Say "I love you" 300% more often
2111. When window shopping, secretly note what your partner likes, and return later to pick up that something special
2112. Discuss what comes to mind for each of you when you think of a "Romantic Rendezvous"

2113. Find a "personal shopper" to help you run romantic errands

2114. Celebrate Beethoven's birthday: December 16

2115. Visit the country where your partner's family came from

---

2116. Use flowers to send *specific* messages of love

2117. Ambrosia symbolizes—Love returned

2118. Amethyst symbolizes—Admiration

2119. Azalea symbolizes—Romance

2120. Camellia symbolizes—Steadfast love

2121. Pink carnations mean—"I'll never forget you"

2122. Cherry blossom symbolizes—Spiritual beauty

2123. Daisies symbolize—Innocence

2124. Gardenias mean—"You're lovely"

2125. Geraniums mean—"A secret rendezvous"

2126. Hazel symbolizes—Reconciliation

2127. Iris symbolizes—A flame of passion

2128. Lilac symbolizes—New love & innocence

2129. Lily symbolizes—Sweetness & purity
2130. Orchids mean—"You're beautiful"
2131. Peach means—"You're unique"
2132. Rosemary symbolizes—Remembrance
2133. Tulips (red) mean—"My perfect lover"
2134. Tulips mean—"You mean everything to me"
2135. Violets mean—Faithfulness

2136. Eat dinner at the most expensive restaurant in town
2137. Choose *fresh* flowers—they'll last *much* longer
2138. If he/she's a fanatical dog/cat lover, get gifts for the pet, too!
2139. "In love and war don't seek counsel." ~ French proverb
2140. Give her a scarf that pictures her favorite flowers
2141. Fill the freezer with twelve boxes of his favorite kind of Girl Scout Cookie
2142. A+ Rating, Romantic Music Artist:

Richard Clayderman

2143. Give him a football signed by his favorite player

2144. Communicate better: Read *A Couples' Guide to Communication*, by John Gottman

2145. Love Coupon: An Evening of Dancing: Kick up your heels for a night on the town!

2146. Have a gourmet picnic—complete with candelabra and music

---

2147. Create a series of gifts and gestures with "crazy in love" as the theme

2148. Note: There are six songs and two movies listed in this book with "crazy" in their titles. Can you find them? Can you use them?

2149. "A love song is just a caress set to music." ~ Sigmund Romberg

2150. Create an audio tape of songs that fit this description

2151. Some suggestions: "Make It with You," Bread

2152. "Lost in Love," Air Supply
2153. Attach to the audio tape a note that is a "caress set to *words*"

2154. Incorporate more music into your day-to-day life together
2155. The Great Ski Weekend Coupon: Included: One snowy mountain, one Swiss chalet, and two days of downhill fun
2156. Mood music: Create a light-hearted mood with the *Picnic Suite* CD by Jean-Pierre Rampal and Claude Bolling
2157. Single guys: Never wrap *anything* in a ring box except an engagement ring
2158. The "Romantic Rowboat" Coupon: Your host will man the oars for a romantic afternoon on a local lake with you
2159. Love Coupon: Good for three wishes. The coupon-giver will be your personal genie. "Your wish is my command!" (Wishes must be legal, affordable, and physically possible to

perform)

2160. Be unconventional
2161. Save one flower from *every* bouquet
he gives you, and create a new
bouquet of dried flowers
2162. Giftwrap all presents in a special way
2163. "The Half-Day-Off-Work" Coupon:
The coupon-giver will arrange with
your employer for a half a day off
work for you
2164. Give him cologne that turns you on
2165. Plan a three-day weekend—as a
surprise for your partner
2166. For parents: Create more time for
yourselves by creating a "Neighborhood
Child-Sharing Program"
2167. For coffee lovers: Buy a gift certificate
from Starbucks

2168–2174
7 Best Love Songs by
Chicago (and/or Peter Cetera)

1. "Glory of Love" (Peter Cetera)
2. "I Don't Wanna Live Without
Your Love"

3. "Just You 'n Me"
4. "The Next Time I Fall" (Peter Cetera and Amy Grant)
5. "Stay the Night"
6. "Will You Still Love Me?"
7. "You're the Inspiration"

2175. Hang a romantic print by Impressionist painter Camille Pissarro
2176. Place a new item of jewelry in her jewelry box—and wait for her to discover it
2177. Toast marshmallows over a campfire
2178. Use a thesaurus to help you describe your lover—beautiful, alluring, angelic, bewitching, charming, comely, divine, enticing, exquisite, magnificent, marvelous, pulchritudinous, resplendent, stunning, sublime
2179. Enjoy a winetasting tour in the Napa Valley
2180. Make a cake from scratch
2181. Always, always, *always* follow your heart
2182. "Often the difference between a

successful marriage and a mediocre one consists of leaving about three or four things a day unsaid."
~ Harlan Miller

2183. Creatively create more time for your relationship

2184. Prioritize your household chores into A, B, and C priorities: Do the A's *now*; do the B's next week, and put off the C's until *next year*!

2185. "Just do it": Be more loving more often

2186. "It's the real thing": Love

2187. "Have it *your* way": Lovemaking

2188. "Fly the friendly skies": Join the Mile High Club!

2189. "Reach out and touch someone": Physically *and* emotionally

2190. "*Try* it—you'll *like* it": If you're out of practice, *try* being more loving— you'll *like* it (It's just as much for *you* as it is for your partner)

2191. The "Couple's Campout" Coupon: Good for a romantic night in the woods. The coupon-giver will supply the tent, sleeping bags, campfire, etc.
2192. Eat dinner at the best Japanese restaurant around
2193. Love Enhancer: Goodwill
2194. When sipping champagne, intertwine your arms
2195. Keep this book handy—so you can refer to it at a moment's notice
2196. Love Enhancer: Attentiveness
2197. Give her diamond earrings by putting them on a teddy bear's ears
2198. Give one pink rose

Favorite Love Songs from 1927
2199. "Can't Help Lovin' Dat Man"
2200. "My Heart Stood Still"
2201. "Why Do I Love You?"

2202. Between lovers: Complete honesty is demanded, assumed, and never questioned
2203. For men married more than ten

years: Propose to your wife *again*—
and give her a BIG diamond ring

2204. A+ Romantic Restaurant Rating: Au
Clocher du Village

2205. Send him/her to a local spa every
Friday after work

2206. Give her socks that picture her
favorite flowers

2207. Photograph your children and
make an album

2208. Give one yellow rose

2209–2231

23 Exercises for Tapping into Your Creativity
People with A+ Relationships are more
creative than average folks. These exercises
will jump-start your creativity

1. Give it a twist: Start with something
   basic, then give it a creative twist

2. Change your routine: Shaking up
   your routine often leads to new ideas

3. Consider every crazy idea that pops
   into your head. You won't use them
   all, but the process *expands* your
   thinking

4.   Give yourself a deadline: Sometimes working under pressure works!

5.   Learn from your mistakes

6.   Go with your strengths: Do what comes *naturally*, go with the flow

7.   Go *counter* to your natural strengths: Try something *different*

8.   Tap into your unconscious mind: There's a lot going on beneath the surface

9.   Challenge the assumptions: Don't assume you know it all!

10. Imagine how *someone else* would do it: How would Einstein create new ideas? Mozart? Walt Disney?

11. Use different "models" of thinking: Think *organically*; think like a *cat*; think like a *millionaire*; think like *Rhett Butler*

12. Re-frame the question: The question might be, "How can I be more loving?" Or it might be, "How can I be more *spontaneous*?"

13. Listen to your intuition/sixth sense/Inner Voice

14. Admit that you're *dissatisfied* with the status quo: It will inspire you to find solutions

15. Don't go it alone! Brainstorm romantic ideas with a group of friends

16. Use random ideas to stimulate different avenues of thinking

17. Change your perspective: See the "Big Picture." Look at the *details*

18. Borrow (then customize) ideas! From movies, books, other couples

19. Face your fears: What's holding you back from being more creative? More loving? More spontaneous? More funloving?

20. Draw pictures; doodle; make diagrams; compile lists

21. Try on a different persona: Think like a kid; think like a member of the opposite sex; think like your partner

22. Withhold judgment: Generate *lots* of ideas before you begin evaluating

23. Have fun; don't take this so seriously; play with ideas; be *wacky*

2232. Read *Love Is Letting Go of Fear*, by Gerald Jampolsky

2233. Serve a cake with birthday candles that won't blow out (Ha!)

2234. Save *hundreds* of the little strips of paper from Hershey's Kisses; give them to her in a jewelry box

2235. Eat dinner at the best English pub around

2236. The Whimsical "Holiday at Home" Coupon: The coupon-giver will treat you to an at-home weekend vacation

2237. Review all the Valentine specials at restaurants the week prior to Valentine's Day

2238. Wish upon a falling star

2239. Give compliments

2240. Clip headline words to create a love note in the format of a ransom note

2241. Visit the Grand Ole Opry

2242. Right after Valentine's Day, stock up on heart-themed wrapping paper and boxes

2243. Send love notes via fax

2244. If you travel a lot: Make a habit of

calling every day *no matter what*

2245. Go on a photo safari

2246. The Official Happy Birthday Coupon:
In addition to providing you with a
birthday cake, candles, balloons,
streamers, and a great surprise gift,
the coupon issuer will happily sing
"Happy Birthday to You"

2247–2257
11 Relationship "Experiments" to Try

Experiment #1: Compliment your partner
once-a-day for thirty days in a row

Experiment #2: Stop nagging for one solid
month

Experiment #3: Listen *without interrupting* for
one week

Experiment #4: Try being *totally supportive* of
your partner for one entire week

Experiment #5: For one solid week, *give
without taking*; ask *nothing* of your
partner

Experiment #6: Program your unconscious
mind to *act* on your loving thoughts
whenever they pop up

Experiment #7: Say nothing negative or
judgmental for three days

Experiment #8: Slow down the pace of your
lovemaking: Take *twice* as long as
usual

Experiment #9: Act as if you feel loving—
even if you don't—for one week. Act
like you did when you first fell in
love

Experiment #10: Tell the truth—no fibs,
white lies, or bending the truth—for
one week

Experiment #11: See who can be more
creatively romantic: Take turns being
"it" for one week each, over a period
of two months

2258. Guys: Do something *with* her that
you hate to do

2259. It only counts as a loving gesture if
you do it cheerfully and without
complaint

2260. Go shopping with her, attend a
movie of her choosing

2261. Support and encourage your partner to stop smoking

2262. Make love on a Sunday afternoon

2263. "It is when we earn love least, that we need it most." ~ Anonymous

2264. Give him a cap from his favorite basketball team

2265. The "Sleep-In-Late" Coupon: You are entitled to sleep 'til noon! Your partner will be responsible for the removal of all disturbances

2266. Enemy of Love: Lack of time

2267. "Who you are shouts so loud, I cannot hear what you're saying." ~ Ralph Waldo Emerson

2268. Eat in the most romantic restaurant in Zurich: Tubli

2269. Go out of your way for your partner

2270. Gather a video library of movies starring his/her favorite actor/actress

2271. Love Coupon: This coupon entitles the holder to one sensuous backrub, performed by the issuer of the Coupon: Time limit: No less than thirty minutes in duration!

2272. As part of foreplay, read aloud to him a sexy passage from an erotic book
2273. Massage her feet

2274–2639
366 Things to Celebrate—
Every Day of the Year Is Special!

January 1: Z Day—Honors those who end up last when placed in alphabetical order!

January 2: Isis Celebration—The goddess of love

January 3: Tom Sawyer's Cat's Birthday

January 4: Tom Thumb's Birthday— Honoring all short people

January 5: Twelfth Night—The last of the Twelve Days of Christmas

January 6: Sherlock Holmes' Birthday

January 7: Flutists celebrate Jean-Pierre Rampal's birthday

January 8: Rock 'n Roll Day & Elvis Presley's Birthday

January 9: National Clean-Off-Your-Desk Day

January 10: Rod Stewart's Birthday

January 11: Naomi Judd's Birthday

January 12: Family Communications Day

January 13: Ha! It's Rip Taylor's birthday

January 14: Faye Dunaway's Birthday

January 15: Hot and Spicy Food
International Day

January 16: National Nothing Day

January 17: No fighting! It's Muhammad
Ali's Birthday

January 18: Winnie the Pooh Day! (A. A.
Milne's Birthday)

January 19: Dolly Parton's Birthday—Play
some country music

January 20: Hat Day

January 21: National Hugging Day

January 22: Linda Blair's Birthday

January 23: Humphrey Bogart's Birthday—
Watch *Casablanca*

January 24: Neil Diamond's Birthday—Sing
out!

January 25: Virginia Woolf's Birthday—A
Room of One's Own Day

January 26: Spouse's Day

January 27: Mikhail Baryshnikov's Birthday

January 28: Backwards Day

January 29: "Today on Oprah…" It's Oprah
      Winfrey's Birthday

January 30: FDR's Birthday

January 31: Carol Channing's Birthday—
      Smile big!

February 1: Clark Gable's Birthday—Watch
      Gone with the Wind

February 2: Groundhog Day

February 3: Norman Rockwell's Birthday—
      Celebrate Americana

February 4: Halfway-Point-of-Winter Day

February 5: Henry "Hank" Aaron's Birthday

February 6: Babe Ruth's Birthday

February 7: Charles Dickens' Birthday

February 8: James Dean's Birthday—Be cool

February 9: Carole King's Birthday

February 10: Jimmy Durante's Birthday

February 11: National Inventor's Day
      (Thomas Edison's Birthday)

February 12: Abraham Lincoln's Birthday

February 13: Chuck Yeager's Birthday

February 14: Valentine's Day

February 15: International Pancake Day

February 16: Sonny Bono's Birthday—I got
      you, Babe

February 17: Montgomery Ward's Birthday

February 18: John Travolta's Birthday

February 19: Temporary Insanity Day

February 20: Frasier Day (Kelsey Grammer's Birthday)

February 21: *The New Yorker Magazine* first published in 1925

February 22: Anniversary of Popcorn (1630)

February 23: Anniversary of the Tootsie Roll (1896)

February 24: Sally Jesse Raphael's Birthday

February 25: George Harrison's Birthday

February 26: And away-y-y we go! Jackie Gleason's Birthday

February 27: Elizabeth Taylor's Birthday

February 28: Anniversary of the final episode of M*A*S*H

February 29: Bachelor's Day

March 1: In the Mood Day (Glenn Miller's Birthday)

March 2: Theodor "Dr. Seuss" Geisel's Birthday

March 3: I Want You to Be Happy Day

March 4: Knute Rockne's Birthday

March 5: Rex Harrison's Birthday

March 6: Michelangelo's Birthday—
    Appreciate art
March 7: Willard Scott's Birthday
March 8: Lynn Redgrave's Birthday
March 9: Panic Day
March 10: Sharon Stone's Birthday
March 11: Johnny Appleseed Day
March 12: Sweet Baby James Taylor's
    Birthday
March 13: Good Samaritan Day
March 14: Ha! Billy Crystal's Birthday
March 15: Judd Hirsch's Birthday
March 16: Jerry Lewis' Birthday
March 17: St. Patrick's Day
March 18: Ham Radio Day
March 19: Glenn Close's Birthday
March 20: Big Bird's Birthday!
March 21: Fragrance Day
March 22: National Goof-Off Day
March 23: Joan Crawford's Birthday
March 24: Steve McQueen's Birthday
March 25: Elton John's Birthday
March 26: Make Up Your Own Holiday Day
March 27: Funky Winkerbean's Birthday
March 28: Beer Brewers Day (August

Anheuser Busch Jr.'s Birthday)

March 29: Oscar Ferdinand Meyer's
Birthday—Hot dog!

March 30: National Doctor's Day

March 31: Anniversary of the Eiffel Tower

April 1: April Fool's Day

April 2: Giovanni Jacopo Casanova's Birthday

April 3: Armenian Appreciation Day

April 4: Arthur Murray's Birthday—Dance!

April 5: Bette Davis' Birthday

April 6: Twinkies Day

April 7: James Garner's Birthday

April 8: Buddha's Birthday

April 9: W.C. Fields' Birthday

April 10: Encourage a Beginning Writer Day

April 11: Barbershop Quartet Day

April 12: Tiptoe through the tulips—it's Tiny
Tim's Birthday

April 13: Thomas Jefferson's Birthday

April 14: Loretta Lynn's Birthday

April 15: Anniversary of the sinking of the
Titanic

April 16: Astronomy Day

April 17: National CPA's Goof-Off Day

April 18: Anniversary of Paul Revere's ride

April 19: Dudley Moore's Birthday

April 20: Jessica Lange's Birthday

April 21: Kindergarten Day

April 22: Earth Day

April 23: William Shakespeare's Birthday

April 24: Barbra Streisand's Birthday

April 25: Meadowlark Lemon's Birthday—
No fighting!

April 26: National Bird Day (John James
Audobon's Birthday)

April 27: Jack Klugman's Birthday—"Odd
couples" celebrate!

April 28: Kiss Your Mate Day

April 29: Duke Ellington's Birthday—Jazz it
up!

April 30: National Honesty Day

May 1: May Day

May 2: Bing Crosby's Birthday

May 3: James Brown's Birthday

May 4: Naked Day

May 5: Tammy Wynette's Birthday

May 6: Sigmund Freud's Birthday

May 7: Beethoven's Ninth Symphony
premiered in 1824

May 8: World Red Cross Day

May 9: The Piano Man, Billy Joel's Birthday

May 10: Fred Astaire's Birthday—Gotta dance!

May 11: Eat What You Want Day

May 12: Limerick Day (Edward Lear's Birthday)

May 13: Stevie Wonder's Birthday

May 14: May the Force be with you on George Lucas' Birthday

May 15: Lyman Frank Baum's Birthday— Follow the Yellow Brick Road

May 16: Liberace's Birthday—Light a candleabra

May 17: Sugar Ray Leonard's Birthday

May 18: Visit Your Relatives Day

May 19: Circus Day

May 20: Cher's Birthday

May 21: National Waitresses Day

May 22: Laurence Olivier's Birthday

May 23: Joan Collins' Birthday

May 24: Bob Dylan's Birthday

May 25: National Tap Dance Day (Bill "Bojangles" Robinson's Birthday)

May 26: John Wayne's Birthday

May 27: Isadora Duncan's Birthday

May 28: Gladys Knight's Birthday

May 29: Bob Hope's Birthday—Thanks for the memories

May 30: Benny Goodman's Birthday

May 31: American Poetry Day (Walt Whitman's Birthday)

June 1: Marilyn Monroe's Birthday

June 2: Jerry Mathers' Birthday

June 3: Tony Curtis' Birthday

June 4: Freddie Fender's Birthday

June 5: World Environment Day

June 6: Kenny G's Birthday

June 7: Jessica Tandy's Birthday

June 8: American Architecture Day (Frank Lloyd Wright's Birthday)

June 9: Senior Citizens Day

June 10: Judy Garland's Birthday

June 11: Jacques Cousteau's Birthday

June 12: Baseball Hall of Fame dedicated in 1939

June 13: Kitchen Klutzes of America Day

June 14: Flag Day

June 15: Magna Carta Day

June 16: Celebrate your own *Love Story* on Erich Segal's Birthday

June 17: Barry Manilow's Birthday

June 18: Paul McCartney's Birthday

June 19: Garfield's Birthday (1978)

June 20: Lionel Richie's Birthday

June 21: Summer Solstice— The First Day of
Summer

June 22: Doughnuts Day

June 23: Midsummer Eve

June 24: Celebration of the Senses Day

June 25: Carly Simon's Birthday

June 26: Go-go celebrate George Michael's
Birthday

June 27: Helen Keller's Birthday

June 28: Gilda Radner's Birthday

June 29: TV Remote Control first introduced
in 1964

June 30: *Gone with the Wind* published in
1936

July 1: Princess Diana's Birthday

July 2: National Literacy Day—Read a
romantic book

July 3: Half -Way Point of the Year—The
183-day mark

July 4: American Independence Day

July 5: Bikini swimsuit premiered in 1946

July 6: Beatrix Potter's Birthday

July 7: Bonanza Bottler Day

July 8: Ringo Starr's Birthday

July 9: Tom Hanks' Birthday—Do something BIG

July 10: Bahamas Independence Day—Plan a vacation there!

July 11: Yul Brynner's Birthday

July 12: Picture this—It's George Eastman's Birthday

July 13: Harrison Ford's Birthday

July 14: Bastille Day

July 15: Linda Ronstadt's Birthday

July 16: Pop some popcorn—It's Orville Redenbacher's Birthday

July 17: Disneyland founded in 1955

July 18: Ha! It's Red Skelton's Birthday

July 19: Vikki Carr's Birthday

July 20: Anniversary of the first Moon landing, 1969

July 21: Ha! It's Robin Williams' Birthday

July 22: Oscar de la Renta's Birthday— Celebrate *in style*

July 23: Woody Harrelson's Birthday

July 24: Amelia Earhart's Birthday

July 25: Merry-Go-Round invented, 1871

July 26: Mick Jagger's Birthday

July 27: Bugs Bunny's Birthday (1940)

July 28: Jacqueline Kennedy Onassis' Birthday

July 29: Wedding of Prince Charles & Diana Spencer

July 30: Paul Anka's Birthday

July 31: Perry Como's Birthday

August 1: Friendship Day

August 2: Carroll O'Connor's Birthday

August 3: Tony Bennett's Birthday

August 4: Champagne invented by Dom Perignon in 1693

August 5: National Mustard Day

August 6: Jamaican Independence Day— Plan a vacation there!

August 7: Garrison Keillor's Birthday

August 8: Dustin Hoffman's Birthday

August 9: Betty Boop's Birthday

August 10: Jimmy Dean's Birthday

August 11: Anniversary of the opening of Mall of America—Shop til you drop!

August 12: Buck Owen's Birthday

August 13: International Lefthanders Day

August 14: National Senior Citizens Day

August 15: Julia Child's Birthday

August 16: *Sports Illustrated* first published in
1954

August 17: Mae West's Birthday

August 18: Bad Poetry Day

August 19: National Aviation Day (Orville
Wright's Birthday)

August 20: Sit Back and Relax Day

August 21: Kenny Rogers' Birthday

August 22: Be An Angel Day

August 23: Hug Your Boyfriend or Girlfriend
Day

August 24: Make a deal with your mate—It's
Monty Hall's Birthday

August 25: Kiss and Make-up Day

August 26: Women's Equality Day—19th
Amendment certified

August 27: Beauty Is in the Eye of the
Beholder Day

August 28: Dream Day—Anniversary of
MLK's "I have a dream" speech

August 29: Michael Jackson's Birthday

August 30: Ted Williams' Birthday

August 31: Gloria Estefan's Birthday

September 1: Lily Tomlin's Birthday
September 2: Jimmy Connors' Birthday
September 3: Charlie Sheen's Birthday
September 4: The Beatles record their first
    single, "Love Me Do"
September 5: Be Late for Something Day
September 6: "Blondie" comic strip debuts in
    1930
September 7: Do It! Day
September 8: First episode of *Star Trek* airs in
    1966
September 9: Hot Dog Day
September 10: Swap Ideas Day
September 11: American Short Story Day
    (O. Henry's Birthday)
September 12: Jesse Owens' Birthday
September 13: Mel Torme's Birthday
September 14: Star Spangled Banner Day
September 15: It's no mystery—It's Agatha
    Christie's Birthday
September 16: Dr. Robert Schuller's Birthday
September 17: John Ritter's Birthday
September 18: Frankie Avalon's Birthday
September 19: Holy Birthday, Batman—It's
    Adam West's Birthday

September 20: Sophia Loren's Birthday
September 21: Tiffany's founded in 1837
September 22: Hobbit Day
September 23: Autumnal Equinox
September 24: F. Scott Fitzgerald's Birthday
September 25: Christopher Reeve's Birthday
September 26: Olivia Newton-John's
        Birthday
September 27: Ancestor Appreciation Day
September 28: Confucius' Birthday
September 29: Jerry Lee Lewis' Birthday
September 30: Johnny Mathis' Birthday
October 1: World Vegetarian Day
October 2: Snoopy's Birthday
October 3: Chubby Checker's Birthday
October 4: Charleton Heston's Birthday
October 5: Ray Kroc's Birthday—Have a Big
        Mac Attack!
October 6: German-American Day
October 7: John Mellencamp's Birthday
October 8: Chevy Chase's Birthday
October 9: John Lennon's Birthday
October 10: Wear a tux—Anniversary of the
        tuxedo in America, 1886
October 11: Ha! *Saturday Night Live's*

premiere, 1975

October 12: Luciano Pavarotti's Birthday—
Sing out!

October 13: Modern Mythology Day

October 14: National Dessert Day

October 15: National Grouch Day

October 16: Winnie the Pooh's Birthday

October 17: Black Poetry Day

October 18: Martina Navratilova's Birthday

October 19: Evaluate Your Life Day

October 20: Dr. Joyce Brothers' Birthday

October 21: Michael Landon's Birthday

October 22: Annette Funicello's Birthday

October 23: Johnny Carson's Birthday

October 24: International Forgiveness Day

October 25: Pablo Picasso's Birthday

October 26: Anniversary of Doonesbury's
premiere in 1970

October 27: Navy Day

October 28: Charlie Daniels' Birthday

October 29: Kate Jackson's Birthday

October 30: Henry "The Fonz" Winkler's
Birthday

October 31: Halloween

November 1: National Author's Day

November 2: Burt Lancaster's Birthday

November 3: Sandwich Day

November 4: Booklover's Day

November 5: Roy Roger's Birthday

November 6: Saxophone Day

November 7: Punsters Day

November 8: Katherine Hepburn's Birthday

November 9: Dr. Carl Sagan's Birthday

November 10: Debut of *Sesame Street*, 1969

November 11: Veterans Day

November 12: Birthday of Princess Grace of Monaco

November 13: *Fantasia* premiered, 1940

November 14: Prince Charles' Birthday

November 15: American Enterprise Day

November 16: Birth of the Blues (W.C. Handy's Birthday)

November 17: Homemade Bread Day

November 18: Mickey Mouse's Birthday

November 19: Jody Foster's Birthday

November 20: Bo Derek's Birthday

November 21: World Hello Day

November 22: Anniversary of the National Hockey League, 1917

November 23: Anniversary of *Dr. Who's*

premiere, 1963

November 24: Dale Carnegie's Birthday

November 25: Old Maid's Day

November 26: Charles Schultz's Birthday

November 27: Jeans Day (Levi Strauss' Birthday)

November 28: Radio debut of the *Grand Ole Opry*, 1925

November 29: Chuck Mangione's Birthday

November 30: Mark Twain/Samuel Clemens' Birthday

December 1: Anniversary of the invention of Bingo, 1929

December 2: Charles Ringling's Birthday

December 3: Andy Williams' Birthday

December 4: Day of the Artisans

December 5: Raise a toast—Prohibition repealed on this day in 1933!

December 6: Ira Gershwin's Birthday

December 7: Johnny Bench's Birthday

December 8: Sammy Davis, Jr.'s Birthday

December 9: Kirk Douglas' Birthday

December 10: Human Rights Day

December 11: Teri Garr's Birthday

December 12: Poinsettia Day

December 13: Dick Van Dyke's Birthday

December 14: The screw was patented in
1798—celebrate as you will

December 15: *Gone with the Wind* premiered
on this day in 1939

December 16: Boston Tea Party Day—Have
a cup of tea

December 17: Wright Brothers Day

December 18: Betty Grable's Birthday

December 19: Robert Urich's Birthday

December 20: Irene Dunne's Birthday

December 21: Anniversary of the first
crossword puzzle in 1933

December 22: Winter Solstice

December 23: Susan Lucci's Birthday

December 24: Christmas Eve

December 25: Christmas Day

December 26: National Whiner's Day

December 27: Marlene Dietrich's Birthday

December 28: Bairn's Day (Unluckiest Day
of the Year)

December 29: Anniversary of the invention
of the bowling ball, 1862

December 30: Bo Diddley's Birthday

December 31: New Year's Eve

2640. Attend the Valentine's Day/mid-winter carnival in Quebec City, Canada

2641. Using resources around you, discover three new romantic ideas per week

2642. "To live is to love—all reason is against it, and all healthy instincts for it." ~ Samuel Butler

2643. Surprise him with a vintage bottle of wine from the year you met

2644. Take a walk down the Avenue of the Stars in Hollywood

2645. Gift resource: Figi's Gift Catalog: (715) 384-6101

2646. Find one romantic idea/concept/gift in today's newspaper

---

2647. Don't give *cash* as a gift

2648. (Unless it's a *lot* of money!)

2649. (Or unless you give it creatively)...

2650. Stack one hundred one dollar bills and wrap them with a red ribbon

2651. Create origami animals made of $100 bills

2652. Fill her purse with quarters

2653–2662
10 Great Beaches of the World

1. Barbuda, West Indies—A+ for *unspoiled*
2. Isla de Cozumel, Mexico—A+ for *lazing*
3. Kea, Greek Islands—A+ for *unspoiled*
4. Mindoro, Philippines—A+ for *beachcombing*
5. Molokai, Hawaii—A+ for *lazing*
6. Mustique, West Indies—A+ for *unspoiled*
7. Naxos, Greece—A+ for *hedonism*
8. North Island, New Zealand—A+ for *lazing*
9. Pamana, Indonesia—A+ for *beachcombing*
10. Sanibel Island, Florida—A+ for *beachcombing*

2663. Love Enhancer: Generosity
2664. Send a single rose to him at work
2665. Wear a ribbon—and nothing else!— and wait under the Christmas tree
2666. Stand in line together at TKTS in

Times Square to get discount tickets
to any Broadway show that's available

2667. A "Lover's Lane" Coupon: This
coupon entitles you to one make-out
session at your local Lover's Lane
(The coupon-issuer is responsible for
providing a car with a roomy back
seat)

2668. Guys: Remember—She usually wants
you to simply *listen* to her

2669. Gals: Remember—He usually want
you to just *appreciate* him

2670. Choose one day of the week, and be
extra, *extra* romantic on that day

2671. Sign your love letters: "Always,
forever, eternally, perpetually,
unceasingly, evermore"

2672. Fold a love note inside her dinner
napkin at home

2673. Go on a spur-of-the-moment
vacation

2674. Buy a "Coupon Book" for local
restaurants and services

2675. Create a "word scramble" puzzle using all romantic words

2676. Butterfly kisses: Where you brush your eyelashes against his/her cheek

2677. Plan surprise anniversary parties

2678. Get an autographed photo of his/her favorite actor

2679. Teach your toddlers to read "Do Not Disturb"—and hang a sign on your bedroom door

---

2680. Integrate his/her lucky number into your life as much as possible…

2681. Get a vanity license plate with that number on it

2682. Get him/her that number of balloons

2683. At hotels, arrange to stay on the "lucky" floor number

2684. At hotels, arrange to get "lucky" room numbers

2685. Get your mate that number of gifts on his/her birthday

2686. Mail him/her that number of roses

2687. Have that number made into a custom piece of jewelry

2688. Use that number in your ATM code

2689. Get a football jersey with that number on it

2690. Play that number in the lottery— You *could* win!

2691. Rent a classic roadster for a day

2692. Create a picture-perfect wedding

2693. Wear "Contradiction" cologne, and show that you're masculine *and* gentle

2694. Always give (and receive) flowers with your *right* hand—it symbolizes positive wishes

2695. "Unconditional love is the most powerful stimulant to the immune system." ~ Bernie Siegal

---

2696. For grandparents only: Write "The Story of Our Life Together"

2697. Self-publish twenty copies of the book

2698. Give copies of this unique keepsake to your family

2699. Choose some daily affirmations

2700. Remember: As couples endure, we trade *newness* and *excitement* for *understanding* and *meaning*

2701. Learn what he/she considers *cool*

Favorite Love Songs from 1928

2702. "Love Me or Leave Me"

2703. "Lover, Come Back to Me"

2704. "She's Funny That Way"

2705. "You're the Cream in My Coffee"

2706. Get a fountain pen so you can write elegant love letters

2707. Aphrodisiac Alert: *Love Potions: A Guide to Aphrodisiacs and Sexual Pleasures*, by Cynthia Merris Watson

2708. Write a love note in a rainbow of colors

2709. For new dads: Give 100% and expect nothing in return for the first three months

2710. "The best way to know God is to love many things." ~ Vincent Van Gogh

2711–2720
10 Songs to Help You Express Your Feelings: *Intense Love & Infatuation*

1. "Can't Take My Eyes Off You," Frankie Valli
2. "Do the Walls Come Down," Carly Simon
3. "Every Breath You Take," The Police
4. "Head Over Heels," Tears for Fears
5. "I Am Waiting," Yes
6. "I Fall to Pieces," Patsy Cline
7. "I Will Always Love You," Whitney Houston
8. "Nights in White Satin," Moody Blues
9. "When a Man Loves a Woman," Percy Sledge
10. "(Your Love Has Lifted Me) Higher and Higher," Rita Coolidge

---

2721. Create a personalized "Sexual-Favor-of-the-Month Club"
2722. "In thy face I see/The map of honor, truth, and loyalty" ~ Shakespeare
2723. Greet her at the airport when she flies

2724. Overdo something. Does he love M&M's? Buy him *fifty pounds* of them!

2725. The "Don't Worry, Be Happy" Coupon: Good for one truly carefree day. The coupon-giver will arrange for a fun-filled day of escape for the two of you

2726. Fill her desk drawers with her favorite candy

2727. FYI: A+ Couples are child*like*, but not child*ish*

2728. Stop taking your partner for granted

2729. Stop suppressing your feelings

2730. Stop reading this book and call your partner *right now* to say "I love you"

2731. Stop arguing over which way the toilet paper should roll

2732. Stop saying, "I told you so"

2733. Stop smoking cigarettes (You'll be around longer to love)

2734. "Stop and Think It Over," by Dale & Grace

2735. "Stop Draggin' My Heart Around,"

by Stevie Nicks & Tom Petty and the Heartbreakers

2736. Visit a butterfly aviary
2737. Enemy of Love: Lack of awareness
2738. Give her a scarf that illustrates her hobby
2739. Apologize to your partner for being too busy to pick her up at the airport—then surprise her by showing-up there

---

2740–2748
9 Ways to Love a Cancer
(22 June–22 July)

1. Cancer is a *water* sign: Cater to his/her dreamy, romantic nature
2. Gift tip: Luxurious
3. Deluxe soaps and creams, lush music are appreciated
4. Often appreciates antiques
5. As Cancer is ruled by the moon, items with a moon motif
6. Lilies; trees in general
7. Smooth and creamy foods

8.   The beauty and romance of Venice
9.   Wrap gifts in silver/gray for your
      Cancer

2749.   As part of foreplay, read aloud to her
        an erotic poem
2750.   Enemy of Love: Temper

2751.   For everything there is a season, and
        a time for every matter of the heart:
2752.   A time for passion, and a time for
        patience,
2753.   A time for him to lead, and a time
        for her to lead,
2754.   A time to talk, and a time to listen,
2755.   A time for sex, and a time for love,
2756.   A time to hold on, and a time to let go,
2757.   A time to learn, and a time to teach,
2758.   A time to stand firm, and a time to
        compromise,
2759.   A time for masculinity, and a time for
        femininity,
2760.   A time to shout for joy, and a time to
        express your fears,
2761.   A time for yourself, and a time for

your mate,

2762. A time for tradition, and a time for change,

2763. A time for you as a couple, and a time for you as a family.

2764. [Read Ecclesiastes 3: 1-8]

2765. Send him to a Fantasy Baseball Camp

2766. For your math lover: There's an *awesome* love poem written in the language of mathematics in "Trurl's Electronic Bard" in the book *The Cyberiad*, by Stanislaw Lem

2767. Stay at the fanciest hotel in New Orleans: The Soniat House

2768. Love Coupon: Good for one "choreographed" lovemaking session! Choose your favorite romantic/erotic music, and then make love to match its mood and rhythms

---

2769–2781
13 Unusual-But-Romantic Places to Have a Memorable Dinner Together

1. In a greenhouse full of flowers

2. At the foot of a beautiful waterfall
3. On a hillside in Venice
4. Under a giant redwood tree
5. Aboard a friend's yacht
6. At midnight in your backyard
7. At the foot of Mount Everest
8. At the top of the Empire State Building
9. In a hot air balloon
10. In a meadow under the stars
11. At the brink of a butte in Montana
12. In the shadow of the Eiffel Tower
13. In a cable car in the Alps

2782. FYI: Women tend to like: Lingerie in *pastels*
2783. FYI: Men tend to like: Lingerie in *black* or *red*

2784. As a secret surprise: Study a book on massage techniques
2785. Go apple picking together in the Fall
2786. Give her socks that picture her favorite animal
2787. Bake her a cake

2788. "Oh love, as long as you can love"
~ Ferdinand Freiligrath

2789. The Decadent "Dinner-In-Bed"
Coupon: Forget *breakfast* in bed—
you're being treated to an elegant
dinner in bed sometime this week

2790. Eat dinner at the restaurant with the
best food

2791. On Monday: Give one red rose with
a lyric from a Beatles song

2792. On Tuesday: Give one red rose with a
lyric from a Billy Joel song

2793. On Wednesday: Give one red rose
with a lyric from a Barbra Streisand
song

2794. On Thursday: Give one red rose with
a lyric from a Moody Blues song

2795. On Friday: Give one red rose with a
lyric from a Billie Holiday song

2796. On Saturday: Give one red rose with
a lyric from a Frank Sinatra song

2797. On Sunday: Give one red rose with a
lyric from a song that *you* composed

2798. Guys: Be nice to her during her menstrual periods
2799. Be aware of the dates
2800. Don't joke about it
2801. Honor femininity

2802. Get tickets to see Cirque du Soleil—be enchanted together!
2803. Serve his favorite dessert
2804. Read & learn: *The Anatomy of Relationships*, by M. Argyle & M. Henderson
2805. "The only way to speak the truth is to speak lovingly." ~ Henry David Thoreau
2806. Serve her tea in her favorite mug
2807. Hire a neighbor kid to cut the lawn; use that time *romantically*
2808. Use sparklers instead of candles on his/her birthday cake
2809. Attend a Sunday afternoon band concert in the park
2810. Have a picnic in the living room in front of the fireplace

2811. Words that *men* love to hear: "I *want* you"

2812. Words that *women* love to hear: "I *need* you"

2813–2835
23 Characteristics of a True Romantic

1. Taps into his/her creativity regularly
2. Is just a *little bit* "naughty"
3. Takes love seriously—
4. But has a great sense of humor
5. Makes his/her intimate love relationship a top priority
6. Makes romantic gestures without ulterior motives
7. Is flexible
8. Celebrates sexuality
9. Understands the importance of little touches, brushes, caresses
10. Appreciates his/her partner's uniqueness
11. Celebrates both the *masculine* and the *feminine*
12. Is a pretty good mind reader
13. Sees the world in a slightly offbeat way

14. Maintains a deep, spiritual connection with his/her partner
15. Is spontaneous
16. Defines him/herself as a "lover"— regardless of other roles
17. Remembers important dates and anniversaries
18. Continuously learns and grows
19. Is in touch with his/her feelings
20. Pursues new and different experiences
21. Gives of himself/herself without expectations
22. Does lots of *little* things
23. Gives without being asked

2836. Steal a kiss
2837. Give it back

2838. As a secret surprise: Sign him/her up for sailing lessons
2839. The "Cinderella" Coupon: Redeemable for one elegant night of dining and dancing. Void after midnight!
2840. Collect souvenirs from every vacation

2841. It's the Great Pumpkin, Charlie Brown! Give a gift on Halloween

2842. Surprise him with the CD from *Phantom of the Opera*, by Andrew Lloyd Weber

2843. For the spiritually-minded: *Embracing Each Other: Relationship as Teacher, Healer & Guide,* by Hal Stone & Sidra Winkelman

---

2844. Monday: Arrive home with a bottle of champagne

2845. Tuesday: Arrive home with one flower picked from a field

2846. Wednesday: Arrive home with love in your heart

2847. Thursday: Arrive home with tickets to *something*

2848. Friday: Arrive home with dinner from a take-out restaurant

2849. Saturday: Arrive home with a romantic movie on video

2850. Sunday: Arrive home with one piece of fine chocolate

2851. Surprise her with a vintage bottle of wine from the year of your wedding

2852. The Second Honeymoon Coupon! You choose the *type* of vacation, your partner chooses the *location*. You choose the length of vacation, your partner chooses the departure date

2853. Leave a trail of your clothes, leading from the front door to your bedroom

2854. Honor your partner's cultural heritage

2855. Let a Billie Holiday song express your feelings for you

2856. Drink coffee at the best café

2857. Have a picnic on the roof

2858. Take a Japanese flower arranging course together

2859. The "Extra Birthday" Coupon: Without having to get older, your partner will supply you with gifts and cake. No candles needed

---

2860–2927
68 Hit Songs with "Love" in Their Titles
1.   "A Little More Love," Olivia

Newton-John

2. "A Woman Needs Love (Just Like You Do)," Ray Parker, Jr. & Raydio
3. "All 4 Love," Color Me Badd
4. "All Out of Love," Air Supply
5. "Another Sad Love Song," Toni Braxton
6. "April Love," Pat Boone
7. "Baby I Love Your Way," Big Mountain
8. "Baby I Love Your Way/Freebird Medley (Free Baby)," Will to Power
9. "Because I Love You (The Postman Song)," Stevie B
10. "Because of Love," Janet Jackson
11. "Best of My Love," The Emotions
12. "Bye Bye Love," Everly Brothers
13. "Caribbean Queen (No More Love on the Run)," Billy Ocean
14. "Come and Get Your Love," Redbone
15. "Cradle of Love," Billy Idol
16. "Dedicated to the One I Love," The Shirelles
17. "Do You Love Me," The Contours

18. "Everybody Loves Somebody," Dean Martin
19. "Friendly Persuasion (Thee I Love)/Chains of Love," Pat Boone
20. "Greatest Love of All," Whitney Houston
21. "Have I Told You Lately That I Love You," Ricky Nelson
22. "I Love a Rainy Night," Eddie Rabbitt
23. "I Love Your Smile," Shanice
24. "I Wanna Dance With Somebody (Who Loves Me)," Whitney Houston
25. "I Want to Know What Love Is," Foreigner
26. "I'd Do Anything for Love (But I Won't Do That)," Meat Loaf
27. "I'd Really Love to See You Tonight," England Dan & John Ford Coley
28. "I'll Never Love This Way Again," Dionne Warwick
29. "I'm in Love Again," Fats Domino
30. "If I Ever Fall in Love," Shai
31. "It Must Have Been Love," Roxette

32. "Jump (For My Love)," Pointer Sisters
33. "Love Hangover," Diana Ross
34. "Love Is a Battlefield," Pat Benatar
35. "Love Is Alive," Gary Wright
36. "Love Is," Vanessa Williams & Brian McKnight
37. "(Love Is) Thicker than Water," Andy Gibb
38. "Love Letters in the Sand," Pat Boone
39. "Love Machine (Part 1)," The Miracles
40. "Love on the Rocks," Neil Diamond
41. "Love Rollercoaster," Ohio Players
42. "Love Theme from *Romeo and Juliet*," Henry Mancini
43. "Love to Love You Baby," Donna Summer
44. "Love Will Keep Us Together," The Captain & Tennille
45. "Love Will Never Do (Without You)," Janet Jackson
46. "Making Love Out of Nothing at All," Air Supply

47. "Muskrat Love," The Captain & Tennille
48. "My True Love," Jack Scott
49. "Real Love," Mary J. Blige
50. "Send One Your Love," Stevie Wonder
51. "Sending All My Love," Linear
52. "Show Me Love," Robin S.
53. "So Much in Love," All-4-One
54. "Sometimes Love Just Ain't Enough," Patty Smyth
55. "That's the Way Love Goes," Janet Jackson
56. "This Guy's in Love with You," Herb Alpert
57. "To Know Him Is to Love Him," The Teddy Bears
58. "To Sir with Love," Lulu
59. "What Is Love," Haddaway
60. "What's Love Got to Do With It," Tina Turner
61. "When a Man Loves a Woman," Michael Bolton
62. "Why Do Fools Fall in Love," The Teenagers & Frankie Lymon

63. "Will You Love Me Tomorrow," The
    Shirelles
64. "Woman in Love," Barbra Streisand
65. "You Give Love a Bad Name," Bon
    Jovi
66. "Young Love," Sonny James
67. "Young Love," Tab Hunter
68. "(Your Love Has Lifted Me) Higher
    and Higher," Rita Coolidge

2928. Wear a T-shirt from his alma mater
2929. "Love is not the dying moan of a
      distant violin—it's the triumphant
      twang of a bedspring."
      ~ S.J. Perelman
2930. Love with all your soul
2931. Picnic in a secluded spot—and make
      love afterward
2932. Wear "Opium" cologne—And show
      him why he should be addicted to
      you
2933. Learn what he/she considers *relaxing*
2934. While at work, imagine your partner
      in a sexy outfit . . . then call her
2935. Learn the waltz

2936. Take your music lover to the Buddy Holly Museum, in Lubbock, Texas: (800) 692-4035
2937. Get an autographed photo of his/her favorite singer
2938. Make love in the living room
2939. Give her a scarf in shades of her favorite color
2940. Take private dance lessons together
2941. Give the gift of Pez
2942. Give her socks in shades of her favorite color

2943–2954
The 12 Birthstones— and Their Symbolic Meanings

Accompany the jewelry with a poem about the symbolic meaning of his or her birthstone:

January: Garnet—*faith & constancy*
February: Amethyst—*happiness & sincerity*
March: Aquamarine—*courage & hope*
April: Diamond—*innocence & joy*
May: Emerald—*peace & tranquillity*
June: Pearl—*purity & wisdom*

July: Ruby—*nobility & passion*
August: Sardonyz—*joy & power*
September: Sapphire—*truth & hope*
October: Opal—*tender love & confidence*
November: Topaz—*fidelity & friendship*
December: Turquoise—*success & understanding*

2955. A Romantic Movie Coupon: Choose
one: *Out of Africa, Somewhere in Time,
Splendor in the Grass, Top Hat,
Casablanca, Tootsie, Key Largo,
Moonstruck*

2956. Order long-stem chocolate roses! Call
(415) 383-8887

2957. The "Convenience Store" Coupon:
Your partner will run to the local
store for you at a moment's notice

2958. Save placemats from all the
restaurants you visit

2959. Go for a walk someplace where you
can see a beautiful skyline

2960. Give one rose for every month you've
been together

2961. Hide a diamond ring in a box of
Cracker Jacks

2962. Go on vacation without luggage: Buy everything you need *there*—including clothes!

2963. The "Create-A-Date" Coupon: Where? Wherever you want. When? Whenever you want. The coupon-giver pays all expenses and guarantees you a great time

2964. "The applause of a single human being is of great consequence."
~ Samuel Johnson

2965. Buy her an antique armoire for her lingerie

2966. Send her one dozen roses at work

2967. Lie—in bed together on a Saturday morning

2968. Cheat—on your budget, just a little bit: Go on a big date

2969. Steal—time from your other responsibilities: Give it to your mate

---

2970. Get "namesake gifts"—

2971. If her name is *Lucy*, get her an *I Love Lucy* T-shirt

2972. If his name is *Tommy*, get the CD *Tommy* by The Who

2973. If her name is *Barbara*, get some Barbie doll paraphernalia

2974. If his name is *Charlie*, get him some *Peanuts* books

2975. If her name is *Patricia*, get her some Peppermint Patties

2976. If his name is *Arnold*, get all of Schwarzenegger's movies

2977. If her name is *Gloria*, get a copy of "Gloria," by Laura Branigan

2978. If his name is *George*, get him a copy of the book *Curious George*

2979. Massage his hands

2980. FYI: Phenylethylamine: A possibly aphrodisiac chemical present in chocolate

2981. The "Knight in Shining Armor" Coupon—in which he will rescue you from Saturday errands and whisk you away for a romantic evening together

2982. Create a perpetual bouquet: Bring

home one flower a day, for a
solid month

2983. Enemy of Love: Jealousy
2984. Learn to tango (it takes two)
2985. Give *fragrant* flowers: Camellia,
Peonies, Lavender
2986. Love Enhancer: Sense of Humor

2987. The anticipation is often just as
much fun as the event or gift itself
2988. Tell her to reserve a specific future
date, but don't tell her *why*
2989. Drop hints about an upcoming
surprise event
2990. Use the song "Anticipation," by Carly
Simon, to help build the suspense

2991–3002
12 *Unusual* Gift Tips for Lovers

1. Buy one blue gift, two red gifts, and
one green gift
2. Find two gifts for under $5, three
gifts for $20-$25, and one gift for
$50-$100

3. Get two sentimental gifts, one gag gift, and one practical gift
4. Get one gift in a toy store, one in a hardware store, and one in a grocery store
5. Get one gift that will appeal to the *mind*, and one gift that appeals to the *sense of beauty*
6. Find one gift that will stimulate his/her sexuality, and one that will stimulate good memories
7. Get one gift for each sense—sight, hearing, touch, smell, and taste
8. Get one gift that represents the past, the present time, and the future
9. Give one gift to use in the morning, one to use in the afternoon, and one to use at night
10. Get one gift for the outdoors, and one gift for the indoors
11. Get one gift that will make him/her laugh, and one gift that will bring tears to his/her eyes
12. Get one gift for each season

3003. Find a restaurant with a spectacular view

3004. Use a thesaurus to help you describe your feelings of love: Infatuated, crazy, frantic, frenetic, frenzied, intoxicated, mad

3005. Learn to jitterbug

3006. Give her theater tickets taped to the CD of the show

3007. After you've bought a new house, give her a house key wrapped in a jewelry box

3008. Give him a baseball signed by his favorite player

3009. Have at least three dozen candles on hand at all times

3010. Serve him coffee in his favorite mug

3011. Give him a cap from his favorite baseball team

3012–3039
28 Ways to *Take Care* of the One You Love

1. Purge your house of all fatty foods if he/she's on a diet

2. Install a home security system

3. Sign your partner up for AAA
4. Install dead bolt locks on her apartment doors
5. Buy fire extinguishers for your home
6. Teach him how to sew on a button—
7. But do it for him when he's home
8. Install an alarm system in her car
9. Bring homemade chicken soup when she's sick
10. Make sure your cars have jumper cables and flares
11. Have a complete First Aid Kit for your home and car
12. Don't let him over-exert himself lifting heavy things
13. Send her to a self-defense class
14. See a chiropractor every once in a while
15. Have your cars serviced regularly
16. Sprinkle salt on the icy steps and sidewalk
17. Wire an extra set of keys under her car for her
18. Post a variety of emergency numbers by each phone

19. Check the air in your car tires
20. Take a CPR class together
21. Get him "The Club" to protect his car
22. Hire a kid to shovel the snow from your driveway (protect her back and heart!)
23. Wear safety helmets when riding bicycles
24. Change the oil in her car
25. Install safety reflectors on your bicycles
26. Teach your partner how to drive in bad weather conditions
27. Take an Outward Bound excursion together
28. Take martial arts classes together

3040. Spend this month's cigarette money on romance (which is healthier?)
3041. Increase the number of compliments you give your partner by 100%

3042. Toast one another every time you hold a wine glass

3043. Toast your good fortune in having found each other

3044. Have an "aphrodisiacs only" picnic
3045. Take a music appreciation class together
3046. Play "She loves me, she loves me not," with a daisy
3047. Give her jade jewelry
3048. "Only little boys and old men sneer at love." ~ Louis Auchincloss
3049. Give him a tie that illustrates his hobby
3050. Go for a stroll in the park

3051. Express your faith together
3052. Meet with others of the same faith regularly
3053. Live your faith day-to-day

3054. Pamper her
3055. Paint her toenails
3056. Brush her hair
3057. Cook breakfast, lunch, and dinner for her

3058. Do a load of laundry
3059. Nuzzle her neck

3060. Give her a basketball signed by her favorite player
3061. Learn more about his favorite sport
3062. Say this and mean it: "I'm sorry"
3063. Visit Fanny Farmer and select gifts for each other
3064. Toast your many happy years together
3065. Get some tasty ideas from *The Creative Breakfast*, by Ellen Klavan
3066. Gals: Greet him at the door wearing high heels, a garter belt, and stockings
3067. Provide more memory for her computer
3068. Read *How to Stay Lovers for Life: Discover a Marriage Counselor's Tricks of the Trade*, by Sharyn Wolf
3069. Never, never, *never* betray a confidence
3070. "We can judge others or we can love others—but we can't do both."
   ~ Anonymous

3071. String streamers in the family room,
       just for fun
3072. Order pizza with all the toppings *she*
       likes best

3073. Give your partner 100% of
       everything he/she *needs*
3074. Give your partner 50% to 75% of
       everything he/she *wants*

3075. Flirt
3076. Kiss
3077. Touch
3078. Hug
3079. Caress
3080. Tease
3081. Whisper
3082. Cuddle
3083. Nuzzle

3084. Take a photography class together
3085. Take a camera with you wherever
       you go
3086. Model for one another
3087. Take *erotic* photos of each other!

3088. Photograph *yourself*—and give the photos to your partner

---

3089. Kiss every square inch of his body
3090. Celebrate your anniversary
3091. Giftwrap with *real flowers* instead of bows
3092. Take the day off work to celebrate his/her birthday
3093. A "Putt Putt" Coupon: Good for one round of miniature golf. Coupon-giver pays the golfing fees; the loser of the game pays for snacks
3094. Have extra sets of car keys and house keys handy
3095. Listen to your Inner Voice
3096. Some help for your love letters: "Without you I'd be—lost, lonely, devastated, annihilated, eradicated, ruined, adrift, nowhere, frittered."
3097. Create an Easter basket full of romantic I.O.U.s hidden in plastic eggs

---

3098. Create a "love" themed gift...

3099. Give the book *Love*, by Leo Buscaglia

3100. And the song "Love Is a Many Splendored Thing," by The Four Aces

3101. And the movie *Can't Buy Me Love*

3102. And the book *Love Is Letting Go of Fear*, by Gerald Jampolsky

3103. And the song "Love Me Tender," Elvis Presley

3104. And the movie *For Love or Money*

3105. And the book *The Secret Language of Love,* by Megan Tresidder

3106. And the song "Love Is," by Vanessa Williams & Brian McKnight

---

3107. "A man is rich according to what he gives, not what he has."
~ Henry Ward Beecher

3108. Learn what he considers *adventurous*

3109. "Life is like a ten-speed bike. Most of us have gears we never use."
~ Charles M. Schulz

3110. Millionaires need love, too: Give him/her a $25,000 coupon redeemable at Tiffany's

3111. Visit a local public garden together
3112. Have all of her jewelry professionally cleaned and polished
3113. "Treat your wife like a thoroughbred and she'll never be a nag."
  ~ Bumper Sticker
3114. Keep this book hidden from your partner: Use it as your romantic "secret weapon"

3115–3127
13 Fun/Whimsical Love Songs

1. "Can't You Hear My Heartbeat," Herman's Hermits
2. "Crazy Little Thing Called Love," Queen
3. "Groovy Kind of Love," Phil Collins
4. "Hello Goodbye," The Beatles
5. "I Think I Love You," The Partridge Family
6. "If I Had a Million Dollars," Barenaked Ladies
7. "I'm Gonna Be (500 Miles)," Proclaimers
8. "Let's Call the Whole Thing Off"

9. "Nobody Does It Better," Carly Simon
10. "Silly Love Songs," Paul McCartney and Wings
11. "Sugar, Sugar," The Archies
12. "When I'm Sixty-Four," The Beatles
13. "You're the One That I Want," John Travolta & Olivia Newton-John

---

3128. Plan a lunch date
3129. Send an anniversary greeting via telegram
3130. Get every book featuring his/her favorite comic character
3131. Save the last slice of pizza for him
3132. Give a mug with both of your names on it
3133. Keep a leather-bound Bible with your names embossed on the cover
3134. Take turns—*every night*—giving each other a back rub

3135. Collect ticket stubs from every movie you attend
3136. Collect postcards from all your vacations

3137. Add to her collection of stuffed animals
3138. Add to his collection of rare magazines
3139. Add to his stamp collection
3140. Add to her coin collection

3141–3161
The 21 Most Romantic Movies of All Time

1. *An Affair to Remember*
2. *The Bodyguard*
3. *Bull Durham*
4. *Casablanca*
5. *Dirty Dancing*
6. *Doctor Zhivago*
7. *Flashdance*
8. *From Here to Eternity*
9. *Ghost*
10. *Gone with the Wind*
11. *Intersection*
12. *The Last of the Mohicans*
13. *An Officer and a Gentleman*
14. *Prelude to a Kiss*
15. *Shadowlands*
16. *Somewhere in Time*

17. *Titanic*
18. *Top Gun*
19. *Untamed Heart*
20. *The Way We Were*
21. *When Harry Met Sally*

3162. Present him with silver jewelry
3163. Give equipment for his/her favorite hobby
3164. Plan little surprises
3165. Eat dinner at the best Vietnamese restaurant around
3166. Work on your listening skills
3167. The Music-Lover's Coupon: Good for one CD by your favorite musical artist—courtesy of the coupon-giver
3168. "Love is a flower and you its only seed." ~ Amanda McBroom
3169. Celebrate "Wife Appreciation Day" (a made-up holiday; *you* choose when!)
3170. Dress up like Santa and entertain your children
3171. Gather several heart-shaped boxes in February and save them for later

3172. For an adventure vacation: Above the Clouds Trekking: (800) 233-4499
3173. Take ballroom dancing classes together
3174. Get a "Silly Slammer" toy to help you express your feelings

---

3175. Frame your wedding vows
3176. Frame her favorite poem
3177. Frame his favorite song lyrics
3178. Frame an autumn leaf
3179. Frame a lock of her hair
3180. Frame your wedding invitation
3181. Frame your marriage license
3182. Frame a greeting card he sent you
3183. Frame a love note from her

3184. Be interested
3185. Be interesting

3186. Give a mug representing his/her hobby
3187. Give a bottle of wine from the state in which your partner was born
3188. Make love dressed in your finest lingerie

3189. Tour Chocolate World in Hershey, Pennsylvania. Call (717) 534-4900

3190. Resource: *The Day-By-Day Celebration Book*, by John Kremer

3191. Take a wine tasting class together

3192. "The word love has by no means the same sense for both sexes, and this is one cause of the serious misunderstandings that divide them."
~ Simone de Beauvoir

3193. The gift: A 14-karat gold key-shaped pendant

3194. The note: "You hold the key to my heart"

3195–3270
76 Top Love Song Duets

1. "A Whole New World," Peabo Bryson & Regina Belle

2. "After All," Cher & Peter Cetera

3. "Ain't No Mountain High Enough," Marvin Gaye & Tammi Terrell

4. "Ain't Nothing Like the Real Thing," Marvin Gaye & Tammi Terrell

5. "All I Ever Need Is You," Sonny & Cher
6. "All My Life," Linda Ronstadt & Aaron Neville
7. "Baby (You've Got What It Takes)," Dinah Washington & Brook Benton
8. "Beauty and the Beast," Celine Dion & Peabo Bryson
9. "The Beat Goes On," Sonny & Cher
10. "Can't We Try," Dan Hill & Vonda Sheppard
11. "Close My Eyes (Forever)," Lita Ford & Ozzy Osbourne
12. "Close Your Eyes," Peaches & Herb
13. "The Closer I Get to You," Roberta Flack & Donny Hathaway
14. "Dancing in the Street," Mick Jagger & David Bowie
15. "Deep Purple," Donny & Marie Osmond
16. "Deep Purple," Nino Tempo & April Stevens
17. "Easy Lover," Philip Bailey & Phil Collins
18. "Ebony and Ivory," Paul McCartney

& Stevie Wonder

19. "Friends and Lovers," Gloria Loring & Carl Anderson

20. "The Girl Is Mine," Michael Jackson & Paul McCartney

21. "Guilty," Barbra Streisand & Barry Gibb

22. "Her Town Too," James Taylor & J.D. Souther

23. "Hey Paula," Paul & Paula

24. "How Do You Do," Mouth & McNeal

25. "(I Believe) There's Nothing Stronger Than Our Love," Paul Anka & Odia Coates

26. "I Can't Help It," Andy Gibb & Olivia Newton-John

27. "I Finally Found Someone," Bryan Adams and Barbra Streisand

28. "I Got You Babe," Sonny & Cher

29. "I Just Can't Stop Loving You," Michael Jackson & Siedah Garrett

30. "I Knew You Were Waiting (For Me)," Aretha Franklin & George Michael

31. "I Like Your Kind of Love," Andy Williams & Peggy Powers
32. "I'm Leaving It Up to You," Dale & Grace
33. "I'm Leaving It (All) Up to You," Donny & Marie Osmond
34. "If I Could Build My Whole World Around You," Marvin Gaye & Tammi Terrell
35. "Islands in the Stream," Kenny Rogers & Dolly Parton
36. "It's Only Love," Bryan Adams & Tina Turner
37. "Kookie, Kookie (Lend Me Your Comb)," Edward Byrnes & Connie Stevens
38. "Leather and Lace," Stevie Nicks & Don Henley
39. "Let It Be Me," Jerry Butler & Betty Everett
40. "Love Is Strange," Mickey & Sylvia
41. "Mockingbird," Carly Simon & James Taylor
42. "Morning Side of the Mountain," Donny & Marie Osmond

43. "The Next Time I Fall," Peter Cetera & Amy Grant
44. "No More Tears (Enough Is Enough)," Barbra Streisand & Donna Summer
45. "On My Own," Patti LaBelle & Michael McDonald
46. "One Man Woman/One Woman Man," Paul Anka & Odia Coates
47. "Playboy," Gene & Debbe
48. "Put a Little Love in Your Heart," Annie Lennox & Al Green
49. "Set the Night to Music," Roberta Flack & Maxi Priest
50. "Shake Your Groove Thing," Peaches & Herb
51. "Should've Never Let You Go," Neil Sedaka & Dara Sedaka
52. "Solid," Ashford & Simpson
53. "Somethin' Stupid," Nancy Sinatra & Frank Sinatra
54. "Somewhere Out There," Linda Ronstadt & James Ingram
55. "Stumblin' In," Suzi Quatro & Chris Norman

56. "Suddenly," Olivia Newton-John & Cliff Richard
57. "Surrender to Me," Ann Wilson & Robin Zander
58. "Then Came You," Dionne Warwick & the Spinners
59. "This Old Heart of Mine," Rod Stewart & Ronald Isley
60. "To All the Girls I've Loved Before," Julio Iglesias & Willie Nelson
61. "Tonight, I Celebrate My Love," Peabo Bryson & Roberta Flack
62. "Too Much, Too Little, Too Late," Johnny Mathis & Deniece Williams
63. "True Love," Elton John & Kiki Dee
64. "Unforgettable," Natalie Cole & Nat King Cole
65. "What Have I Done to Deserve This?" Pet Shop Boys & Dusty Springfield
66. "What Kind of Fool," Barbra Streisand & Barry Gibb
67. "Where Is the Love," Roberta Flack & Donny Hathaway
68. "Wild Night," John Mellencamp &

Me'shell NdegéOcello

69. "With You I'm Born Again," Billy Preston & Syreeta
70. "Yah Mo B There," James Ingram & Michael McDonald
71. "Yes, I'm Ready," Teri DeSario & KC
72. "You and I," Eddie Rabbitt & Crystal Gayle
73. "You're a Special Part of Me," Diana Ross & Marvin Gaye
74. "You're All I Need to Get By," Marvin Gaye & Tammi Terrell
75. "Young Lovers," Paul & Paula
76. "Your Precious Love," Marvin Gaye & Tammi Terrell

3271. Get married *again* (to your current spouse)
3272. Create a fun and meaningful rededication ceremony
3273. Read *Weddings for Grownups,* by Carroll Stoner
3274. Read *I Do: A Guide to Creating Your Own Unique Wedding Ceremony,* by Sydney Barbara Metrick

3275. Read *Weddings by Design,* by Richard Leviton

3276. Enemy of Love: Arrogance
3277. Remind yourself to be more loving
3278. Use your brain to help your heart: Read *Jump Start Your Brain*, by Doug Hall
3279. Ignore "call waiting" when talking with her on the phone
3280. Once-a-month: Have dinner brought in by a caterer
3281. Look for the unstated assumptions in your relationship—they often block your creativity and passion
3282. Perform a favor for her mother
3283. Do "The Twist"
3284. Learn what he/she considers *romantic*
3285. Give a subscription to the magazine that covers his/her hobby
3286. A+ Romance Rating: Hotel Gritti Palace, in Venice, Italy
3287. Have a wine and cheese picnic
3288. Stroll along the city streets

Favorite Love Songs from 1929

3289. "Am I Blue?"
3290. "I'll Always Be in Love with You"
3291. "I'm Just a Vagabond Lover"
3292. "More Than You Know"
3293. "My Kinda Love"
3294. "Till We Meet Again"
3295. "You Do Something to Me"

3296. Don't assume you know everything there is to know about your partner
3297. Don't assume "your way" is always right
3298. Don't assume you know all the best sexual techniques
3299. Don't assume you know what's on his/her mind

3300–3309
10 Most Romantic Spots in America

1. Big Sur, California
2. Charleston, South Carolina
3. Grand Canyon, Arizona
4. La Jolla, California
5. Maui, Hawaii

6. Nantucket, Massachusetts
7. New Orleans, Louisiana
8. Niagara Falls, New York
9. San Francisco, California
10. Sedona, Arizona

3310. Get in touch with your sense of adventure
3311. Get in touch with your sense of humor
3312. Get in touch with your feelings
3313. Get in touch with your dreams
3314. Get in touch with your creativity
3315. Get in touch with your inner child
3316. Get in touch with your mate
3317. Get in touch with your hopes for the future
3318. Get in touch with your Inner Child
3319. Get in touch with your Inner Teenager
3320. Get in touch with your Inner Romantic

3321. "To fear love is to fear life."
~ Bertrand Russell

3322. Kiss every square inch of her body—
S-L-O-W-L-Y

3323. The Wacky "Half-Birthday"
Celebration Coupon: You are entitled
to celebrate your half-birthday—*the
day exactly six months after* your official
birthday. Included: cake and candles,
ice cream and presents

3324. Generate one new romantic gesture
every day for a year

3325. Propose on Valentine's Day

3326. Hide a love note in his/her napkin at
a restaurant

3327. Flowers that match nicknames:
Buttercup, Poppy, Sweet Pea

3328. Never, never, *never* say "What's for
dinner?" before saying "I love you"

3329. "I will act as if I do make a
difference." ~ William James

3330. Hang a homemade flag with a big red
heart on it in front of your home (as
a code that you want to make love)

3331. Spend a weekend in New York City

3332. View your life as a story, and strive
for a happy ending

3333.   Go on a *fourth* honeymoon

3334.   List the three best lessons in love you
        learned from your parents

3335.   Write a letter to your parents
        thanking them for these lessons

3336.   Unlearn the worst relationship habit
        you learned from your parents

3337.   Unlearn the dumbest attitude about
        love you learned from TV

3338.   Gals: Unlearn the "Men are from
        Mars" attitude: He's an *individual*, not
        a stereotype

3339.   Guys: Unlearn the "Women are from
        Venus" attitude: All women are *not*
        the same

3340.   The Ultimate Picnic Coupon: You
        are entitled to an all-out, elegant,
        dinner picnic. Included: 3 course
        meal, fine wine, candles, and music.
        Proper dress required

3341.   Give her a crystal bud vase

3342.   "The heart has reasons that reason

does not understand." ~ Jacques Bossuet

3343. Practice daily affirmations to improve your attitude and outlook

3344. Enemy of Love: Poor timing

3345. Skim the Yellow Pages, looking for companies that might help you in your romantic endeavors

3346. Toast your partner while out with friends

3347. Pre-order her favorite meal and drinks when out for dinner

3348. Send loving thoughts to your lover via ESP

3349. Know *all* of you partner's sizes!

3350. Visit Verona, Italy (A+ Romantic City, and setting of *Romeo and Juliet*)

3351–3358
8 Tips for Married Men

1. Flirt with your wife

2. Don't tell mother-in-law jokes

3. Never, never, *never* refer to your wife as "My Old Lady"

4. Refer to your wife as "My Bride"

5. Don't abandon your role as "lover" after you take on the role of "husband"

6. Do your fair share of the household chores

7. Be a loving role model for your children

8. Don't take your wife for granted

3359. Learn to browse and shop for romantic gifts via the Internet

3360. Plan your future together

3361. "We love the things we love for what they are." ~ Robert Frost

---

3362. For Halloween, dress as a *famous couple*—

3363. (Pick a new couple every year!)—

3364. Rhett Butler & Scarlett O'Hara

3365. Romeo & Juliet

3366. Fred & Wilma

3367. Adam & Eve

3368. Antony & Cleopatra

3369. Tom Sawyer & Becky

3370. Napoleon & Josephine

3371. Raggedy Ann & Andy
3372. Lil' Abner & Daisy May
3373. Barbie & Ken
3374. Cupid & Psyche

3375. Sing "your song" to him or her
3376. Surprise her with a bud vase with one red rose
3377. Learn what he/she considers *soothing*
3378. Celebrate Valentine's Day on the 14th of every month
3379. Buy her gold jewelry
3380. Learn to two-step
3381. Surprise her with an elegant jewelry box
3382. "Too much of a good thing is wonderful." ~ Mae West
3383. Give her an umbrella in shades of her favorite color

3384. Dance cheek-to-cheek
3385. Sleep cheek-to-cheek

3386. Buy an antique bed—
3387. Wear Victorian lingerie—

3388. Trade all electric lights for candles—
3389. Play music by Mozart and Debussy—
3390. And create a weekend of old-fashioned romantic love

3391. Learn to country line dance
3392. Ask a local travel agent to alert you to special vacation deals
3393. Volunteer together for a community organization
3394. "Perhaps that is what love is—the momentary or prolonged refusal to think of another person in terms of power." ~ Phyllis Rose
3395. Share an inspirational passage from a favorite book
3396. Wrap yourself as a Christmas gift and wait under the tree
3397. Love Enhancer: Commitment
3398. Send him an invitation: "Needed: An audience of one for an intimate Lingerie Fashion Show"

3399. English: "I adore you"
3400. French: "Je t'adore"

3401. Italian: "Ti adoro"
3402. German: "Ich mag dich sehr"
3403. Spanish: "Te adoro"
3404. Portugese: "Eu te adoro"

3405. Buy her lingerie that turns you on
3406. Buy him an outfit that turns you on
3407. Watch a movie that turns you on
3408. Talk about what he/she does that most turns you on
3409. Suggest a new sexual activity that turns you on

3410. Play "Role Reversal"—do each other's chores this weekend
3411. Play "Role Reversal"—when you next make love

3412. Learn more about the emotional and psychological aspects of sex
3413. Love Coupon: An All-Sports Weekend! The coupon-issuer will pay for and accompany you to any pro sporting event taking place in your vicinity within the next month

Favorite Love Songs from 1930

3414. "Body and Soul"
3415. "Embraceable You"
3416. "Love for Sale"
3417. "What Is This Thing Called Love?"
3418. "You Brought a New Kind of Love to Me"

3419. Give equipment for his/her favorite sport
3420. Rent a limousine to be at her service for a solid week
3421. "There is no fear in love, but perfect love casts out fear." ~ 1 John 4:18

3422–3432
11 Rules for Fighting Fair

1. Stick to the issue
2. Stay in the present
3. Say what you feel when you feel it
4. Don't generalize
5. Don't accuse
6. Don't threaten
7. Get all of your emotions out
8. But don't use emotion as a weapon

9. Don't say anything you'll regret
10. Compromise, but don't negotiate
11. Work toward resolution

3433. Celebrate your anniversary every
      month
3434. Kiss the back of his neck
3435. Dance—and sing—in the rain
3436. Prepare dinner together wearing
      matching aprons—and nothing else!
3437. "Love cannot be bought except with
      love." ~ John Steinbeck
3438. Enjoy a little "Afternoon Delight"

3439. "Happiness and love are just a choice
      away." ~ Leo Buscaglia
3440. Remember: While love *is* an emotion,
      it is also a *choice*
3441. Choose—very specifically—to act
      like newlyweds for one day
3442. Choose—very consciously—to make
      the most of every waking hour today
3443. Choose—with care—the words you
      say to your lover

3444. Hide a love note in a bottle of vitamins
3445. Invite her to try some "Vitamin L"

3446. Spend an evening stargazing together
3447. Romantic music alert: Michael Bolton CDs: *All That Matters; The One Thing*

3448. Write three paragraphs on "I Remember When We First Met"
3449. Write it in the style of a romance novel
3450. Or write a poem with the same title
3451. Present it to your partner on the anniversary of your meeting

---

3452–3463
12 Things Lovers Can Do—If They Try

1. You can give without losing anything
2. You can change without losing your uniqueness
3. You can grow without growing apart
4. You can compromise without compromising *yourself*
5. You can open up without being judged

6. You can disagree without arguing
7. You can feel without losing control
8. You can be affectionate without being sexual
9. You *can* keep the passion alive in a long-term relationship
10. You can be mature without losing the child inside of you
11. You can listen without having to solve the problem
12. You can be in a couple without losing your individuality

3464. Give her perfume that turns you on
3465. Businessperson's Tip: Your mate is the most important "customer" you'll ever have!
3466. "Who, being loved, is poor?"
  ~ Oscar Wilde

3467. Guys: Stop judging, stop correcting, stop lecturing
3468. Gals: Stop nagging, stop complaining, stop whining

3469. Give her a ruby ring…

3470. Along with "Rubylove," by Cat Stevens

3471. Wrapped in ruby red wrapping paper

3472. Learn sign language together

3473. Communicate intimate messages across crowded rooms

3474. Read *The Joy of Signing*, by Lottie Riekoff

3475. Or *A Basic Course in American Sign Language*, by Tom Humphries

---

3476. Connect love, creativity and spirituality: Read *The Artist's Way: A Spiritual Path to Higher Creativity*, by Julia Cameron

3477. "The most useless day is that in which we have not laughed." ~ Charles Field

3478. Give her Ralph Lauren "Romance" perfume

3479. Begin planning your 50th anniversary—during your honeymoon

3480. Buy gifts during end-of-season sales

3481–3498
18 Things That Come in "Twos"—
Ideas for Couples

1. Bicycles built-for-two
2. Double sleeping bags
3. Two-seater sports cars
4. A Chinese pu-pu platter for two
5. Mozart's Sonata in D Major for Two Pianos, K. 448
6. Two-person kayaks
7. Two-for-the-price-of-one specials at stores
8. Two-for-the-price-of-one specials at restaurants
9. Duets: "Endless Love," Luther Vandross & Mariah Carey
10. Loveseats
11. Stravinsky's Concerto for Two Pianos
12. Singing songs in two-part harmony
13. Doubles solitaire
14. Wedding rings
15. Double beds
16. See-saws

17. Double-scoop ice cream cones
18. Two-person hot tubs

3499. Celebrate with a bottle of scented massage oil
3500. A "Quickie Picnic" Coupon: The coupon-issuer will provide the wine, cheese, blanket, transportation, and fascinating conversation
3501. Scatter rose petals over your bed
3502. At every event, save the "Anniversary Waltz" for the two of you
3503. Buy her that special something that she's always wanted, but wouldn't buy for herself

---

3504–3510
7 Items for a Lifetime Romantic Checklist

1. Improve your relationship in a *specific* way, once-a-month, *forever*
2. Make love in Paris
3. Do something *so outrageous* that it becomes a story your family will tell for *generations*
4. Never forget a *single* anniversary,

birthday, or Valentine's Day

5. Celebrate your 25th anniversary by renewing your wedding vows
6. Give a gift that is so special it becomes a keepsake/family heirloom
7. Make love one thousand times

3511. Kidnap him/her!
3512. Drive around till he/she's disoriented
3513. Then go to that favorite restaurant
3514. Or away for a surprise romantic weekend

3515. Cater to your cat lover
3516. Get a subscription to *Cat Fancy Magazine*: (714) 855-8822
3517. Visit the "Cat Cabinet" museum in Amsterdam, Holland

3518. Take dancing lessons
3519. Create a collage from your favorite photos of the two of you
3520. Give one red rose
3521. Attend Oktoberfest in Germany: (212) 661-7200

3522. Order fancy foods from the Norm Thompson catalog: (800) 547-1160

Favorite Love Songs from 1931

3523. "Dancing in the Dark"
3524. "Dream a Little Dream of Me"
3525. "Goodnight Sweetheart"
3526. "I Found a Million-Dollar Baby"
3527. "Where the Blue of the Night"

3528. A "Fantasy Island" Coupon: The coupon-giver agrees to play along with any sexual fantasy your fertile imagination can invent. Not voided by any decency laws whatsoever

3529. "Love is strongest in pursuit; friendship in possession."
    ~ Ralph Waldo Emerson

3530. Give one dozen yellow roses

3531. Buy blank greeting cards—Express your love in your own words

3532. Burn incense

3533. Create one *simple* ritual—maybe around dinner

3534. Create one *elaborate* ritual—maybe around your anniversary

3535. Create one *meaningful* ritual—for when one of you leaves on a trip

3536. Create one *silly* ritual—for brightening a bad mood

3537. Create one *intimate* ritual—as part of foreplay

3538. Create one *family* ritual—for including and acknowledging your kids

---

3539. Guys: Always open her car door for her

3540. Gals: Always lean over and unlock his car door for him

3541. "Everyone on the planet is given the same weekend. Some people just use it better."
    ~ An ad for the *Wall St. Journal*

3542. Take a weekend drive with no map and no agenda

3543. Do all your chores during the week: Free-up your weekend for love!

3544. Take a weekend vacation at home
3545. Take a three-day weekend every
three months

3546. "To love deeply in one direction
makes us more loving in all others."
~ Madame Swetchine
3547. Blow her a kiss
3548. Build intimacy: Read *Passage to
Intimacy*, by Lori H. Gordon
3549. Program yourself to be more loving
3550. Massage his aching shoulders

Favorite Love Songs from 1932
3551. "April in Paris"
3552. "How Deep Is the Ocean?"
3553. "You're an Old Smoothie"
3554. "You're Getting to Be a Habit
with Me"

3555. Design a family coat-of-arms
3556. Eat dinner at the restaurant with the
best service
3557. Find obscure recordings by his/her
favorite singer

3558. Create a custom crossword puzzle that has romantic messages in it

3559. Give her *anything* in one of those distinctive turquoise Tiffany's boxes

3560. The "Jewelry, Jewelry, Jewelry!" Coupon: This amazing coupon is redeemable at any jewelry store anywhere in the world. Good for a truly outrageous purchase. You choose your gift. The coupon-issuer pays the bill. Up to $_____.

3561. Serve a cheap champagne with your next TV dinner

3562. Eat dinner at the best pizza joint in town

3563. "The only abnormality is the incapacity to love." ~ Anaïs Nin

Favorite Love Songs from 1933

3564. "Heartaches"

3565. "Honeymoon Hotel"

3566. "Let's Fall in Love"

3567. "Smoke Gets in Your Eyes"

3568. Learn a foreign language together

3569. "To speak of love is to make love."
~ Honore de Balzac

3570. Play "All-Day Foreplay"

3571. Pack a picnic basket, and have lunch in his office

3572. "To get the full value of joy you must have someone to divide it with."
~ Mark Twain

3573. A+ Romance Rating: The music CD *Let's Talk About Love*, by Celine Dion

3574. Teach your grandchildren everything you know about love

3575. Take a hike in the mountains

3576. Wear matching friendship rings to remind you that you're *friends* as well as lovers

3577. On your anniversary bake a cake with the appropriate number of candles

3578. "We can forgive as long as we love."
~ La Rochefoucauld

3579. Eat dinner at the best Italian restaurant around

3580. Take a walk in the rain

3581. Work on your *friendship* as well

as your *love*

3582. Read *Love & Friendship*,
by Allan Bloom

3583–3602
The 20 Most Romantic
Country Songs of All Time

1. "Blue," LeAnn Rimes
2. "Diamonds and Dirt," Rodney Crowell
3. "Dream On, Texas Ladies," John Michael Montgomery
4. "Everything I Love," Alan Jackson
5. "Flame in Your Eyes," Alabama
6. "He Stopped Loving Her Today," George Jones
7. "Hello Darlin'," Conway Twitty
8. "I'll Always Love You," Dolly Parton
9. "It's Your Love," Tim McGraw & Faith Hill
10. "Look at Us," Vince Gill
11. "Love Me Like You Used To," Tanya Tucker
12. "Love Will Find Its Way to You," Reba McEntire

13. "Love Without End, Amen," George Strait
14. "Stand By Your Man," Tammy Wynette
15. "Take the Ribbon from Your Hair," Tammy Smith
16. "The Dance," Garth Brooks
17. "This Night Won't Last Forever," Sawyer Brown
18. "To Be Loved By You," Wynonna
19. "Unchained Melody," Rodney McDowell
20. "You Win My Love," Shania Twain

3603. Send him flowers from "a secret admirer"
3604. "When love beckons you, follow him, though his ways are hard and steep." ~ Kahlil Gibran
3605. Give *fragrant* flowers: Casablanca Lilies, Stephanotis
3606. A "Day at the Races" Coupon: Good for a fun day at the racetrack or ballpark. Tickets and refreshments included

3607. Enemy of Love: Laziness

3608. Love Coupon: One romantic dinner at home. Prepared by the coupon-issuer. Proper dress required

3609. "A happy marriage is a long conversation which always seems too short." ~ André Maurois

3610. *Many* couples in long-term A+ Relationships express this thought. Perhaps—just *perhaps*—we should believe them

3611. Experiment: View your relationship as a *conversation*: It involves give-and-take; expressing yourself; listening; responding

3612. Visit a spiritually meaningful place, like Rome

3613. Daydream together

3614. Contact the Institute for Relationship Therapy: (800) 729-1121

3615. If you share the same literary tastes, organize a book discussion group

3616–3625
10 Ways to Love a Leo
(23 July –23 August)

1. Leo is a *fire* sign: Cater to his/her passionate, sexual nature
2. Gift tip: Small and expensive
3. Expensive perfumes and colognes
4. Gold jewelry, and gold-colored items
5. The flamboyant side of Leos will love surprise parties
6. As the sun rules Leo, items with a sun motif
7. Sunflowers; bay trees
8. Elegant and sophisticated foods
9. The charm of medieval Prague
10. Wrap gifts in golden tones

3626. For one full day, don't use *words*, but *touch*, to express your love
3627. Always have scented candles on hand
3628. Write a special toast to your partner
3629. Flaunt your sexuality

Recommended *1st* Anniversary Gifts
3630. Traditional: *Paper* • Modern: *Clocks* •

Godek's: *Lingerie*

Recommended 2nd Anniversary Gifts

3631. Traditional: *Cotton* • Modern: *China* • Godek's: *French lingerie*

Recommended 3rd Anniversary Gifts

3632. Traditional: *Leather* • Modern: *Crystal* • Godek's: *Roses*

Recommended 4th Anniversary Gifts

3633. Traditional: *Fruit* • Modern: *Appliances* • Godek's: *Champagne*

Recommended 5th Anniversary Gifts

3634. Traditional: *Wood* • Modern: *Silver* • Godek's: *Perfume*

Recommended 6th Anniversary Gifts

3635. Traditional: *Iron* • Modern: *Wood* • Godek's: *Books*

Recommended 7th Anniversary Gifts

3636. Traditional: *Copper* • Modern: *Desksets* • Godek's: *Wine*

Recommended 8th Anniversary Gifts

3637. Traditional: *Bronze* • Modern: *Linen* • Godek's: *Time*

Recommended 9th Anniversary Gifts

3638. Traditional: *Pottery* • Modern: *Leather* • Godek's: *Music CDs*

Recommended *10th* Anniversary Gifts

3639. Traditional: *Aluminum* • Modern:
Diamond jewelry • Godek's: *Silk*

Recommended *11th* Anniversary Gifts

3640. Traditional: *Steel* • Modern: *Fashion
jewelry* • Godek's: *Software*

Recommended *12th* Anniversary Gifts

3641. Traditional: *Linen* • Modern: *Pearls* •
Godek's: *Toys*

Recommended *13th* Anniversary Gifts

3642. Traditional: *Lace* • Modern: *Furs* •
Godek's: *Umbrellas*

Recommended *14th* Anniversary Gifts

3643. Traditional: *Ivory* • Modern: *Gold
jewelry* • Godek's: *Furniture*

Recommended *15th* Anniversary Gifts

3644. Traditional: *Crystal* • Modern: *Watches*
• Godek's: *Chocolate*

Recommended *16th* Anniversary Gifts

3645. Godek's: *Lingerie*

Recommended *17th* Anniversary Gifts

3646. Godek's: *Lingerie*

Recommended *18th* Anniversary Gifts

3647. Godek's: *Lingerie*

Recommended *19th* Anniversary Gifts

3648. Godek's: *Lingerie*

Recommended *20th* Anniversary Gifts

3649. Traditional: *China* • Modern: *Platinum* • Godek's: *Gemstones*

Recommended *21st* Anniversary Gifts

3650. Godek's: *Cedar*

Recommended *22nd* Anniversary Gifts

3651. Godek's: *Pine*

Recommended *23rd* Anniversary Gifts

3652. Godek's: *Maple*

Recommended *24th* Anniversary Gifts

3653. Godek's: *Mahogany*

Recommended *25th* Anniversary Gifts

3654. Traditional: *Silver* • Modern: *Silver* • Godek's: *Poetry*

Recommended *26th* Anniversary Gifts

3655. Godek's: *Frivolous*

Recommended *27th* Anniversary Gifts

3656. Godek's: *Serious*

Recommended *28th* Anniversary Gifts

3657. Godek's: *Cheap*

Recommended *29th* Anniversary Gifts

3658. Godek's: *Expensive*

Recommended *30th* Anniversary Gifts

3659. Traditional: *Pearl* • Modern: *Diamond*

• Godek's: *Sapphire*

Recommended *31st* Anniversary Gifts

3660.   Godek's: *Educational*

Recommended *32nd* Anniversary Gifts

3661.   Godek's: *Practical*

Recommended *33rd* Anniversary Gifts

3662.   Godek's: *Simple*

Recommended *34th* Anniversary Gifts

3663.   Godek's: *Complex*

Recommended *35th* Anniversary Gifts

3664.   Traditional: *Coral* • Modern: *Jade* •
         Godek's: *Pearl*

Recommended *36th* Anniversary Gifts

3665.   Godek's: *A round-the-world cruise*

Recommended *37th* Anniversary Gifts

3666.   Godek's: *Computers*

Recommended *38th* Anniversary Gifts

3667.   Godek's: *Balloons*

Recommended *39th* Anniversary Gifts

3668.   Godek's: *Leather*

Recommended *40th* Anniversary Gifts

3669.   Traditional: *Ruby* • Modern: *Ruby* •
         Godek's: *Theater tickets*

Recommended *41st* Anniversary Gifts

3670.   Godek's: *Candy*

Recommended *42nd* Anniversary Gifts
3671. Godek's: *Leather*
Recommended *43rd* Anniversary Gifts
3672. Godek's: *Her choice*
Recommended *44th* Anniversary Gifts
3673. Godek's: *His choice*
Recommended *45th* Anniversary Gifts
3674. Traditional: *Sapphire* • Modern:
        Sapphire • Godek's: *Emerald*
Recommended *46th* Anniversary Gifts
3675. Godek's: *Timepieces*
Recommended *47th* Anniversary Gifts
3676. Godek's: *Calligraphy*
Recommended *48th* Anniversary Gifts
3677. Godek's: *Fruit*
Recommended *49th* Anniversary Gifts
3678. Godek's: *Something heavy*
Recommended *50th* Anniversary Gifts
3679. Traditional: *Gold* • Modern: *Gold* •
        Godek's: *Paris*
Recommended *51st* Anniversary Gifts
3680. Godek's: *Violets*
Recommended *52nd* Anniversary Gifts
3681. Godek's: *Sculpture*
Recommended *53rd* Anniversary Gifts

3682. Godek's: *Something masculine*

Recommended 54th Anniversary Gifts

3683. Godek's: *Something feminine*

Recommended 55th Anniversary Gifts

3684. Traditional: *Emerald* • Modern:
Emerald • Godek's: *Gold*

Recommended 56th Anniversary Gifts

3685. Godek's: *Red*

Recommended 57th Anniversary Gifts

3686. Godek's: *Blue*

Recommended 58th Anniversary Gifts

3687. Godek's: *Yellow*

Recommended 59th Anniversary Gifts

3688. Godek's: *Green*

Recommended 60th Anniversary Gifts

3689. Traditional: *Diamond* • Modern:
Diamond • Godek's: *Sapphire*

Recommended 61st Anniversary Gifts

3690. Godek's: *Outdoor-oriented*

Recommended 62nd Anniversary Gifts

3691. Godek's: *Indoor-oriented*

Recommended 63rd Anniversary Gifts

3692. Godek's: *Sex-oriented*

Recommended 64th Anniversary Gifts

3693. Godek's: *Sports-oriented*

Recommended 65th Anniversary Gifts

3694.   Godek's: *Pearl*

Recommended 67th Anniversary Gifts

3695.   Godek's: *Traditional*

Recommended 68th Anniversary Gifts

3696.   Godek's: *Modern*

Recommended 69th Anniversary Gifts

3697.   Godek's: *Purple*

Recommended 70th Anniversary Gifts

3698.   Godek's: *Diamond*

Recommended 71st Anniversary Gifts

3699.   Godek's: *Venice*

Recommended 72nd Anniversary Gifts

3700.   Godek's: *Antiques*

Recommended 73rd Anniversary Gifts

3701.   Godek's: *Her choice*

Recommended 74th Anniversary Gifts

3702.   Godek's: *Rolls Royce*

Recommended 75th Anniversary Gifts

3703.   Godek's: *If you make it this far you get to start all over again!*

3704.   Surf the Internet for romantic ideas

3705.   Give her your car key on a gold chain with a note: "You drive me wild!"

3706. Cover the ceiling with helium balloons
3707. Rent costumes to inspire and enhance a fantasy weekend
3708. Take a limo ride
3709. Buy lots of *little* diamonds for one another

3710. Watch cloud formations
3711. Watch your children grow
3712. Watch your love grow
3713. Watch out for each other's best interests
3714. Watch your partner's favorite TV show
3715. Watch him or her mature
3716. Watch your relationship deepen
3717. Watch time go by
3718. Watch your favorite movie together—for the 10th time
3719. Watch an eclipse of the sun
3720. Watch an eclipse of the moon
3721. Watch the clock turn to midnight on New Year's Eve
3722. Watch your pennies so you can buy

that special gift

3723. Watch your weight so you stay healthy

3724. A "Couch Potato" Coupon: You're entitled to a solid weekend of sitting in front of the TV, while the coupon-giver caters to all of your junk food needs

3725. "The little things? The little moments? They aren't little."
~ Jon Kabat-Zinn

3726. Take an extra five minutes in bed to welcome each other to a new day

3727. Mood music: Create a comfortable, jazzy mood with the *Chase the Clouds Away* CD by Chuck Mangione

---

3728. Prescription for romance: Hug!

3729. Minimum dosage: Maintenance level: two per day

3730. Average dosage: Happiness level: four per day

3731. Recommended dosage: Passionate level: ten per day

3732. Words that *men* love to hear: "I *believe* in you"

3733. Words that *women* love to hear: "I *cherish* you"

3734. Match your love notes to your flowers

3735. "The red rose is my passion for you; the pink rose is my commitment to you; the yellow rose is the sunshine you've given me"

3736. "One flower for each day I'll be away from you (I'm glad it's a *small* bouquet)"

3737. "She loves me—She loves me not—She *loves* me!"

3738. Give him a Mont Blanc pen so he can write love letters to you in style!

3739. Buy snacks at the best café

3740. Drink a bottle of rare French wine together

Favorite Love Songs from 1934

3741. "I Get a Kick out of You"

3742. "Let's Fall in Love"
3743. "The Very Thought of You"
3744. "You and the Night and the Music"
3745. "You're the Top"

3746. A "Chocoholic" Coupon: You are entitled to a massive no-holds-barred celebration of chocolate! Included: an *extraordinary* amount of chocolate
3747. Eat dinner at the best German restaurant around
3748. Tour the great vineyards of France
3749. When traveling, mail a greeting card every day you're gone

---

3750. Write a letter together to your grandchildren
3751. And one to your great, great, great grandchildren

3752–3760
9 Songs to Help You Express Your Feelings: *Desire & Sexual Attraction*

1. "Afternoon Delight," Starland Vocal Band

2. "Feel Like Makin' Love," Bad Company
3. "I Want Your Sex," George Michael
4. "Kiss You All Over," Exile
5. "Let's Spend the Night Together," Rolling Stones
6. "Natural Woman," Aretha Franklin
7. "Sexual Healing," Marvin Gaye
8. "Slave to Love," Bryan Ferry
9. "The Sweetest Taboo," Sade

3761. Get *front row center* seats for her favorite performer
3762. Tell her about the event, *but not about the seats*

3763. Fill her shoes with penny candy
3764. A "Saturday Night Fever" Coupon: Dance your cares away this Saturday night. Proper dress required
3765. Enemy of Love: TV
3766. Learn what he/she considers *sexy*
3767. Take an extra five minutes to reconnect after a day at work
3768. Sing "your song" to your lover at a

Karaoke bar

3769. Strategically dab perfume on intimate places on your body

3770. "The ideal day never comes. Today is ideal for him who makes it so."
~ Horatio Dresser

3771. Put notes on household products...

3772. Joy dishwashing liquid: "Every day with you is a *joy*"

3773. Cheerios: "Just knowin' you love me cheers me up"

3774. Old Spice: "You spice up my life"

3775. Ritz Crackers: "Let's 'Put on the Ritz' tonight"

3776. A roll of Lifesavers: "You're a lifesaver"

3777. Caress soap: "Let's do this tonight"

3778. Hershey's Kisses: "I'll trade you *these* for some of *yours*"

3779. Think-up your *own* suggestive notes to attach to Snickers Bars...

3780. Hershey's kisses

3781. Mounds candy bars

3782. Fire Balls

3783. Enjoy an autumn hayride together

3784. As a secret surprise, learn to cook a gourmet meal

3785. Catch a new act at a local comedy club

3786. Take a horse-drawn carriage ride

3787. Give a balloon bouquet

3788. Locate a nearby meadow where you can pick wildflowers

3789. Give him movie tickets taped to its soundtrack on CD

3790. "The road to the heart is the ear." ~ Voltaire

3791. Give her ice capades tickets inside a pair of ice skates

3792. Make two *incredible* banana splits

3793. Enclose pressed flowers with a love note

3794. Find a "romantic hideaway" bed-and-breakfast to call your own

3795. Buy him a T-shirt picturing his favorite rock group

3796. Read aloud to each other

3797. Go for a midnight stroll on the beach

3798. Give him a cap from his favorite

football team

3799. Jump-start your creativity: Read *Drawing on the Right Side of the Brain*, by B. Edwards

3800. "The giving of love is an education in itself." ~ Eleanor Roosevelt

3801. "When you look for the good in others, you discover the best in yourself." ~ Martin Walsh

3802. Teach your children everything you know about love

3803. Discuss what each of you finds *erotic*

3804. Discuss what each of you finds *sexy*

3805. What would you be willing to *try?*

3806. Give her a stuffed animal with a note attached...

3807. Teddy bears: "I can't bear being away from you"

3808. Stuffed lions: "I'm roarin' to get you"

3809. Stuffed pigs: "I'm hog wild over you"

3810. Stuffed tigers: "You're grrrrrreat!"

3811. Stuffed monkeys: "Let's monkey around"

3812. Gals: Get a classic, matching set of bra, panties, garter belt, and stockings—in *black*

3813. Gals: Get a classic, matching set of bra, panties, garter belt, and stockings—in *white*

3814. Great inspiration and great motivation come from the *heart*, not from the *head*

3815. "The only true gift is a portion of yourself." ~ Ralph Waldo Emerson

3816. The Truly Romantic "Wedding Rededication" Coupon: Good for a small ceremony in which you renew your wedding vows

---

Favorite Love Songs from 1935

3817. "Begin the Beguine"

3818. "Cheek to Cheek"

3819. "Lovely to Look At"

3820. "These Foolish Things Remind Me of You"

3821. Update your ideas of gender differences

3822. Integrating your mind and body will help your heart. Learn about "Awareness Through Movement" at The Feldenkrais Guild: (800) 775-2118

3823. Eat in the most romantic villa in Venice: Academia

3824–3849
An A to Z List to Inspire Your Love

Ask your partner to pick a letter. He or she has twenty-four hours in which to perform a loving gesture based on any of the key words below:

A is for Attitude, Available, Accept, Ardor, Accolades, Admire, A' La Mode, Anniversary, Ambrosia, Ardent, Athens, Australia

B is for Boudoir, B&Bs, Buttercups, Beaches, Blue, Boston, Bicycling, Broadway, Brandy, Bubblebaths, Bahamas

C is for Champagne, Creativity, Candlelight, Candy, Chocolate, Convertibles, Casablanca, Cognac, Caviar, Chivalry, Crabtree & Evelyn

D is for Diamonds, Dinner, Daffodils,
   Dancing, Dating, Dolls, Dirty dancing

E is for Enthusiasm, Energy, Excitement,
   Emeralds, Earrings, Elvis, Exotic,
   Expensive

F is for Flirting, Fantasies, Feminine,
   Faithful, France, Fruits, Frenching,
   Foreplay

G is for Gardenias, Godiva, Get-aways,
   Glenn Miller, Gourmet, Greece

H is for Hearts, Humor, Hugs, Hide-aways,
   Horses, Hershey's Kisses, Hyatt

I is for Intimacy, Intrigue, Italy, Inns,
   Ingenuity, Ice cream, Ice skating,
   Interdependent, Imaginative,
   Invitation

J is for Java, Jasmine, Jell-O, Journey, Joyful,
   Jingle bells

K is for Kissing, Kinky, Kittens, Koala Bears

L is for Love, Laughing, Love Letters, Lilacs,
   Lace, Leather, Leo Buscaglia,
   Lobsters, Lovemaking, Lovesongs

M is for Monogamy, Marriage, Masculine,
   M&M's, Massage, Movies, Mistletoe,
   Mozart

N is for Negligee, Naughty, Nibble, Nighttime, Nubile, Novelty, Nurture, Nymph, Naples, Nightcap, Nape, Nepal

O is for Orgasm, Opera, Oprah, Orchid, Outrageous, Outdoors

P is for Passion, Poppies, Poetry, Persimmons, Paris, Polkas, Panties, Pizza, Photos, Pearls, Picnics, Playfulness, Purple

Q is for Quaint, Quality, Queen, Quebec, Question, QE2, Quiche, Quiver

R is for Rendezvous, Roses, Rubies, Red, Reading, Rome, Rituals, Riviera, Restful, Rapture, Rio, Rainbows

S is for Sex

T is for Talking, Teasing, Tulips, Titillating, Theater, Togetherness, Toasts, Toys, Trains, Trinidad

U is for Uxorious, Undress, Undulate, Urges, Unexpected, Union, Under the Spreading Chestnut Tree, Unabashed feelings

V is for Violets, Venice, Venus, Valentines, Vegetables, Victoria's Secret

W is for Wine, Wisteria, Walking Hand-in-
   hand, Weddings
X is for X-Rated, Xerographic, Xylophones,
   Xmas
Y is for Yes, Yellow, Yin & Yang, Young-at-
   heart
Z is for Zany, Zeal, Zings, Zodiac, Zurich

3850. Get in touch with your own body—
   it will enhance your enjoyment of sex
3851. Beware of "relationship entropy": The
   tendency of couples to drift apart if
   energy isn't added to the relationship
3852. For coffee lovers: Buy a variety of
   coffee beans
3853. Pledge your love in writing
3854. Practice "emotional foreplay"

3855. A "Professional Sporting Event"
   Coupon: You are entitled to two
   tickets to any professional sporting
   event taking place within 100 miles
3856. Prepare a bucket of steaming water so
   he can soak his aching feet
3857. "The way to love anything is to

realize that it might be lost"
~ G.K. Chesterton

3858. Massage her neck muscles

3859. The "Weekend Movie Marathon"
Coupon: You choose a theme, and
the coupon-issuer will rent six movies
that fit the theme, pop the popcorn,
and be your weekend movie date

3860–3866
7 Lists for Lovers

A+ Couples don't leave things to *chance*, they
write things down

1. Create with your partner: A "Wish
List"—For *things* you want

2. A "Dream List"—For *places* you want
to visit

3. A "Fantasy List"—For sensual and
sexual desires

4. A "Date List"—For activities,
restaurants

5. A "Hollywood List"—For films you
want to see

6. A "Home Improvement List"—For
ways to enhance your environment

7. A "Self-Improvement List"—For ways in which you want to grow

---

3867. Admit it when you're wrong
3868. Love with all your heart
3869. Remember and re-create the feeling of passion you had for your partner when you first met
3870. "The object of love is to serve, not to win." ~ Woodrow Wilson
3871. Love Coupon: Good for a $100 shopping spree in the nearest lingerie shop (or lingerie catalog)

3872. Take the day off work—and spend most of the day in bed together
3873. Give him a tie that illustrates his favorite sports team
3874. Fill her jewelry box with one hundred tiny love notes
3875. The "Shoot Your TV" Coupon: You are entitled to one week in which your partner devotes all of his or her TV time to *you*
3876. Learn what he/she considers *touching*

3877–3895
19 Ways to Earn Your "MBA"
(Masters of Bedroom Amore)

1. Focus on fondling
2. Ask your partner to direct you—*very specifically*—in how they like to be touched
3. Talk candidly about the differences between *sexy* and *sensual*
4. Read one book by Dr. Ruth
5. Guys: Talk more
6. Gals: Touch more
7. Practice: Talking "dirty" while making love
8. Practice: Talking *seductively* in bed
9. Experiment with fantasies
10. Experiment with reading erotica
11. Experiment with sensual, sexy, and outright X-rated movies
12. Try putting yourself in your partner's shoes (figuratively *and* literally!)
13. Spend one solid hour exploring various kissing techniques
14. Guys: Be *vulnerable*—without being a *wimp*

15. Gals: Be *confident*—without being *overbearing*
16. Turn your "bedroom" into a "boudoir"
17. Remember: Practice makes perfect
18. Try loosening up those vocal cords during sex
19. Try loosening up those inhibitions during sex

3896. Celebrate New Year's Eve surrounded by good friends
3897. Go to Las Vegas for the great entertainment
3898. "Where there is great love there are always great miracles." ~ Willa Cather
3899. Mindset: Love is a matter of *skills*, not a matter of luck or fate
3900. Eat dinner at the best French restaurant around
3901. Have lunch at the best local dive
3902. For your movie buff: An endless supply of popcorn
3903. Bring dinner home when he/she's really busy

3904–3917
14 Ways to Put the *Zing* Back in Your Relationship

1. Give her a bottle of champagne as a "Thank You" for doing some everyday chore
2. Gals: Promise him a week of ESPN (Exceptional Sex Practiced Nightly)
3. Revive chivalry
4. Place a romantic message on a local billboard
5. Locate a copy of the 1935 hit song "Zing! Went the Strings of My Heart"
6. Dress to please your partner—while going out in public
7. Seduce him
8. Dress to please your partner—while home alone together
9. Make a giant greeting card from a large cardboard box
10. Write a little note: "My sexiest memory of you is…"
11. Fly to Paris for the weekend
12. Leave written clues that lead him to a hidden gift

13. Rent a Harley motorcycle for a freewheeling vacation
14. Leave a subtly suggestive message on the answering machine

---

3918. Simple Sex Rule #1: Guys are fast, gals are slow
3919. Simple Sex Rule #2: Guys are visual—*show* him
3920. Simple Sex Rule #3: Gals are auditory—*tell* her

3921. Create a sexy "Five-Sense Evening," during which you and your lover stimulate all five of each other's senses
3922. Make love to her *the way she wants to be made love to*
3923. Make his/her friends *your* friends
3924. Expand your definition of love every year
3925. "Life for every person should be a journey in jubilance!"
  ~ Charles Fillmore
3926. Make love in a semi-public place
3927. Create a memento wall: Paste-up

favorite mementos, movie stubs, programs, etc.

3928. Daily affirmation: "I will appreciate what I have"

3929. Throw *great* parties together...
3930. Become famous for your Halloween costume balls
3931. Host wine tasting parties
3932. Host beer tasting parties
3933. Have a summertime beach party
3934. Gather good friends for dinner once a month
3935. Host a New Year's Eve costume ball
3936. Have monogrammed place mats made
3937. Host an elegant garden party
3938. Host an Academy Awards party

3939. When traveling apart, write one paragraph expressing how much you miss him/her; mail it
3940. Rent an RV for a cross-country road trip
3941. When traveling, mail a different postcard every day you're gone

3942. "When you've exhausted all possibilities, remember this: you haven't." ~ Robert Schuller

3943. Wear matching Japanese kimonos

3944–3962
19 Romantic Movies Starring
the All-Time Great Romantic Couples

1. *Red Dust* (Gable & Harlow)
2. *Hold Your Man* (Gable & Harlow)
3. *Flying Down to Rio* (Astair & Rogers)
4. *Top Hat* (Astaire & Rogers)
5. *Maytime* (MacDonald & Eddy)
6. *Sweethearts* (MacDonald & Eddy)
7. *Love Finds Andy Hardy* (Garland & Rooney)
8. *Girl Crazy* (Garland & Rooney)
9. *That Forsyte Woman* (Garson & Pidgeon)
10. *Scandal at Scourie* (Garson & Pidgeon)
11. *To Have and Have Not* (Bogart & Bacall)
12. *Fire Over England* (Leigh & Olivier)
13. *21 Days Together* (Leigh & Olivier)
14. *Cleopatra* (Taylor & Burton)

15. *The Sandpiper* (Taylor & Burton)
16. *The Long, Hot Summer* (Newman & Woodward)
17. *Paris Blues* (Newman & Woodward)
18. *Woman of the Year* (Hepburn & Tracy)
19. *Without Love* (Hepburn & Tracy)

3963. Learn what he/she considers *exciting*
3964. Eat dinner at the restaurant with the best wine list
3965. Save your love letters in a shoebox
3966. Fall in love all over again
3967. "There is no greater invitation to love than loving first." ~ St. Augustine
3968. The Sweets-for-the-Sweet Coupon: You are entitled to a twelve-pound pile of any three kinds of candy that you specify
3969. Write a tiny note somewhere on your skin with ink, and ask your lover to look for it!

3970. Collect and record several "birthday" and age-related songs on audio tape
3971. *Happy Birthday*, Stevie Wonder

3972. *Happy Birthday*, New Kids on the Block
3973. *Happy Birthday*, Altered Images
3974. *Birthday*, The Beatles
3975. *Happy Birthday to You*, Bing Crosby
3976. *Happy Birthday to You*, Eddy Howard
3977. *Happy Birthday to You*, Sunsetters
3978. *Happy, Happy Birthday, Baby*, Tune Weavers
3979. *I Wish I Were 18 Again*, George Burns
3980. *When I'm Sixty-Four*, The Beatles
3981. *Young at Heart*, Frank Sinatra

3982–3998
17 Quirky Questions That Open a Window into Your Lover's Personality

Sometimes the best route into the psyche is a roundabout route. Ask your lover these questions:

1. If you could be a comic strip character, who would you be?
2. If your name were to appear in the dictionary, how would you define yourself?
3. If you could create the perfect job for

yourself, what would it be?

4. Who are your heroes? (Fictional *and* real)

5. If you had three wishes, what would they be?

6. Could you live for a year in a tent with your partner (without going crazy)?

7. How many self-help books have you read in your lifetime?

8. If you could accomplish one crazy stunt that would land you in the Guinness Book of World Records, what would it be?

9. Would you rather be really, really smart, or really, really good looking?

10. If you could be a super hero, who would you be?

11. If you were Rick, in the movie *Casablanca*, would you have let Ilsa leave at the end?

12. If you had just one more day to live, how would you live that day?

13. What one thing did your parents *always* yell at you for?

14. What one part of your body would you like to change?
15. Would you ever go skinny-dipping?
16. What three historical figures would you like to have a conversation with?
17. Did Francesca do the right thing in *Bridges of Madison County*?

3999. Give a case of his/her favorite wine
4000. "The art of being wise is the art of knowing what to overlook."
    ~ William James
4001. Give him rock concert tickets taped to the group's latest CD
4002. For your movie buff: His/her favorite movie on video
4003. "The best proof of love is trust."
    ~ Dr. Joyce Brothers
4004. Have a love quote embroidered on her pillowcase
4005. A "Coffee, Tea & Me" Coupon: Good for coffee or tea served to you anywhere in your home, at a time of your choosing
4006. Learn to polka

4007. **Stop** complaining!
4008. **Look** lovingly into your lover's eyes
4009. **Listen** attentively

4010. Buy a box of kids' valentines
4011. Mail *hundreds* of them to your lover
4012. Mail one-a-day for several months
4013. Mail them all at once
4014. Fill his briefcase with them
4015. Tape them all over her car
4016. Fill the sink with them
4017. Fill her pillow with them

4018. Prescription for romance:
       Compliment him/her
4019. Repeat every four to six hours

4020. "There is no remedy for love but to
       love more." ~ Henry David Thoreau
4021. Drip honey on your lover's body; lick
       it off
4022. Give him balloons to match his age
4023. Take a walk in the park
4024. Spoil him for a solid week
4025. "A man is never so weak as when a

> woman is telling him how strong he is." ~ Anonymous

4026. Learn to square dance (not just for squares)
4027. Eat in the most romantic inn in Copenhagen: Skovshoved
4028. Give him Godiva Chocolates to satisfy his sweet tooth
4029. Make a life-sized cardboard cut-out of yourself

4030–4041
12 Sexy Tips—For Gals Only

1. On *his* birthday, give *yourself* some lingerie
2. Read a few men's magazines—for some insight into the male psyche
3. Greet him at the door wearing sexy lingerie
4. Wear a red bow tie and matching heels—and nothing else
5. Mail him a pair of your sexiest panties and attach a sexy note
6. Reminder: Most mens' sex hormone

levels are highest in the morning

7. Pose on a bed of black silk sheets wearing white silk lingerie
8. Pose on a bed of white silk sheets wearing black silk lingerie
9. Seduction music: "I Wanna Be Loved By You," by Marilyn Monroe
10. Never, never, *never* fake it
11. Greet him at the front door wearing your wedding gown
12. Be his "Calendar Girl": Paste pictures of yourself in a swimsuit calendar

---

4042. Romantic music alert: Earl Klugh CDs: *Heartstrings; Love Songs; Ballads*
4043. French kiss
4044. "Where love is concerned, too much is not even enough."
~ P.A.C. de Beaumarchais
4045. Great relationships require equal parts of passion, commitment, and intimacy
4046. Commission a custom quilt to include a variety of designs symbolizing your life together

4047. Send him a perfumed love letter
4048. Learn to like your in-laws!
4049. Spend a weekend on Nantucket
Island

4050. Collect CDs of romantic music from
romantic movies…
4051. *Against All Odds*
4052. *Doctor Zhivago*
4053. *Out of Africa*
4054. *Romeo and Juliet*
4055. *Sleepless in Seattle*
4056. *Somewhere in Time*
4057. *The Bodyguard*
4058. *Titanic*
4059. *Top Gun*

4060–4064
5 Songs to Help You Express Your Feelings: *New Love*

1. "We've Only Just Begun," The Carpenters
2. "(I've Been) Searchin' So Long," Chicago
3. "Puppy Love," Paul Anka

4. "The First Time Ever I Saw Your Face," Roberta Flack
5. "All My Loving," The Beatles

4065. Tease
4066. But don't mock
4067. Tickle
4068. But don't torture

4069. Take a moonlit stroll
4070. Give a sexy massage
4071. Make a habit of dropping into a card shop once a month
4072. Have sex on the big boardroom table in the executive conference room of your mate's office
4073. Practice yoga together
4074. A birthday resource: *The Oxford Book of Ages*, edited by Anthony Samson
4075. A "Quickie" Coupon: This rare and highly-prized coupon entitles you to sex with the coupon-giver *immediately* upon the handing this coupon back to him or her (No excuses accepted)
4076. "Therefore encourage one another

and build each other up."
~ 1 Thessalonians 5:11

Favorite Love Songs from 1936

4077. "I've Got You Under My Skin"
4078. "Let Yourself Go," Fred Astaire
4079. "Love Is Like a Cigarette," Eddy Duchin
4080. "The Night Is Young and You're So Beautiful"
4081. "No Regrets," Billie Holiday
4082. "The Way You Look Tonight," Fred Astaire

4083. "A kiss is an application for a better position." ~ Jeff Rovin
4084. The Joy of Sex Coupon: The coupon-giver provides the book. You choose the page. You both enjoy yourselves and each other as you follow the instructions on that page
4085. Surprise her with a crystal vase full of flowers
4086. Enemy of Love: Lack of understanding

4087. For your bird lover: *Bird Talk Magazine:* (714) 855-8822

4088. Pinch his butt when no one is looking

4089–4188
100 Love Songs Recorded by Frank Sinatra

1. "Almost Like Being in Love"
2. "At Long Last Love"
3. "Can I Steal a Little Love"
4. "Crazy Love"
5. "Don't Take Your Love From Me"
6. "End of a Love Affair"
7. "Everybody Ought to Be in Love"
8. "Everybody Love Somebody"
9. "Falling in Love With Love"
10. "Farewell, Farewell to Love"
11. "Give Her Love"
12. "Half as Lovely"
13. "Hallelujah, I Love Her So"
14. "Hello Young Lovers"
15. "Hey Jealous Lover"
16. "How Are You Fixed for Love"
17. "I Am Loved"

18. "I Believe I'm Gonna Love You"
19. "I Can't Believe That You're in Love with Me"
20. "I Can't Stop Falling in Love with You"
21. "I Fall in Love Too Easily"
22. "I Fall in Love With You Ev'ry Day"
23. "I Got a Gal I Love"
24. "I Love My Wife"
25. "I Love Paris"
26. "I Love You"
27. "I Love You (Version #1)"
28. "I Love You (Version #2)"
29. "I Loved Her"
30. "I Wish I Were in Love Again"
31. "I Wish You Love"
32. "I Would Be in Love Anyway"
33. "If I Ever Love Again"
34. "If I Loved You"
35. "It's a Lovely Day Tomorrow"
36. "I've Got a Love to Keep Me Warm"
37. "I've Never Been in Love Before"
38. "Just One Way to Say I Love You"
39. "The Last Call for Love"
40. "Let's Fall in Love"

41. "Like Someone in Love"
42. "Look of Love"
43. "Love and Marriage"
44. "Love Is a Many Splendored Thing"
45. "Love Is Here to Stay"
46. "Love Is Around The Corner"
47. "Love Isn't Just for the Young"
48. "Love Lies"
49. "Love Locked Out"
50. "Love Looks So Well on You"
51. "Love Me"
52. "Love Me As I Am"
53. "Love Me Tender"
54. "Love Means Love"
55. "Love Walked In"
56. "A Lovely Moonlit Night"
57. "Lovely Way to Spend an Evening"
58. "Lover"
59. "Love's Been Good to Me"
60. "Melody of Love"
61. "Mind If I Make Love To You"
62. "Moon Love"
63. "My Love For You"
64. "My One and Only Love"
65. "Once I Loved"

66. "Once in Love with Amy"
67. "The One I Love"
68. "One Love"
69. "One Love Affair"
70. "P.S.: I Love You"
71. "People Will Say We're in Love"
72. "Prisoner of Love"
73. "Secret Love"
74. "So in Love"
75. "So Long My Love"
76. "Somewhere My Love"
77. "Take My Love"
78. "Taking a Chance on Love"
79. "Tell Her You Love Her"
80. "Tell Her You Love Her Each Day"
81. "That's How Much I Love You"
82. "Then Suddenly Love"
83. "This Is My Love"
84. "This Love of Mine"
85. "This Was My Love"
86. "To Love and Be Loved"
87. "Two in Love"
88. "What Is This Thing Called Love"
89. "What Now My Love"
90. "When I Stop Loving You"

91. "When I'm Not Near the Girl I Love"
92. "When Somebody Loves You"
93. "When Your Lover Has Gone"
94. "Wives and Lovers"
95. "You Brought a New Kind of Love to Me"
96. "You My Love"
97. "You'd Be So Easy to Love"
98. "You'll Always Be the One I Love"
99. "Your Love for Me"
100. "You're Nobody 'Til Somebody Loves You"

4189. Write a *really* sexy, suggestive personal ad in the newspaper—in code!
4190. Rent every movie that stars his favorite actress
4191. Take a cooking class together
4192. Wear matching bathrobes
4193. Love Coupon: Entitling you to an afternoon of watching clouds together
4194. Give a subscription to a favorite magazine
4195. The "Lazy Love" Coupon: This

coupon entitles you to a sensuous, luxurious, extended lovemaking session with the coupon-issuer. Time requirement: At least 3 hours

4196. Extend your vacation budget by staying in cheap motels

4197. Keep every love letter and note from your lover

4198. Decorate with stuffed Poohs, Piglets, and Tiggers

4199. Re-write "The Twelve Days of Christmas"—and give *all* the gifts!

4200. Copy a romantic poem onto fancy parchment paper

4201. Have it framed

4202. Hang it on the wall and wait for your partner to notice it

---

4203. Have dinner at home by candlelight

4204. Heck, have *breakfast* by candlelight!

4205. Make every Monday "Extra Kisses Day"

4206. Make every Tuesday "Gift Day"

4207. Make every Wednesday "Partner Appreciation Day"

4208. Make every Thursday "Love Is About the Little Things Day"

4209. Make every Friday evening "Date Night"

4210. Make every Saturday "Sexual Exploration Day"

4211. Make every Sunday a "Spiritual Connection Day"

4212. Take a massage class: Learn to do it *right*

4213. Vacuum kiss (suck the air out of your mouths; separate with a "pop")

4214. "Grow old with me! The best is yet to be." ~ Robert Browning

4215. Have breakfast at the best diner

4216. Daily affirmation: "I will be aware of my feelings of love"

4217. Run a road race to raise money for charity

4218. Make a habit of browsing in a lingerie shop once a season

4219. Take a drawing class together
4220. Pose nude for each other
4221. Act out a sexy artist/model fantasy

4222. Pray together
4223. Play together

4224. When traveling, hide a love letter under his/her pillow and tape a photo of yourself to the TV screen
4225. Leave three greeting cards hidden around the house
4226. Mail a greeting card on your way to the airport
4227. Mail another greeting card as soon as you arrive at your destination

---

4228. "Men are all alike in their promises. It is only in their deeds that they differ." ~ Moliere
4229. Clip ads that show gift ideas you want to consider
4230. FYI: While men aren't typically as *verbal*, they are often more *action-oriented* than women

4231. Create a start-up screen for her computer that displays a romantic message
4232. Make romance a *habit*
4233. "To fall in love is awfully simple, but to fall out of love is simply awful."
~ Anonymous

Favorite Love Songs from 1937

4234. "I've Got My Love to Keep Me Warm"
4235. "In the Still of the Night"
4236. "Shall We Dance?" Fred Astaire
4237. "Somebody to Care for Me," Deanna Durbin
4238. "Thanks for the Memory"
4239. "Where or When"

4240. Remember, a little exhibitionism never hurt anyone
4241. Turn the *ordinary* into the *special*
4242. Surprise your partner at work with an *armful* of flowers
4243. Send teddy bears
4244. Take turns shooting portrait photos

of each other; try to capture the true *essence* of each other's personality

4245. Explore Greek temples
4246. Learn to sing a love song duet
4247. When traveling, mail a little love note every day you're gone
4248. A "Dancing Lesson" Coupon: Good for one dancing lesson given by a professional at a dance studio. The coupon-giver will participate with both left feet
4249. Go to popular vacation spots off-season

7 Songs to Help You Express Your Feelings: *Suggestive*

4250. "In the Mood," Glenn Miller
4251. "Lay Lady Lay," Bob Dylan
4252. "Light My Candle," from the Broadway musical *Rent*
4253. "Makin' Whoopee!" (1928)
4254. "Physical," Olivia Newton-John
4255. "So Deep Within You," Moody Blues
4256. "We've Got Tonight," Kenny Rogers & Sheena Easton

4257. Learn to disco
4258. Turn everyday events into "little celebrations"
4259. Name your computer hard drive after her
4260. Planning doesn't destroy spontaneity, it creates opportunity
4261. The Saturday Night Date Coupon: Where? Wherever you want. When? You decide. The coupon-giver guarantees a great time and will pay all expenses up to $50
4262. "Vulnerability is always at the heart of love." ~ Leo Buscaglia

---

4263. Write little love notes
4264. Write long, passionate love letters to one another
4265. Write poetry
4266. Write a "Thank You" note for something your partner's done for you
4267. Write notes on Post-It Notes and stick them around the house
4268. Write notes on rolls of toilet paper

4269. Write a list of ten gifts you know your partner would love

4270. Write a list of ten places your partner would love to go

4271. Write a list of ten places where you'd like to take your partner

4272. Write a list of ten activities you know your partner would enjoy

4273. Write a note using candy conversation hearts

4274. Write love notes on the refrigerator using Magnetic Poetry

4275. Write a love note using a Scrabble game

4276. Give your partner a *gift*: Something that he or she *wants*

4277. Give your partner a *present*: Something that *you* want him or her to have

---

4278. "The only love worthy of the name, ever and always uplifts." ~ George MacDonald

4279. Send a Valentine's Day card in *August*

4280. Lingerie, lingerie, lingerie!
4281. A satin camisole and matching tap pants
4282. Matching bra and panty sets
4283. An elegant peignoir
4284. Teddies
4285. Boxer shorts with big red hearts on them
4286. Garter belts and stockings
4287. A bustier
4288. Silk pajamas
4289. An outfit like the one worn by this month's Playmate of the Month

---

4290. Use "multi-tasking" as a strategy to save time
4291. But be totally focused on your mate during intimate times

---

4292. Go for it in a BIG way: Be *outrageously* romantic!
4293. Take a ride in a convertible together

Favorite Love Songs from 1938
4294. "Falling in Love with Love"

4295. "I Married an Angel," Larry Clinton
4296. "Jeepers Creepers"
4297. "This Can't Be Love"
4298. "Two Sleepy People," Bob Hope & Shirley Ross
4299. "You Go to My Head," Kay Kyser
4300. "You Must Have Been a Beautiful Baby"

4301. Write a letter saying you're a researcher for the new edition of *The Joy of Sex*, and you need her help with your studies
4302. Don't *ever* give your partner reason to be jealous
4303. Surprise her with sachets for her lingerie drawers
4304. Write a list: "33 Romantic Things I'm Going to Do for You This Year"

4305. Take a romantic cruise . . .
4306. Abercrombie & Kent Int'l.: (800) 323-7308; www.abercrombiekent.com
4307. American Canadian Caribbean Line:

(800) 556-7450;
www.accl-smallships.com

4308. American Hawaii Cruises:
(800) 765-7000; www.cruise-
hawaii.com

4309. Bergen Line: (800) 323-7436;
www.bergenline.com

4310. Carnival Cruise Lines:
(800) 227-6482; www.carnival.com

4311. Celebrity Cruises: (800) 437-9111;
www.celebrity-cruises.com

4312. Classical Cruises: (800) 252-7745

4313. Clipper Cruise Line: (800) 325-0010;
www.clippercruise.com

4314. Club Med Cruises: (800) 258-2633

4315. Commodore Cruise Line:
(800) 237-5361;
www.commodorecruise.com

4316. Costa Cruise Lines: (800) 332-6782;
www.costacruises.com

4317. Crystal Cruises: (800) 820-6663

4318. Cunard Line: (800) 728-6273;
www.cunardline.com

4319. Disney Cruise Line: (800) 939-2784;
www.disneycruise.com

4320. First European Cruises:
(888) 983-8767; www.first-
european.com

4321. Holland America Line:
(800) 426-0327;
www.hollandamerica.com

4322. Norwegian Cruise Line:
(800) 327-7030; www.ncl.com

4323. Orient Lines: (800) 333-7300

4324. Premier Cruises: (800) 990-7770;
www.premiercruises.com

4325. Regal Cruises: (800) 270-7245;
www.regalcruises.com

4326. Royal Caribbean Int'l.:
(800) 327-6700;
www.royalcaribbean.com

4327. Sea Air Holidays: (800) 732-6247;
www.seaairholidays.com

4328. Star Clippers: (800) 442-0551;
www.star-clippers.com

4329. Tall Ship Adventures:
(800) 662-0090;
www.tallshipadventures.com

4330. Windjammer Barefoot Cruises:
(800) 327-2601;

www.windjammer.com

4331. Windstar Cruises: (800) 626-9900; www.windstarcruises.com

---

4332. Re-create the fun and excitement you had in early stages of your relationship

4333. Secretly place a "Valentine ad" in a theater playbill for a show you're going to attend together

4334. Mindset: "Couple-Thinking:" View yourself primarily as a member of a couple

4335. "Respect is love in plain clothes." ~ Frankie Byrne

4336. Buy her a T-shirt picturing her favorite movie star

4337. Enemy of Love: Repetition

4338. Plan a picnic in a garden

4339. Send a written invitation inside a picnic basket

4340. Include the CD *In the Garden*, by Eric Tingstad & Nancy Rumbel

4341–4352
12 Reasonable and Unreasonable Expectations for Couples

1. Don't expect perfection
2. Do expect honesty
3. Don't expect him/her to read your mind
4. Do expect him/her to anticipate you
5. Don't expect infatuation to last forever
6. Do expect true love to last forever
7. Don't expect to live happily ever after without working at it!
8. Do expect to live lovingly ever after
9. Don't expect him/her to be reasonable all the time
10. Do expect him/her to control his/her emotions most of the time
11. Don't expect to be "in sync" all of the time
12. Do expect to forgive one another on a regular basis

4353. "If you can dream it you can do it."
~ Walt Disney

4354. Identify your dreams…what do you *want*? (To live happily ever after? To create a loving family?)
4355. Share your dreams with your mate
4356. Focus your love, your energy, and your intentions on your dream

4357. Guys: Buy her an *entire* outfit.
4358. Include: Elegant lingerie, a gorgeous dress, a matching scarf, a matching piece of jewelry, and shoes
4359. (Have her best girlfriend advise you!)
4360. Make sure you get all the sizes *perfect*
4361. Spread the outfit on the bed
4362. Along with a written invitation to dinner

4363. Retain your personal style while accommodating your mate
4364. Recognize that one mode of expression isn't enough
4365. When he gets up in the middle of the night: Roll onto his side of the bed, then demand a sexual favor before you'll move over

4366–4375
10 Ways to Love a Virgo
(24 August–23 September)

1. Virgo is an *earth* sign: Cater to his/her grounded, practical nature
2. Gift tip: Natural and elegant
3. Objects made of wood
4. Plants and flowering bushes make great gifts
5. Gardening tools and books
6. Prefers natural foods to sweets
7. Buttercups; hazelnut trees
8. Visually-appealing foods
9. The elegance of Paris
10. Wrap gifts in blue for your Virgo

4376. "Why it is better to love than be loved? It is surer." ~ Sacha Guitry

4377. Place a *standing order* with a florist: Never forget another anniversary!

4378. A "Wednesday Night Date" Coupon: Renewable every week for 2 years

4379. Start some *good* habits: Read *Habits of the Heart*, by Robert Bellah

4380. Write a list: "12 Things About You That Make Me Smile"

4381. Type it up on your computer using fancy fonts

4382. Give it to him/her along with a photo of you smiling

4383–4393
11 Ways to Affair-Proof Your Relationship

1. Be best friends as well as lovers
2. Don't nag
3. Laugh together often
4. Make love often
5. Don't wear sloppy clothes to bed
6. Don't let problems go unresolved
7. Keep your partner among your top three priorities
8. Let the infatuation fade, but keep the *passion* alive
9. Never relinquish your role as your mate's "lover"
10. Make some sacrifices but don't martyr yourself for his/her sake
11. Weave love, sex, and romance into the fabric of your daily lives

4394–4404
11 Places to Take Your
Water-Loving Lover Snorkeling

1. Bahamas, Out Islands
2. Bonaire Marine Park, Netherlands Antilles
3. Delos, Greece
4. Gulf of Aqaba, Red Sea
5. Heron Island, Australia
6. La Jolla, California
7. Looe Key, Florida
8. Madang, Papau, New Guinea
9. Providentiales, Turks and Caicos
10. Santa Barbara Island, California
11. Stingray City, Grand Cayman

4405. Cater to the kid in him...
4406. Go to an amusement park together
4407. Vacation at a dude ranch in the American West
4408. Go to a pro baseball game together

4409. "On life's vast ocean diversity we sail, Reason the card, but passion is the gale" ~ Alexander Pope

4410. The "Hero" Coupon: Redeemable for two hero sandwiches (also known as "grinders" and "submarine sandwiches" in different regions of the country) and two sodas

4411. Keep two lovebirds—named after the two of you

4412. Visit a spiritually meaningful place, like Jerusalem

4413. Listen closely for the song in her heart

4414. Learn to sing that song of love together

4415. Sing that song back to her when she forgets

4416. Don't buy her cheap lingerie—

4417. Unless you plan to rip it off her body during passionate lovemaking

---

4418. Enemy of Love: Mismatched partners

4419. Begin each day with a prayer

4420. "I am, in every thought of my heart, yours." ~ Woodrow Wilson

4421. "Service isn't a big thing. It's a million little things." ~ Anonymous

4422. Take an extra five minutes to give thanks for each other at the end of the day

---

4423. Brainstorm as many romantic ideas as you can in fifteen minutes

4424. Generate ideas that are serious and silly

4425. Practical and ridiculous

4426. Expensive and cheap

4427. Meaningful and sexy

4428. Generate ideas for gifts and gestures...

4429. And places to go and things to do

4430. Admit it when you're wrong

4431. Do-It-Yourself Romantic Afternoon: 1 canoe, 1 lazy day, 2 star-struck lovers

---

4432. Be patient with each other's style of communication...

4433. Some people (typically men)

communicate *to get information*

4434. Some people (typically women) communicate *to make emotional connection*

4435. Some people (typically men) use communication as a way to *compete*

4436. Some people (typically women) use communication as a way to *cooperate*

4437. For parents only: Enough already! Escape from your kids for five hours!

4438. "Remember when you were at your best? Now be there again!"
    - Anonymous

4439. Identify the worst "Relationship Rut" you are in—and resolve to get *out*!

4440. Mindset: Love is an *art*, not a *science*

4441. Quit trying to do it *perfectly*! Just keep trying!

4442–4537
96 Great Date Movies

1. *A Star Is Born* (♥♥♥♥♥ Romance Movie Rating)

2. *About Last Night* (♥)

3. *The Accidental Tourist* (♥♥♥)
4. *Act of Love* (♥)
5. *The African Queen* (♥♥♥)
6. *Aladdin* (♥♥)
7. *Algiers* (♥♥)
8. *All About Eve* (♥♥)
9. *The American President* (♥♥♥)
10. *Anna Karenina* (♥♥)
11. *A Place in the Sun* (♥♥♥)
12. *Basic Instinct* (♥♥♥♥♥) (Erotic)
13. *Beauty and the Beast* (♥♥♥♥)
14. *Braveheart* (♥♥)
15. *Breakfast at Tiffany's* (♥♥♥♥)
16. *Brief Encounter* (♥♥)
17. *Butch Cassidy and the Sundance Kid* (♥♥♥♥)
18. *Camelot* (♥♥♥)
19. *Camille* (♥♥)
20. *Carlito's Way* (♥♥)
21. *Chapter Two* (♥♥)
22. *Circle of Friends* (♥♥)
23. *Color of Night* (♥♥) (Erotic)
24. *Dances with Wolves* (♥♥♥)
25. *Dance with Me* (♥♥)
26. *Dark Victory* (♥♥♥)

27. *Don Juan DeMarco* (♥♥)
28. *Dying Young* (♥♥♥♥♥)
29. *The Enchanted Cottage* (♥♥♥♥)
30. *The English Patient* (♥♥♥)
31. *Ever After* (♥♥♥)
32. *Firelight* (♥♥♥♥)
33. *Forget Paris* (♥♥)
34. *Four Weddings and a Funeral* (♥♥♥)
35. *French Kiss* (♥♥♥)
36. *Gigi* (♥♥♥)
37. *Grease* (♥♥♥)
38. *The Heiress* (♥♥)
39. *Holiday Inn* (♥♥♥♥♥)
40. *Intermezzo* (♥♥♥)
41. *IQ* (♥♥)
42. *Key Largo* (♥♥♥♥♥)
43. *The King and I* (♥♥♥♥♥)
44. *The Lady in Red* (♥♥♥)
45. *Last of the Mohicans* (♥♥♥)
46. *Legends of the Fall* (♥♥)
47. *Like Water for Chocolate* (♥♥♥♥)
48. *Lonesome Dove* (♥♥)
49. *The Long Hot Summer* (♥♥♥♥)
50. *Lovers—A True Story* (♥♥♥)
51. *The Mask of Zorro* (♥♥♥♥)

52. *Michael* (♥ ♥)
53. *The Mirror Has Two Faces* (♥ ♥ ♥)
54. *Moonstruck* (♥ ♥ ♥ ♥ ♥)
55. *Mr. Skeffington* (♥ ♥ ♥)
56. *Muriel's Wedding* (♥ ♥)
57. *My Fair Lady* (♥ ♥ ♥ ♥)
58. *9 1/2 Weeks* (♥ ♥ ♥ ♥ ♥) (Erotic)
59. *Notorious* (♥ ♥)
60. *Now, Voyager* (♥ ♥ ♥ ♥)
61. *Oklahoma!* (♥ ♥ ♥)
62. *On Golden Pond* (♥ ♥ ♥)
63. *One Fine Day* (♥ ♥ ♥)
64. *Only You* (♥ ♥)
65. *Out of Africa* (♥ ♥ ♥ ♥)
66. *Polish Wedding* (♥ ♥)
67. *Pretty Woman* (♥ ♥ ♥)
68. *Raintree County* (♥ ♥ ♥)
69. *Rebel Without a Cause* (♥ ♥)
70. *Roman Holiday* (♥ ♥ ♥)
71. *Sabrina* [with Bogart & Hepburn] (♥ ♥ ♥ ♥)
72. *Sabrina* [with Julia Ormand & Harrison Ford] (♥ ♥ ♥)
73. *Saturday Night Fever* (♥ ♥)
74. *Scent of a Woman* (♥ ♥)

75. *Seems Like Old Times* (♥ ♥ ♥)
76. *Sense and Sensibility* (♥ ♥ ♥)
77. *Singin' in the Rain* (♥ ♥ ♥ ♥)
78. *Six Days, Seven Nights* (♥ ♥ ♥)
79. *Sleepless in Seattle* (♥ ♥ ♥ ♥ ♥)
80. *Sommersby* (♥ ♥ ♥ ♥)
81. *Speechless* (♥ ♥ ♥ ♥)
82. *Splendor in the Grass* (♥ ♥ ♥ ♥)
83. *Star Wars* (♥ ♥)
84. *Suddenly Last Summer* (♥ ♥)
85. *Summertime* (♥ ♥ ♥)
86. *The Philadelphia Story* (♥ ♥ ♥ ♥)
87. *The Wedding Singer* (♥ ♥ ♥)
88. *To Have and Have Not* (♥ ♥ ♥)
89. *Top Hat* (♥ ♥ ♥)
90. *Up Close and Personal* (♥ ♥)
91. *Waterloo Bridge* (♥ ♥ ♥)
92. *West Side Story* (♥ ♥ ♥ ♥ ♥)
93. *White Christmas* (♥ ♥ ♥)
94. *Why Do Fools Fall in Love* (♥ ♥ ♥)
95. *Wuthering Heights* (♥ ♥ ♥ ♥)
96. *You Light Up My Life* (♥ ♥ ♥)

4538. If you live in the city, take a drive in the country

4539. If you live in the country, visit the nearest city
4540. If you're landlocked, visit the coast
4541. If you're coastal, find a mountain to hike
4542. If you're shy, join Toastmasters together
4543. If you have two left feet, take dance lessons
4544. If you're afraid of flying, take a cross-country trip by train

---

4545. Listen better
4546. Call often
4547. Play more
4548. Work less
4549. Talk quietly

4550. Surf www.bestvideo.com: Movies on video via mail
4551. The Splash-Filled "Bubblebath-For-Two" Coupon: Included: Candlelight, champagne, bubblebath, and one wet and willing partner

Favorite Love Songs from 1939

4552. "All the Things You Are"
4553. "I Concentrate on You"
4554. "If I Didn't Care"
4555. "Some Like It Hot," Gene Krupa

4556. Get serious about being more creative: Read *Mental Aerobics*, by B. Alexis Castorri
4557. Buy him a new set of tires for his car
4558. Arrange Sunday brunch at home (serve a *gourmet feast* for your partner)

4559. Clip newspaper comics that reflect your relationship
4560. A "Peanuts" comic about Charlie Brown's unrequited love
4561. A "Blondie" comic about Dagwood's bumbling but true love
4562. A "Rose Is Rose" comic about making daily life romantic
4563. A "Single Slices" comic about the adventures of singledom
4564. A "Zippy" comic about some bizarre aspect of love

4565. Mail one of these comics to your partner
4566. Tape some comics to the refrigerator door
4567. Fold a comic into his/her wallet

4568–4593
26 Relationship Skills to Master—
If You Want an A+ Relationship

Take the "Relationship Report Card": Grade yourself and your partner
(A+ through F, like in school):

1. Affection _____
2. Arguing skills _____
3. Attitude _____
4. Commitment _____
5. Communication _____
6. Considerate _____
7. Couple thinking _____
8. Creativity _____
9. Empathy _____
10. Flexibility _____
11. Friendship _____
12. Generosity _____
13. Gift-giving skills _____

14. Honesty _____
15. Household management _____
16. Listening skills _____
17. Lovemaking _____
18. Patience _____
19. Playfulness _____
20. Romance _____
21. Self-awareness _____
22. Self-esteem _____
23. Sense of humor _____
24. Sensitivity _____
25. Spontaneity _____
26. Tolerance _____

A Guide to Grading:

A = Passionate, exciting, fulfilling; not perfect but clearly excellent

B = Very good, solid, better-than-most, consistent, improving

C = Average, adequate, acceptable, okay, ho-hum, static

D = Below average, dismal, unhappy, bad but not hopeless

F = Hopeless, dangerous; tried everything, didn't work

♥ You grade yourself and your partner

♥ Get your partner to grade him/
   herself and you
♥ Compare and discuss your grades;
   you'll gain great insight into
   your relationship
♥ Celebrate everything from a B- to an A+
♥ Work to improve your C's and D's

4594. "There is need for variety in sex, but
      not in love." ~ Theodor Reik
4595. Overlook your partner's faults
4596. Toss a coin in a fountain and make
      a romantic wish together

4597. The note: "You are the light of my
      life"
4598. The songs: "You Are the Sunshine of
      My Live," by Stevie Wonder (1973)
4599. "Sunrise Serenade," by Glenn Miller
      (1939)
4600. "You Are My Sunshine" (1940)
4601. "Sunshine of Your Love," by Cream
      (1968)

4602. A gift women want: *Elegant* lingerie

4603. A present men want to give women: *Sexy* lingerie

4604. Never, never, *never* nag. Use positive reinforcement. It really works

4605. Eat dinner at the best Chinese restaurant around

4606. Play Glenn Miller's "In the Mood" to let him know you're in the mood

4607. Enemy of Love: Boredom

Favorite Love Songs from 1940

4608. "All or Nothing at All"

4609. "Come Down to Earth, My Darling," Fats Waller

4610. "The Nearness of You," Dinah Shore

4611. "Pennsylvania 6-5000," Glenn Miller

4612. "Taking a Chance on Love"

4613. "You Stepped Out of a Dream"

4614. Climb Mount Washington

4615. Hire a pianist to play during dinner at home

4616. Give a bouquet of *edible* flowers! (Tiger lilies, zucchini flowers, marigolds)

4617. "Whatever our souls are made of, his and mine are the same."
~ Emily Bronte

4618. Gift & Date Idea: Get the song "Endless Love," by Diana Ross & Lionel Richie—

4619. And rent the movie *Endless Love*, featuring the song

4620–4631
12 Classic Love Songs

1. "All of Me" (1931)
2. "As Time Goes By" (1943)
3. "I Can't Give You Anything but Love" (1928)
4. "I Love You for Sentimental Reasons" (1945)
5. "I'm Getting Sentimental Over You" (1932)
6. "I'm in the Mood for Love" (1935)
7. "Love Is a Many Splendored Thing" (1955)
8. "Love Me Tender," (1956)
9. "The Man I Love" (1924)

10. "Moon River" (1961)
11. "My Funny Valentine" (1937)
12. "Some Enchanted Evening" (1949)

4632. Try being *totally positive* for one entire week
4633. No complaining allowed

4634. Give him his favorite kind of gum
4635. Prove your love through your actions—not your words
4636. "Look at a person's light, not their lampshade." ~ Jerry Jampolsky
4637. Keep a stash of her favorite candy hidden from the kids
4638. Go to London for dinner

4639. Eskimo kiss (rub noses)
4640. Teach your kids about love through the example of your own relationship
4641. Spend a second honeymoon at a picturesque Italian villa
4642. For parents only: Spend an entire afternoon photographing your family
4643. The only time "getting the last word

in" works is when those words are
"I love you"

4644. Go camping instead of going on an
expensive vacation

4645. Create public signals to let your lover
know you're hot for him/her...
4646. Hum "your song" in her ear
4647. Say, "It's getting *awfully hot* in here..."
4648. Scratch your left ear with your right
index finger

4649. Quote a Shakespearian sonnet
4650. Or have one rendered in calligraphy
4651. Sonnet 18 begins, "Shall I compare
thee to a summer's day?"
4652. Re-write the sonnet to make it reflect
the two of you

4653–4669
17 Love Tips for *Parents*

1. Don't refer to each other as "Mom"
and "Dad"
2. Remember: You're still *lovers*, as well
as parents

3. Do make time for each other—At least two dates per month

4. Don't turn yourself into a martyr for the sake of your kids

5. Remember: Parents have a *right* to privacy from their kids

6. Do learn from your children: The joy and wonder of life!

7. Don't feel guilty for wanting to escape from your kids occasionally

8. Do find great babysitters: Train 'em, and pay 'em well!

9. Do find someone who can babysit on *school nights*, too

10. When out on a date together, refrain from talking about the kids

11. Don't smother your kids—They need space, too

12. Take brief vacations away from the kids

13. Do make more time by *streamlining* household chores

14. Have a "quickie" when your kids are watching TV

15. Make love when your kids are napping

16. Don't live your life *for* your kids, but *with* them
17. Do be loving role models for your children

4670. Treat your partner like royalty
4671. Treat her to her favorite sundae
4672. Treat him to his favorite sweet treat
4673. Treat your partner with a sexual surprise

4674. Rollerblade
4675. Stay at the fanciest hotel in Budapest: Gellert
4676. Never, never, *never* forget your partner's birthday
4677. Don't hold your frustrations inside until they explode all at once
4678. Compare your stated priorities with how you actually spend your time
4679. "One advantage of marriage is that, when you fall out of love with her or he falls out of love with you, it keeps you together until you fall in again."
~ Judith Viorst

4680. Play in a playground
4681. Play a romantic fantasy character
4682. Mold Play-Doh into a heart

4683. Count shooting stars together
4684. Count the number of days you've been married
4685. Count the number of days you've been a couple
4686. Count your blessings
4687. Count the number of times you've made love

4688. Togetherness = One milkshake, two straws
4689. Go on a *third* honeymoon

4690. Fly to Hawaii
4691. Fly to Venice
4692. Fly to Paris
4693. Let your imagination fly
4694. Fly in a glider
4695. Fly in a blimp
4696. Fly a kite

Favorite Love Songs from 1941

4697. "Green Eyes," Jimmy Dorsey
4698. "The Anniversary Waltz"
4699. "This Love of Mine," Stan Kenton
4700. "You Made Me Love You,"
Harry James

4701. Give him a cap from his favorite hockey team
4702. "And yet, a single night of universal love could save everything."
~ Roland Giguere
4703. Increase your creativity by taking art lessons: Read *The Art of Staying Together*, by Michael Broder
4704. Celebrate with a special bottle of *very expensive* wine
4705. Fill a bag of M&M's with all green ones—seal it up and give it to your partner
4706. Give fine Belgian chocolate
4707. Get a poster in her favorite artistic style for her office
4708. Upgrade his favorite software

4709–4717
9 Do's and Don'ts of Sexual Fantasies

Exploring sexual fantasies is a great way of spicing up your love live

1. Do go all out—costumes, props, etc.
2. Don't take it too seriously
3. Do "stay in character"
4. Don't share your fantasy escapades with *anyone* else!
5. Do go along with your partner's imagination
6. Don't break the mood
7. Do plan a "story lines"
8. Don't push your shy partner too far or too fast
9. Do stretch your "comfort zone"

4718. Learn from your mistakes

4719. Ask him/her to pick a number between one and ten thousand—then consult this book, and *do* that item!

4720. (If the chosen item is impossible, subtract his/her age from the number and perform *that* number!)

4721–4727

7 Best Love Songs by The Beatles

1. "All My Loving"
2. "And I Love Her"
3. "I Want to Hold Your Hand"
4. "P.S. I Love You"
5. "She's a Woman"
6. "Something"
7. "The Long and Winding Road"

4728. Have breakfast in front of a roaring fire

4729. The "Weekend Getaway" Coupon: Here's the deal: You get to choose the weekend, and the coupon-issuer gets to choose the location

4730. Women: Remember, men like flowers, too!

4731. Sexy movie alert: *The Unbearable Lightness of Being*

4732. Do something wonderful and out of character—surprise him/her!

4733. Thank God for bringing the two of you together

4734. Once you've mastered foreplay, add

"afterplay" to your repertoire

4735. Attend Bible classes together

4736. Sleep in a feather bed and a down comforter

4737. Give him hockey tickets taped to a puck

4738. Buy a case of champagne. Label each of the twelve bottles...

4739. "His birthday"

4740. "Her birthday"

4741. "Christmas/Hanukkah/Holidays"

4742. "Anniversary (of meeting)"

4743. "Anniversary (of wedding)"

4744. "Groundhog Day"

4745. "For a midnight snack"

4746. "Before making love"

4747. "Celebrate a work achievement"

4748. "The first snowfall of the year"

4749. "For making up after a fight"

4750. "The first day of Spring"

4751. "We are shaped and fashioned by what we love." ~ Johann Wolfgang von Goethe

4752. See your relationship as a place to exercise your creativity

4753. Use a flower on the pillow as a signal that you want to make love

4754. Learn a *great* dance routine ala Fred Astaire and Ginger Rogers

4755. Write "I love you" in skywriting

4756. Get a vanity license plate with a secret love code on it

4757. The "101 Kisses" Coupon: Redeemable for 101 Hershey's Kisses. Coupon-giver's treat!

4758. View rainbows by moonlight at Cumberland Falls State Park in Kentucky

4759. Secretly save money for your 50th anniversary celebration

4760. Leave *clues* about where and when you'll meet for a special date

---

4761. "Actions speak louder than words"

4762. Take action right now—don't wait another five minutes!

4763. Turn off the TV, turn on the radio,

and dance in your living room

4764. Pop open a bottle of cheap champagne—*right now*—just to celebrate your love

4765. Include one romantic gesture on your To Do List every week

4766. Act like you did when you first fell in love

4767. Take a walk together after dinner every evening

4768–4770
Your 3 Resources for Expressing Love

1. Time—A very limited resource; this is why it's so precious

2. Money—Also a limited resource; handy for gifts, travel, etc.

3. Creativity—Your *unlimited* resource; fun and energizing, and often makes up for lack of time and money

---

Favorite Love Songs from 1942

4771. "String of Pearls," Glenn Miller

4772. "Paper Doll," The Mills Brothers

4773. "That Old Black Magic"

4774. "We'll Meet Again"
4775. "You'd Be So Nice to Come Home To"

4776. On your anniversary, create a sexual gift based on the number of years you've been together
4777. On your 3rd anniversary—take a three-day "Sexual Holiday"
4778. On your 10th anniversary—give her ten "Orgasm Coupons"
4779. On your 16th anniversary—give him sixteen kisses—on sixteen different body parts

---

4780–4794
15 Ways to Really Be a *Couple* in Public

1. Always make your "entrance" arm-in-arm
2. Wear outfits that match in a subtle way
3. Compliment her in front of her friends
4. Hold her chair for her at the table
5. Whisper your pet name to her
6. PDA
7. Brush against him in a sexually

suggestive way

8. Wear matching baseball caps
9. Open doors for her with an extra little *flourish*
10. Hold hands
11. Give him a seductive smile
12. Order for her when dining out
13. Wink at him from across the room
14. Blow her a kiss
15. Buy her one rose from a street vendor

4795. Give your partner room to breathe, but always be there for him/her
4796. Unlearn: Your superior attitude about being logical and reasonable
4797. Call her at work and say, "Is this the office of the most beautiful woman in the world?"
4798. Remember: Being happy together is a *decision* you make

---

4799–4807
9 Ways to Take Care of His Heart

1. Send him a photo of the two of you that will bring a smile to his face

2. Make love so vigorously that you give him an aerobic workout!

3. Give him *low-fat* chocolates

4. Learn CPR (Cardiopulmonary Resuscitation) together

5. Watch a movie that you know will touch him deeply

6. Exercise with him—and wear a skimpy spandex outfit to get his heart racing!

7. Read *Stress, Diet & Your Heart*, by Dr. Dean Ornish

8. Get him a Nordic-Track

9. Have him reduce the fat in his diet by 75%

4808. "Husbands are like fires—they go out when unattended." ~ Zsa Zsa Gabor

4809. Attend to his wants, his needs, his quirky uniqueness

4810. Don't let your kids consume all of your time and energy

4811. Tonight: Do one little thing that you know would *delight* him

4812–4827
16 Listening Skills for Lovers

1. Give your lover your *undivided* attention
2. Read between the lines—Listen for what's *not* being said
3. Eliminate the phrase "Yes, but…" from your vocabulary
4. Don't interrupt your partner
5. Practice empathy
6. Suspend judgment
7. Make lots of eye contact
8. Listen for the *emotional* content—
9. As well as the *informational* content of what's said
10. Give the benefit of the doubt
11. Listen to *understand*—not to *rebut*
12. Listen with patience
13. Allow there to be silences in your conversations
14. Listen with your heart, not your head
15. Listen carefully to the *tone* of your partner's voice
16. Listen to (watch for) *body* language

4828. Review your priorities monthly: Make sure love is in the top three

4829. Attend the Valentine's Day/mid-winter carnival in St. Paul, Minnesota

4830. "Self-love is not only necessary and good, it is a prerequisite for loving others." ~ Rollo May

4831. Take care of your partner's physical, emotional, and spiritual needs

4832. Celebrate holidays together

4833. Dab his favorite perfume between your breasts

4834–4843
10 Qualities That 5,000 Women Want *Most* in Husbands

1. Sensitivity
2. Romantic
3. Good listener
4. Strong character
5. Empathy
6. Intelligence
7. Shares his feelings
8. Sense of humor
9. Understanding

10. Responsiveness

4844. Dads: Add Mother's Day to your list of Obligatory Romance Days
4845. Moms: Make him "King for a Day" on Father's Day

4846. Favorite gifts for men: Big-screen TVs
4847. Favorite gifts for men: Leather briefcases
4848. Favorite gifts for men: Hobby-related stuff

4849. For your golf nut: You caddy for him/her!
4850. Rent a canoe
4851. Give her symphony tickets taped to the CD of the featured selection
4852. "See everything; overlook a great deal; correct a little."
~ Pope John XXIII
4853. Go camping with rented equipment

4854. Collect mementos of your honeymoon

4855. Create a collage of menus, tickets, postcards, etc., from your honeymoon

4856. Spend a *second* honeymoon in the same place you visited on your *first*

4857. (Same hotel—same *room*!)

4858. Tell the hotel manager: You'll receive extra special treatment!!

4859. Guys: Remember—Cuddling is just as important as sex

4860. Gals: Remember—Sex is just as important as cuddling

4861. Be your mate's biggest fan: Write him/her a fan letter

4862. "Real love begins where nothing is expected in return." ~ Antoine de Saint-Exupery

4863. Visit the New England Carousel Museum: (203) 585-5411

4864. Become famous for your *oddball* parties...

4865. Invite friends over to watch *The*

Wizard of Oz on TV

4866. Dress as football players and cheerleaders for a Super Bowl party
4867. Throw a "scavenger hunt" party
4868. Throw Solstice parties in the Summer and Winter

4869. English: "I want to make love with you"
4870. French: "Je voudrais faire l'amour avec toi"
4871. Italian: "Vorrei far l'amore con te"
4872. German: "Ich möchte mit dir schlafen"
4873. Spanish: "Quiero hacer el amor contigo"
4874. Portugese: "Eu quero fazer amor con você"

4875. Designate one week to improving your communication skills...
4876. Monday: Get *You Just Don't Understand*, by Deborah Tannen
4877. Tuesday: Do two exercises from the book

4878. Wednesday: Talk about the times you felt most connected
4879. Thursday: Identify your biggest communication problem as a couple
4880. Friday: Reverse roles: What insights arise?
4881. Saturday: Practice patience!
4882. Sunday: Communicate with body language only: Make love

4883. Buy her turquoise jewelry
4884. Resource: A "video detective agency"! VideoFinders: (800) 343-4727
4885. Don't be jealous

4886. Be her hero
4887. Be his playmate
4888. Be her friend
4889. Be his confidante
4890. Be her servant
4891. Be his gopher
4892. Be her cheerleader
4893. Be his caddy
4894. Be her fantasy
4895. Be his support

4896–4918
23 Romantic Tips for Guys Only

1. Let her warm her cold feet on you in bed
2. Treat her like a *queen* while she's pregnant
3. Wear a bow tie and cummerbund—and nothing else
4. Put the toilet seat down!
5. Hold her face gently in your hands when you kiss
6. Don't just roll over after making love
7. Never, never, *never* give her *practical* gifts
8. Read a few women's magazines—for some insight into the female psyche
9. If you want her to wear nice lingerie to bed, *you start* by wearing silk boxers
10. Shave on Saturday night
11. Be her birth coach
12. Share the TV remote control with her
13. Get her her *own* TV remote control
14. Don't be a slob in the bathroom
15. Rinse the sink after you shave
16. *Never* compare her to past girlfriends

17. When dining out, *always* order dessert, and let her nibble off your plate

18. Never, never, *never* say, "Yes, dear," just to appease her

19. Send a clever telegram to her parents, asking permission to marry their daughter

20. Never, never, *never* joke about her PMS

21. Quit the macho act when you're with your mate

22. Be her "Calendar Boy": Paste pictures of yourself on a Chippendale calendar for her

23. Bring her the little soaps and shampoos from hotels

4919. Gals: Get a "fantasy photo" taken of yourself for him

4920. Lingerie portraits are most popular

4921. Followed by "fantasy outfit" and nude poses

4922. (This experience may boost your self-esteem, as you'll experience how *made-up* those fashion models are!)

4923. Have a large print made and framed

4924. Present it to him with a grand
unveiling ceremony

4925. (Give him a small print to carry in
his wallet!)

Favorite Love Songs from 1943

4926. "Cross Your Heart," Artie Shaw

4927. "One for My Baby"

4928. "People Will Say We're in Love"

4929. Acknowledge when your partner
is right

4930. Enjoy a sunrise picnic

4931. The Bubblebath-For-Two Coupon:
You know what to do. Void where
prohibited by tiny size of tub

4932. "The heart has its reasons which
reason knows nothing of."
~ Blaise Pascal

4933. Enemy of Love: Lack of respect

4934–4959
26 Fun & Quirky Ways to
Get to Know Each Other Better

1. Share favorite childhood memories

2. Visit your childhood home together
3. "Fantasy Window Shopping:" Talk about *why* you'd buy various items
4. Play "Show and Tell" using a beloved item from your childhood
5. Have your astrological charts analyzed by an expert
6. See what a Ouija Board has to say about your relationship
7. Learn to read Tarot Cards together
8. Visit a gypsy fortune teller together
9. Learn to analyze horoscopes, and do readings for the two of you
10. Have your handwriting analyzed
11. Learn the art of handwriting analysis
12. Visit sites of special meaning to you
13. Share stories of the childhood objects you still own
14. Study and compare your anagrams
15. Share stories from grammar school
16. Share stories from college
17. Share stories about your first job
18. Tell your funniest stories
19. Share your most embarrassing moments

20. Share your moments of great insight
21. Share your most painful moments
22. Share the milestones of your life
23. Talk about your favorite teacher
24. Talk about your heroes
25. Talk about your real-life role models
26. Talk about your fictional role models

4960. On a whim, get a discount fare to Paris for the weekend
4961. Experiment: Dress as sexy as you *dare*, for a date out with him
4962. Use chocolate body paint
4963. "Love is always revolutionary."
    - Andrei Voznesensky
4964. Make love on the kitchen table
4965. Enemy of Love: Prudishness

4966. Classic Gift #1: Flowers
4967. Classic Gift #2: Perfume
4968. Classic Gift #3: Jewelry
4969. Classic Gift #4: Champagne
4970. Classic Gift #5: Chocolate
4971. Classic Gift #6: Lingerie
4972. Classic Gift #7: Dinner

4973. Classic Gift #8: Music
4974. Classic Gift #9: Theater
4975. Classic Gift #10: Art

4976. Classic crooning from Johnny Mathis…
4977. Selected CDs: *All About Love; Wonderful*
4978. *Too Much, Too Little, Too Late*
4979. *In the Still of the Night*

4980. Guys: Do something *for* her that you hate to do
4981. It only counts as a loving gesture if you do it cheerfully and without complaint
4982. Go grocery shopping, wash the dishes, weed the garden

4983. Be patient
4984. Write down your dreams and wishes for your future together
4985. Splurge on a $50 shopping spree at Crabtree & Evelyn
4986. When traveling, give a rose for each

day you'll be away

4987. Stay in a restored palace in Madrid:
Santa Mauro

4988. Treat your thrill-seeker to the best
roller coasters in America...

4989. "The Great Bear" at Hershey Park in
Hershey, Pennsylvania

4990. "Riddler's Revenge" at Six Flags
Magic Mountain in Valencia,
California

4991. "Mamba" at World of Fun in Kansas
City, Missouri

4992. "Journey to Atlantis" at Sea World in
Orlando, Florida

4993. "Batman & Robin" at Six Flags in
Jackson, New Jersey

4994. Gift & Date Idea: Get the song
"When Doves Cry," by Prince—

4995. And rent the movie *Purple Rain*,
featuring the song

4996. And let yourselves be inspired to
create a night of hot sex

4997–5008
The 12 Birthflowers—
and Their Symbolic Meanings

Accompany the bouquet with a note about the symbolic meaning of his/her birthflower:

January: Snowdrop—*purity*
February: Carnation—*courage*
March: Violet—*modesty*
April: Lily—*virtue*
May: Wisteria—*hope*
June: Rose—*simplicity*
July: Daisy—*innocence*
August: Poppy—*peace*
September: Morning Glory—*contentment*
October: Cosmos—*ambition*
November: Chrysanthemum—*cheerfulness*
December: Holly—*foresight*

5009. Spread suntan lotion on her back for her—*slowly and sensuously*

5010. Togetherness = One Walkman, two headsets

5011. "There isn't any formula or method. You learn to love by loving."
~ Aldous Huxley

5012.   Center yourself, both physically and emotionally: Take an "Awareness Through Movement" Feldenkrais class: (800) 775-2118

5013–5147
135 Things You Should Know About Your Partner

Exploring these topics will help you get to know your partner's likes and dislikes a little bit better

Knowing these things will bring you closer together

Knowing these things will also help you express your love more effectively and buy more appropriate gifts

1.   Favorite color
2.   Lucky number
3.   Favorite flower
4.   Favorite author
5.   Favorite book (fiction)
6.   Favorite book (non-fiction)
7.   Favorite fairy tale
8.   Favorite children's book
9.   Favorite Bible passage

10. Favorite saying
11. Favorite proverb
12. Favorite poem
13. Favorite poet
14. Favorite song
15. Favorite singer
16. Favorite musical band
17. Favorite *kind* of music
18. Favorite dance tune
19. Favorite romantic song
20. Favorite slow dance tune
21. Favorite rock 'n roll song
22. Favorite ballad
23. Favorite country song
24. Favorite Gospel song
25. Favorite jazz number
26. Favorite R&B tune
27. Favorite songwriter
28. Favorite magazine
29. Favorite meal
30. Favorite food
31. Favorite vegetable
32. Favorite fruit
33. Favorite cookie
34. Favorite ice cream

35. Favorite kind of chocolate
36. Favorite snack food
37. Favorite restaurant (expensive)
38. Favorite restaurant (cheap)
39. Favorite fast food joint
40. Favorite TV show (current)
41. Favorite TV show (old)
42. Favorite comedian
43. Favorite actor (living)
44. Favorite actor (of any era)
45. Favorite actress (living)
46. Favorite actress (of any era)
47. Favorite movie of all time
48. Favorite adventure movie
49. Favorite erotic movie
50. Favorite romantic comedy
51. Favorite comedy film
52. Favorite action movie
53. Favorite Broadway play
54. Favorite musical
55. Favorite show tune
56. Favorite breed of dog
57. Favorite breed of cat
58. Favorite animal
59. Favorite comic strip

60. Favorite comic character
61. Favorite TV cartoon
62. Favorite TV cartoon character
63. Favorite artist
64. Favorite style of artwork
65. Favorite painting
66. Favorite sculpture
67. Favorite hero/heroine/role model
68. Favorite heroine
69. Role model (actual person)
70. Role model (fictional)
71. Favorite athlete
72. Favorite sport (to watch)
73. Favorite Olympic sport
74. Favorite sports teams
75. Favorite board game
76. Favorite foreplay activity (to receive)
77. Favorite foreplay activity (to perform)
78. Favorite lovemaking position
79. Favorite sexy outfit (for partner)
80. Favorite sexy outfit (for self)
81. Favorite erotic fantasy
82. Favorite time of day to make love
83. Favorite place on your body to be touched erotically

84. Favorite music to make love to
85. Favorite season
86. Favorite time of day
87. Favorite holiday
88. Favorite hobby
89. Favorite type of jewelry
90. Preferred jewelry (silver or gold?)
91. Preferred clothing (for yourself)
92. Preferredclothing (for your partner)
93. Favorite designer
94. Favorite erotic clothing (for yourself)
95. Favorite erotic clothing (for your partner)
96. Dream vacation spot
97. Favorite vacation activity
98. Favorite city
99. Favorite foreign country
100. Favorite wine
101. Favorite champagne
102. Favorite beer
103. Favorite soft drink
104. Favorite way to spend an afternoon
105. Favorite room in your home
106. Favorite woman's perfume
107. Favorite men's cologne

108. Favorite brand of make-up
109. Favorite aroma
110. Favorite fictional character
111. Favorite historical personality
112. Best gift you've ever received
113. Favorite way to relax
114. Favorite way to get energized
115. Favorite store
116. Favorite side of the bed
117. Favorite TV sitcom
118. Favorite TV drama
119. Favorite joke
120. Favorite classical composer
121. Favorite symphony
122. Favorite opera
123. Favorite album/CD
124. Favorite car (make & year)
125. Favorite *color* for a car
126. Favorite country
127. Favorite city
128. Favorite clothing designer
129. Favorite dance
130. Favorite gemstone
131. Favorite pet
132. Best subject in school

133. Favorite Girl Scout cookie
134. Favorite day of the week
135. Favorite month of the year

5148. Give a movie poster picturing his/her favorite actor

5149. "Perform random acts of kindness and senseless acts of beauty."
~ Anne Herbert

5150. Make a habit of visiting a gift shop once every two months

5151. Consciously *choose* to be in a good mood: They're contagious

5152. Every year, get a Christmas tree ornament with special meaning

---

5153. When she's eight months pregnant, have a professional portrait taken of the two of you together

5154. When your baby is six, twelve, and eighteen months old, have family portraits taken

---

5155. Vacation in spots inspired by his/her favorite books and films

5156. If your partner is a fan of *Midnight in the Garden of Good and Evil* visit Savannah, Georgia

5157. Take your *Braveheart* to Scotland

5158. Fans of *Somewhere in Time* vacation at the Grand Hotel, on Mackinac Island, Michigan

5159. Visit the "Anne of Green Gables" house on Prince Edward Island

5160. Baja Expeditions [(800) 843-6967] offers a cruise that follows John Steinbeck's *Log from the Sea of Cortez*

5161. Tour the covered bridges in Madison County, Iowa

5162. Take a Mediterranean "Odyssey," and visit many of the Greek islands

5163. Take inspiration from the film *Casablanca*—and take an exotic vacation to Casablanca, Morocco

---

5164. Write a love poem in haiku style

5165. Take a rollercoaster ride

5166. Eat dinner at the best restaurant in the state

5167. "Happiness is not a state to arrive at,

but a manner of traveling."
~ Samuel Johnson

5168. Give diamonds!
5169. On a whim, get a discount fare to *somewhere* for the weekend

Favorite Love Songs from 1944

5170. "A Lovely Way to Spend an Evening"
5171. "Dream"
5172. "Irresistible You"
5173. "This Heart of Mine," Vaughn Monroe

5174. Never go to bed mad
5175. Never part without kissing
5176. Never insult your partner
5177. Never complain to your family about your mate
5178. Never betray a confidence
5179. Never criticize your partner in public
5180. Never say never

5181–5187
7 Best Love Songs by Diana Ross & The Supremes

1. "Ain't No Mountain High Enough"

2. "Baby Love"
3. "When You Tell Me That You Love Me"
4. "I'm Gonna Make You Love Me" (with the Temptations)
5. "Stop! In the Name of Love"
6. "Touch Me in the Morning"
7. "You Can't Hurry Love"

5188. "You cannot do a kindness too soon—for you never know how soon it will be too late."
~ Ralph Waldo Emerson
5189. Love: Say it, express it, do it—*now!!*
5190. Carpe diem—"Seize the day"
5191. Mail confetti in an envelope along with a note that simply says, "Let's celebrate!"
5192. Hide a love note in his pants pockets

5193. Close your eyes and imagine what your lover looks like
5194. Close your eyes to your partner's shortcomings

5195. Say this: "I love you"
5196. Repeat four times daily for the rest of your life

5197. Write a one-stanza love poem
5198. Give it to your partner on your anniversary
5199. Add one new stanza every year
5200. On your 25th anniversary, have it rendered in calligraphy
5201. On your 50th anniversary have it set to music and recorded!

5202. Open your heart and soul to each other
5203. Learn to play "Heart and Soul" on the piano

5204. Go to Rome for dinner
5205. Remember: People do what they do out of either love or fear

---

5206–5226
The 21 Most Romantic
Broadway Musicals of All Time

1. *A Little Night Music*

2. *Aspects of Love*
3. *Brigadoon*
4. *Carousel*
5. *Fiddler on the Roof*
6. *Funny Girl*
7. *Grease*
8. *Guys and Dolls*
9. *Hello Dolly*
10. *Kiss Me Kate*
11. *Man of La Mancha*
12. *My Fair Lady*
13. *Oklahoma*
14. *Phantom of the Opera*
15. *Show Boat*
16. *Sound of Music*
17. *South Pacific*
18. *Sweet Charity*
19. *The Fantastics*
20. *The King and I*
21. *West Side Story*

5227. Present her with a fine gold locket with your photo inside
5228. Enemy of Love: Generic gestures
5229. Blindfold her and make slow,

sensual love to her

5230. Give your heart
5231. Give it a chance
5232. Give her your entire income tax refund
5233. Give him your best sexy smile
5234. Give in to your feelings
5235. Give without expecting anything in return
5236. Give in during an argument
5237. Give up your inhibitions
5238. Give your partner the benefit of the doubt
5239. Give all you've got

5240–5252
13 Sexy Games for Lovers to Play

1. Strip poker
2. Strip chess
3. Nude Twister
4. I Dare You
5. Scrabble Sex
6. One-A-Day
7. Naughty Charades

8. Talk Dirty to Me
9. Elevator Challenge
10. Taking Turns
11. In Public
12. Instant Gratification
13. Delayed Gratification

5253. Create "signals" to let your lover know you're in the mood for love...
5254. Play anything by Billie Holiday on the stereo
5255. Have "your song" playing when he/she returns home
5256. For men: Casually say, "I think I'll shave tonight..."
5257. A pillow that says "TONIGHT" on one side, and "LATER" on the other

---

5258. Start with Elizabeth Browning's poem, "How do I love thee, let me count the ways"
5259. Re-write it in your own words
5260. Write a numbered list of all the ways you love your partner

5261. "Love is a talkative passion."
~ Bishop Wilson

5262. Spend a lazy Sunday afternoon together

5263. "You never know till you try to reach them how accessible men are; but you must approach each man by the right door." ~ Henry Ward Beecher

---

5264–5272
9 Ways to Love a Libra
(24 September–23 October)

1. Libra is an *air* sign: Cater to his/her light, funloving nature
2. Gift tip: Romantic and elegant
3. Libras love games
4. Lingerie
5. Get a wide selection of romantic music
6. Hydrangeas; apple trees
7. Delicate or sweet foods
8. The exotic beauty of Egypt
9. Wrap gifts in bright blue and pink

5273. Go horseback riding together

5274. Listen to the CD *Amore: The Great Italian Love Arias*
5275. Rent a yacht and crew for a Caribbean cruise
5276. For your golf nut: A dozen new golf balls

5277. Take your mate somewhere *special*…
5278. Has she seen all of her favorite singers *in concert*?
5279. Has he heard all of his favorite symphonies played *live*?
5280. Has she been to the *best* restaurant in her *favorite* city?
5281. Has he seen his favorite team play *live*?
5282. Has she been to the *Broadway opening* of a new play?
5283. Has he been to the birthplace of his favorite actor?

5284. Overwhelm him/her
5285. Honor him/her
5286. Romance him/her
5287. Woo him/her
5288. Date him/her

5289. Feed him/her
5290. Stimulate him/her
5291. Nurture him/her
5292. Understand him/her
5293. Support him/her
5294. Calm him/her
5295. Surprise him/her
5296. Delight him/her

5297. Favorite gifts for women: Bath oils
5298. Favorite gifts for women: Scented lotions
5299. Favorite gifts for women: Potpourri
5300. Favorite gifts for women: Designer purses

5301–5304
4 of the Funniest (Yet True!) Things Ever Said About Love

1. "People who throw kisses are hopelessly lazy." ~ Bob Hope
2. "It all comes down to who does the dishes." ~ Norman Mailer
3. "Love is the triumph of imagination over intelligence." ~ H. L. Mencken

4. "Why does a woman work ten years to change a man's habits, and then complain that he's not the man she married?" ~ Barbra Streisand

---

5305. For your beach bunny: Vacations at the America's best beaches . . .
5306. Cannon Beach, Oregon
5307. Kapalua Beach, Maui, Hawaii
5308. Main Beach, East Hampton, New York
5309. East Beach, Santa Barbara, California
5310. Grayton Beach, Florida
5311. Sandspur, Bahia Honda Key, Florida

5312. Get to know your partner better by asking quirky questions—like, "If you were stranded on a desert island . . ."
5313. What three music CDs would you most like to have with you?
5314. What would you miss the most?
5315. How long do you think you would survive?
5316. Would you wear clothes?
5317. What three books would you want to bring?

Favorite Love Songs from 1945

5318. "Autumn Serenade"
5319. "If I Loved You"
5320. "The More I See You," Carmen Cavallaro
5321. "Sentimental Journey," Doris Day
5322. "There, I've Said It Again," Vaughn Monroe
5323. "This Heart of Mine," Judy Garland

5324. Enemy of Love: Bad attitude
5325. Rent a big screen TV for watching *Casablanca*
5326. Give him a truly wild tie
5327. Remember: A vacation is just a trip, but a honeymoon is a state-of-mind

---

5328. Giftwrap a wishbone in a jewelry box
5329. The note: "Wish you were here."

5330. Be curious
5331. Be kind
5332. Be giving

5333. Be courteous
5334. Be generous
5335. Be creative
5336. Be spontaneous
5337. Be funloving

5338. Give your partner choices:
5339. Classic or avant-garde?
5340. Conservative or outrageous?
5341. Public or private?
5342. Expensive or cheap?
5343. Modern or antique?
5344. Here or there?
5345. Loud or soft?
5346. Big or small?
5347. Light or dark?
5348. Fast or slow?
5349. Today or tomorrow?
5350. Active or lazy?
5351. One or many?
5352. Gold or silver?
5353. Now or later?
5354. Right or left?
5355. Red or blue?
5356. Day or night?

5357. Cover the entire floor of your living room with balloons

5358. Play "footsie" under the table at an elegant restaurant

5359. Enemy of Love: Lack of role models

5360. Spend an entire *day* in bed together

5361. "To love is to receive a glimpse of heaven." ~ Karen Sunde

---

5362. While on vacation, tell everybody that you're *newlyweds* (You'll be treated *extra* special)

5363. In Italy, point to yourselves and say "Novelli sposi"

5364. In China, say "Xin hun"

5365. In Denmark, say "Nygifte"

5366. In France, say "Nouveaux mariés"

5367. In Germany, say "Hochzeitspaar"

5368. In Greece, say "Nionymphi"

5369. In Japan, say "Shin kon"

5370. In Portugal, say "Récem casados"

5371. In Russia, say "Novobrachnoe"

5372. In Spain, say "Recéin casado"

5373. In Sweden, say "Nygifta"

5374. Pick seven random dates throughout the year, and make them *special* in a unique or odd way
5375. Label Day #1: "Play Day"
5376. Label Day #2: "Music Day"
5377. Label Day #3: "Food Day"
5378. Label Day #4: "Sex Day"
5379. Label Day #5: "Red Day"
5380. Label Day #6: "Humor Day"
5381. Label Day #7: "Surprise Day"
5382. Create three more "special days" that cater to your lover's interests

---

5383. Make reservations at a local bed-and-breakfast for Valentine's Day *a year in advance*
5384. The "Ultimate Full-Body Massage" Coupon: The coupon-issuer will give you a *one-hour, professional-style, full-body* massage
5385. Return to the spot with the most romantic view you've ever experienced
5386. "The loving are the daring."
~ Baynard Taylor

5387. Call him at work and tell him *in explicit detail* how you're going to make love to him tonight

---

5388. Be prepared! Always have on hand:
5389. A bottle of champagne
5390. Some candles
5391. A little "trinket gift"
5392. A romantic greeting card
5393. A humorous greeting card
5394. A lingerie gift
5395. A CD of romantic music

5396. Take a horse-drawn carriage ride through Central Park in New York
5397. "Love is the silent saying and saying of a single name." ~ Mignon McLaughlin
5398. Fall asleep holding hands
5399. Visit www.hahaha.com for info on the Montreal comedy festival
5400. Give him mud flaps for his truck featuring his favorite cartoon character
5401. For parents only: Read a book on parenting together

5402. Mail him a pack of matches. Attach a note: "I'm hot for you"

5403. Whenever you buy new lingerie, model it for him

5404–5410
7 Songs to Help You Express Your Feelings: *Loneliness & Missing You*

1. "Far Away," Carole King
2. "I Miss You," Klymaxx
3. "I Miss You Like Crazy," Natalie Cole
4. "Missing You Now," Michael Bolton
5. "Missing You," Jim Reeves
6. "Wishing You Were Here," Chicago
7. "You've Lost That Lovin' Feeling," Daryl Hall & John Oates

---

5411. Lower your inhibitions

5412. Raise your expectations of yourself

5413. Make time to be alone together

5414. Turn off the TV, phone, and pager

5415. Escape from work, chores, and the computer

5416. Isolate yourselves from kids and pets

5417. Try being *totally accepting* of your
partner for one entire week—
5418. No criticizing allowed
5419. Try being completely *non-judgmental*
for one entire week—
5420. No preaching allowed

5421. If your mate is "past-oriented,"
he/she appreciates the sentimental
and nostalgic—
5422. Save things, find mementos, focus on
meaningful gestures
5423. If your mate is "now-oriented,"
he/she appreciates spontaneity and
creativity—
5424. Be adventurous, be flexible, do lots of
little things
5425. If your mate is "future-oriented,"
he/she appreciates planning and
anticipation—
5426. Create surprises, plan ahead, make
grand gestures

5427–5438
12 Ways to *Overdo It* for Your Lover

1. Write a love poem—and compose one new stanza *every week*
2. Get *every recording ever made* by his favorite musical group
3. Make a little loving gesture *every day for a solid year*
4. Get *every book* ever written by her favorite author
5. Get *every movie* starring his favorite actor
6. Get twenty-five pounds of her favorite candy
7. Take her to see the movie *Titanic*—fifteen times
8. Make love to him every night—until he asks you to stop
9. Give her twelve dozen roses on Valentine's Day
10. Write a list: "101 Reasons Why You're the Greatest"
11. Write each reason on a separate square of paper
12. Wrap them in a fancy gift box

5439. Remember: Your friendship will get you through when the love falters

5440. A "Quickie Back Massage" Coupon: Performed by the coupon-giver. Must be performed *immediately* upon relinquishment of this coupon

5441. Loosen up! Have *fun* in your relationship

5442. "The smallest good deed is better than the grandest good intention." ~ Duguet

5443. Wear scented body lotion

5444. Write a letter together to be opened by your children when they're fifty years old

5445. Make a distinction between "making love" and "having sex"—and make sure you include *both* in your repertoire

5446. Enemy of Love: Stinginess in general

5447. Serve breakfast in bed

5448. Send her a menu from the fancy restaurant you're taking her to

5449–5475
27 Ways to "Get It" by Mail

While you do have to shop, you don't necessarily have to go "shopping"

1. African Market Catalog (arts, clothing): (888) 846-2858
2. Croke's Comedy Catalog (ha!): (888) 222-9304
3. Divali Candelights Co. (elegant candles): (888) 834-8254
4. For Counsel (for lawyers!): (800) 637-0098
5. Golf House (duffer's gifts): (800) 336-4446
6. Hot off the Ice (NHL gifts): (800) 446-8423
7. Into the Wind (kites 'n stuff): (800) 541-0314
8. Levinger (reader's tools): (800) 544-0880
9. The Lighter Side (funny stuff): (813) 747-2356
10. Littleton Coin Company (¢): (800) 258-4645
11. Nature Company (cool & natural):

(800) 227-1114

12. Neiman Marcus (clothing & related):
    (800) 825-8000
13. Recollections (nostalgic):
    (908) 747-3858
14. Rick's Movie Graphics (posters 'n
    stuff): (800) 252-0425
15. Seasons (fun stuff): (800) 776-9677
16. Sexy Shoes (*high* heels):
    (517) 734-4030
17. The Smithsonian (curious items):
    (800) 322-0344
18. Sporty's Catalog (sports-related):
    (800) 422-2770
19. Stave Puzzles (jigsaw puzzles):
    (802) 295-5200
20. Sundance (western & rustic):
    (800) 422-2770
21. Tailwinds (aviation): (800) 992-7737
22. Vermont Teddy Bear Co. (hand-
    made!): (800) 829-2327
23. Victorian Papers (elegant papers):
    (800) 800-6647
24. Williams-Sonoma (cook's tools):
    (800) 541-2233

25. Wireless (cool stuff): (800) 669-9999
26. The Wood Workers' Store (practical tools): (800) 279-4441
27. Worldwide Games (games & puzzles): (800) 888-0987

5476. Catch her eye—and tell her you adore her
5477. "Can't Take My Eyes Off You," by Frankie Valli
5478. "These Eyes," by The Guess Who
5479. "For Your Eyes Only," by Sheena Easton

Favorite Love Songs from 1946
5480. "Come Rain or Come Shine"
5481. "Doin' What Comes Natur'lly"
5482. "Prisoner of Love," Perry Como

5483. Include her favorite stuffed animal in many of your romantic gestures
5484. Put love notes in a teddy bear's paws
5485. Put new jewelry on it
5486. Secretly pack it in her suitcase
5487. Mail it to her at work

5488. Hold it hostage for romantic favors

5489–5500
His Name in a Song:
12 Hits Named for Guys

1. "Arthur's Theme (Best That You Can Do)," Christopher Cross
2. "Bennie and the Jets," Elton John
3. "Big Bad John," Jimmy Dean
4. "Bobby's Girl," Marcie B
5. "Daniel," Elton John
6. "Danny's Song," Anne Murray
7. "Frankie," Connie Francis
8. "Hats Off to Larry," Del Shannon
9. "Johnny Angel," Shelley Fabares
10. "Louie Louie," The Kingsmen
11. "Michael," The Highwaymen
12. "Mickey," Toni Basil

5501. *Can This Marriage be Saved?* by Margery Rosen
5502. *Do I Have to Give Up Me to Be Loved By You?* by Jordan & Margaret Paul
5503. *Is There Sex After Marriage?* by Carol Botwin

5504. *If Love Is the Answer, What Is the Question?* by Uta West

5505. *Is This Where I Was Going?* by Natasha Josefowitz

5506. *Why Can't Men Open Up?* by Steven Naifeh & Gregory White Smith

5507. *Why Did I Marry You, Anyway?* by Arlene Modica Matthews

---

5508. Kiss hello

5509. Kiss goodbye

5510. Kiss a message in Morse Code

5511. Kiss a part of his/her body you've never kissed before

5512. Kiss in public

5513. Kiss and make up

5514. Kiss and "get down"

5515. Surf www.vsom.com: European and Asian films on video, from Video Search of Miami

5516. Hire a professional photographer to take tasteful-yet-sexy photos of you for your mate

5517. Start with the romantic basics, then

give 'em a twist! Your own creativity is
your greatest romantic resource

5518. Coordinate background music and
special events
5519. Play Glenn Miller's "String of Pearls"
when giving a string of pearls
5520. Play Barry Manilow's "Looks Like We
Made It" when you've come through
a rough time
5521. Play Simon and Garfunkel's "Bridge
Over Troubled Waters" to thank your
partner for being there for you
5522. Play Bad Company's "Feel Like
Makin' Love" when...well, *you* know
5523. Play Kenny Rogers' "Through the
Years" during a special anniversary
celebration
5524. Play Harry Connick, Jr.'s version of
"It Had to Be You" during an
engagement party

5525. The "Multiple-Choice" Coupon:
Choose one: 1) One soothing
massage, 2) One romantic movie

date, or 3) Dinner for two at a romantic restaurant

5526. Write love notes on the kitchen blackboard

5527. Go on a picnic

5528. Give her perfume—

5529. And create a date to match its name:

5530. "Passion" perfume: Be passionate—And plan an evening of lovemaking

5531. "Tropics" perfume: Be exotic—Plan a vacation to tropical Trinidad

5532. "Destiny" perfume: Be prophetic—Write a poem about why it's your *destiny* to be together

---

5533. Splurge on a $25 shopping spree at The Warner Brothers Store

5534. Give a balloon in his/her favorite color

5535. Kiss her gently to wake her

5536. Hire a local performer to serenade her on your behalf

5537. "Love at the lips was touch as sweet as I could bear." ~ Robert Frost

5538. Enemy of Love: Selfishness
5539. Send an envelope full of nothing but love stamps
5540. Live *passionately* (*work* passionately, *play* passionately, *love* passionately)
5541. Take a holistic look at your lives and your love at the Chopra Center for Well Being, in La Jolla, California: (619) 551-7788

5542. Themed gifts & date: A bottle of "Incognito" perfume
5543. And a CD by the group Incognito: *Positivity* or *Beneath the Surface*
5544. And create a *mysterious* date: Wear a disguise and go to a dim restaurant

---

5545–5562
18 "His" and "Hers" Ideas

1. "His" and "Hers" matching motorcycles
2. "His" and "Hers" matching T-shirts
3. Have "His" and "Hers" overnight bags packed at all times
4. "His" and "Hers" matching coffee mugs

5. "His" and "Hers" monogrammed bath towels
6. Carve "His" and "Hers" jack-o-lanterns at Halloween
7. "His" and "Hers" rocking chairs
8. "His" and "Hers" bicycles
9. Get "His" and "Hers" mobile phones
10. "His" and "Hers" Porsches (Millionaires need love, too)
11. "His" and "Hers" VW Bugs (Love for the rest of us)
12. "His" and "Hers" tennis rackets
13. "His" and "Hers" matching silk pajamas
14. "His" and "Hers" matching heart-shaped tattoos!
15. Special "His" and "Hers" Christmas tree ornaments
16. "His" and "Hers" monogrammed towels
17. "His" and "Hers" bottles of red and white wine
18. "His" and "Hers" matching beach towels

5563. Don't mistake lust for love
5564. (There's nothing *wrong* with lust; just recognize the difference)
5565. When you feel *love*, act on it
5566. Likewise, when you feel *lust*, act on *that!*

5567. Forgive
5568. Forget

5569. Have the courage to open yourself up to your partner
5570. Have the courage to work through your tough issues
5571. Read *The Courage to Love*, by Edith Weigert
5572. Read *Notes on Love and Courage*, by Hugh Prather
5573. Read *The Courage to Create*, by Rollo May
5574. Remember: Love just *happens*, but your have to *create* a relationship

---

Favorite Love Songs from 1947
5575. "A Fellow Needs a Girl"

5576. "Almost Like Being in Love"
5577. "But Beautiful You," Tex Beneke
5578. "Everything I Have Is Yours," Billy Eckstine
5579. "Mam'selle"
5580. "Near You," Francis Craig
5581. "That's My Desire," Frankie Laine

5582. Write a love poem that uses her *name* as the major rhyme
5583. Write a *hot-hot-hot* note to him; seal it in three envelopes; place it under his windshield wiper
5584. Celebrate birthdays
5585. Blindfold him and make wild love to him
5586. "I'd rather have roses on my table than diamonds on my neck."
   ~ Emma Goldman
5587. Make reservations at the best restaurant in town for Valentine's Day *a year in advance*
5588. Surprise him with a boxful of candy conversation hearts

5589. From a pack of playing cards, give her the Two of Hearts, along with a note: "Our two hearts beat as one."

5590. Give him the Three of Hearts: "Three reasons why I gave my heart to you…"

5591. Give her the Four of Hearts: "Here's where we're going on our next four dates…"

5592. Give him the Five of Hearts: "I'll pick you up promptly at five tonight for a little surprise…"

5593. Give her the Queen of Hearts, and make her Queen for a Day

---

5594. Put a dollar in a jar every time you make love

5595. Use the money on your 50th wedding anniversary

5596–5607
12 Red Hot Books to Set Your Sex Life Ablaze

1. *101 Nights of Grrreat Sex*, by Laura Corn

2. *The Couples' Guide to Erotic Games*, by Gerald Schoenewolf
3. *For Each Other: Sharing Sexual Intimacy*, by Lonnie Barbach
4. *Hot Monogamy*, by Patricia Love
5. *In the Mood*, by Doreen Virtue
6. *The Kama Sutra of Vatsyayana*, edited by W. G. Archer
7. *Masters and Johnson on Sex and Human Living*, by William Masters & Virginia Johnson
8. *The Metaphysics of Sex*, by J. Evola
9. *Red Hot Love Notes for Lovers*, by Larry James
10. *Secrets of Better Sex*, by Joel Block
11. *Super Marital Sex: Loving for Life*, by P. Pearsall
12. *Sex Secrets*, by Brian Chichester

5608. Buy her favorite candy bar
5609. Create a traffic ticket: A citation for "speeding away" with your heart
5610. Practice: The philosophy of "Walk a mile in his/her shoes"; learn empathy
5611. "Kissing power is stronger than will

power." ~ Abigail Van Buren
5612. Rent a cabin in the woods

5613–5620
8 Insights About Arguing

1. Become more aware of what's really going on, and you'll both benefit greatly
2. Arguing about money is rarely about money—It's about *power*
3. Arguing about sex is rarely about sexuality—It's about *intimacy*
4. Arguing about chores is rarely about chores—It's about *fairness*
5. Arguing about the kids is rarely about the kids—It's about *control*
6. Arguing about jealousy is rarely about fidelity—It's about *maturity*
7. Arguing about work is rarely about the work—It's about *time*
8. Arguing about relatives is rarely about them—It's about *expectations*

5621. If she's very practical-minded, *don't* send cut flowers

5622. Send *silk* flowers instead
5623. Or flowering plants
5624. Or give her a gift certificate to her favorite shop
5625. Or just give her cash

Favorite Love Songs from 1948

5626. "A—You're Adorable"
5627. "It's Magic," Doris Day
5628. "My Darling, My Darling," Jo Stafford
5629. "My Happiness," Ella Fitzgerald
5630. "So in Love"

5631. Prescription for romance: Say "I love you" three times in the morning, and three times in the evening
5632. Repeat dosage every day for the rest of your life

5633. Always have a stash of wrapping paper
5634. And matching bows
5635. And a selection of cool boxes

5636–5647
The 12 Star Signs of the Zodiac
and Their Basic Personality Traits

Knowing your partner's attributes will let you
show your love in a custom-made way

Use your own inborn traits to help you
express your love naturally

Aries (20 March–20 April): Courageous,
energetic, loyal

Taurus (21 April–21 May): Sensible,
peaceful, stable

Gemini (22 May–21 June): Unpredictable,
lively, charming, witty

Cancer (22 June–22 July): Secure, home-
loving, graceful, strong

Leo (23 July–23 August): Idealistic,
honorable, loyal

Virgo (24 August–23 September): Shy,
sensitive, values knowledge

Libra (24 September–23 October):
Diplomatic, charming, stylish

Scorpio (24 October–22 November):
Compassionate, proud, determined

Sagittarius (23 November–21 December):
Bold, impulsive, adventurous

Capricorn (22 December–20 January):
Resourceful, self-sufficient,
responsible
Aquarius (21 January–18 February): Bold,
emotional under cool exterior
Pisces (19 February–19 March): Imaginative,
sympathetic, romantic

5648. The Delicious "Midnight Snack"
Coupon: The coupon-giver will fix
you a snack of your choosing and
serve it to you no matter how late at
night it is
5649. Togetherness = Sitting side-by-side in
diner booths
5650. "A wedding anniversary is the
celebration of love, trust, partnership,
tolerance, and tenacity. The order
varies for any given year."
~ Paul Sweeney
5651. Serve dessert in bed
5652. Read *Massage: Principles & Techniques*,
by Gertrude Beard
5653. Learn what he/she considers
scandalous!

5654. Have a "love note conversation" consisting entirely of song titles!

5655. Him: "I'm in the mood for love"

5656. Her: "Some enchanted evening"

5657. Him: "I want to hold your hand"

5658. Her: "I can't give you anything but love"

5659. Him: "Why do I love you?"

5660. Her: "Opposites attract"

5661. Don't get stuck in any *one* mode of expressing your love...

5662. You need both communication *and* quiet times

5663. Be *spontaneous* sometimes, and *well-planned* other times

5664. Celebrate your *similarities* and honor your *differences*

5665. Use *surprises* as well as *rituals*

5666–5675
10 Qualities That 5,000 Men *Dislike* Most in Wives

1. Nagging
2. Overly emotional

3. Dogmatic
4. Fickle
5. Not enough sex
6. Procrastinating
7. Manipulative
8. Angry
9. Siding with the kids
10. Talking too much

5676–5681
6 Songs to Help You Express Your Feelings: *Anniversaries & Celebrations*

1. "Always and Forever," Heatwave
2. "The Anniversary Song," Richard Tucker
3. "Celebration," Kool & The Gang
4. "Forever and Ever, Amen," Randy Travis
5. "More Today Than Yesterday," Spiral Staircase
6. "Our Love Is Here to Stay"

5682. The gift: A poster of her dream vacation location
5683. The note: "Some day, my love"

5684. Take a walk on the beach
5685. Celebrate Valentine's Day *one day early*

5686. English: "You're so sexy"
5687. French: "Tu es très sexy"
5688. Italian: "Sei molto sexy"
5689. German: "Du bist sehr sexy"
5690. Spanish: "Eres muy sexy"
5691. Portugese: "Você é muito sexi"

5692. Buy him a puppy
5693. Go away on vacation
5694. "Where we do not respect, we cease to love." ~ Benjamin Disraeli
5695. The Completely Caffeinated "Coffee Date" Coupon: Choose your favorite coffee café and get ready to put on a buzz

---

5696. Dedicate one week to exploring your emotions. Focus on one specific emotion per day
5697. Sunday: Tenderness
5698. Monday: Joy
5699. Tuesday: Nostalgia

5700. Wednesday: Wonder
5701. Thursday: Peace
5702. Friday: Passion
5703. Saturday: Love

5704. On his 32nd birthday: Bake and number 32 chocolate chip cookies
5705. Invite 32 people to his birthday party
5706. Give him 32 kisses
5707. Give him a 32-minute-long backrub
5708. Call him at 32 minutes past the hour, every hour, to say "I love you"
5709. Give him a sports jersey with the number 32 on it
5710. Present him with a list of "32 Reasons Why You're the Best"

5711. The gift: An elegant wristwatch
5712. The inscription: "I always have time for you"

Favorite Love Songs from 1949
5713. "Candy Kisses," George Morgan
5714. "Diamonds Are a Girl's Best Friend"
5715. "Lovesick Blues," Hank Williams

5716. "Mona Lisa"
5717. "My Foolish Heart"

5718. Make a sudden, radical change in how you express your love ("Quantum Romance")
5719. Make small, gradual changes in your love style ("Process Romance")

5720. Dedicate yourself to improving your relationship skills:
5721. Create your own *personalized* Couples Curriculum
5722. Get your lover to join you in this year-long experiment in life improvement
5723. Create a one-year course by choosing twelve topics (Communication, Sexuality, Creativity, Spontaneity, etc.) and focus on one topic each month
5724. Find books that address these topics and read them together
5725. Create your own "homework" assignments

5726. You may want to repeat the "Sexuality" segment *several* times

---

5727. Try a little foot reflexology on your lover: Read *The Complete Guide to Foot Reflexology*, by Kevin & Barbara Kunz

---

5728. Hold a surprise birthday party for your partner

5729. And for the truly adventurous: Hold a surprise wedding

5730. Choose gemstones according to their *color*, to help express your feelings:

5731. Choose a gemstone to match his/her eyes

5732. Choose a *combination* of different gems in his/her favorite color

5733. Write a poem that incorporates the symbolism of the gem

5734. Get jewelry that incorporates his/her birthstone

5735. Custom-design a piece of jewelry that combines *your* birthstone and your *lover's* birthstone

5736. Use the birthstones of all of your *children*

5737. Red: Ruby, garnet, tourmaline, spinel, red beryl, coral

5738. Blue: Sapphire, tanzanite, topaz, zircon, tourmaline, spinel, aquamarine

5739. Green: Emerald, garnet, peridot, sapphire, jade, andalusite

5740. Purple: Amethyst, sapphire, tanzanite, spinel, garnet

5741. Pink: Tourmaline, sapphire, spinel, kunzite, morganite, pearl, coral

5742. Yellow: Citrine, sapphire, topaz, fore opal, garnet, tourmaline

5743. Brown: Topaz, andalusite, smoky quartz, tourmaline

5744. White: Moonstone, pearl, diamond

5745. Words that *men* love to hear: "You're the *greatest*"

5746. Words that *women* love to hear: "I *adore* you"

5747. If your partner is a perfectionist,

identify *specific things* you're willing to do *perfectly*—if he/she will stop expecting you to be perfect all the time

5748.   Host an at-home movie film festival

5749–5770
22 Creative Ways to
Celebrate Valentine's Day

1.   Devote yourself 100% to each other on Valentine's Day
2.   Rent a local hotel's Honeymoon Suite
3.   Take the day off work on Valentine's Day
4.   One day simply *isn't* enough! Celebrate for a *solid week!*
5.   Buy *several boxes* of kids' valentines, and *flood* your partner with them!
6.   Give your partner one card *every hour on-the-hour*
7.   Make a batch of heart-shaped cookies
8.   Make a giant Valentine card on the back of a travel poster—
9.   And have vacation travel tickets (to that location) taped to the poster

10. Plan *a solid day's worth* of romantic music
11. Stay at a local bed & breakfast
12. Send *ten* Valentine's Day cards
13. Send a *hundred* Valentine's Day cards!
14. Spend the *entire day* watching romantic movies
15. Give your modern gal a piece of antique jewelry
16. Bake a heart-shaped cake—
17. And decorate it with red frosting and heart-shaped sprinkles
18. Spend *every* Valentine's Day together—no matter what!
19. Send a Valentine's Day card each day for a week
20. Send a Valentine's Day card each day for a month
21. Find the best "Lovers' Package" at a local hotel
22. Spend the *entire day* in bed together

Favorite Love Songs from 1950

5771. "A Bushel and a Peck"
5772. "Be My Love," Mario Lanza

5773. "I Wanna Be Loved," The Andrews Sisters
5774. "It's So Nice to Have a Man Around the House"

5775. Hold a picnic by starlight *and* candlelight—outside at midnight
5776. Gals: Practice that sultry, throaty voice that guys like so much

---

5777–5784
8 Ways to Love a Scorpio
(24 October–22 November)

1. Scorpio is a *water* sign: Cater to his/her dreamy, romantic nature
2. Gift tip: Natural and sensuous
3. Bath accessories and scented items
4. Quality leather items and adornments
5. Honeysuckle; hawthorn
6. Sharp and tangy foods
7. The jazz and passion of New Orleans
8. Wrap gifts in maroon for your Scorpio

5785. Give two red roses
5786. Secretly fill a bottle of 7-Up with champagne
5787. Write "I love you" in the dust on the coffee table

5788–5803
16 of the Best Ski Resorts

Skiing: The only relationship activity where it's acceptable to go *downhill*

1. Aspen, Colorado
2. Bear Mountain, California
3. Big Sky, Montana
4. Jackson Hole, Wyoming
5. Mammoth Mountain, California
6. Mont Tremblant, Quebec, Canada
7. Purgatory Resort, Durango, Colorado
8. Sierra-At-Tahoe, California
9. Snowbird, Utah
10. Snowmass, Colorado
11. Steamboat, Colorado
12. Sugarbush, Vermont
13. Sun Valley, Idaho
14. Telluride, Colorado
15. Vail, Colorado

16. Whistler/Blackcomb, British Columbia, Canada

5804. Go to a carnival or fair together
5805. Take a roll of quarters for playing games
5806. Win a teddy bear for her
5807. Declare a moratorium from your diet—have some cotton candy

---

5808. Guys: Exchange a little of your rugged individualism for relationship building
5809. Gals: Trade some of your empathy for assertiveness

5810. Fill her purse with bubble gum
5811. Start the day in a special way: Recite a prayer or affirmation together
5812. Use a portable reading light when reading in bed
5813. Enemy of Love: Rigid attitudes
5814. Get her some Jimmy Buffett tunes to prepare for a Florida Keys vacation

---

5815. Enjoy a week in Acapulco
5816. Put your feelings on paper

5817. Declare *peace* in the "Battle of the Sexes"

5818–5824
7 Best Love Songs by Celine Dion

1. "Beauty and the Beast" (with Peabo Bryson)
2. "Because You Loved Me"
3. "If You Asked Me"
4. "Let's Talk About Love"
5. "Tell Him"
6. "The Power of Love"
7. "When I Fall in Love" (with Clive Griffin)

5825. Dote on your dog lover
5826. Get a subscription to *Dog World Magazine*: (312) 726-2802
5827. Visit the Dog Museum, near St. Louis: (314) 821-3647

5828–5852
25 Love Tips for Business Executives

1. For salesmen in love: Treat her better than your best customer
2. For VPs in love: Prepare a

"Relationship Annual Report" for your mate

3. For advertising execs in love: Create an ad campaign that expresses your love

4. For stockbrokers in love: If there were a "Dow Jones Romance Average," how well are your "relationship stocks" doing?

5. For PR execs in love: Create a love-related "PR stunt" for your partner

6. For managers in love: Are you managing your *relationship* as well as you're managing your *career*?

7. For Regional Managers: If your partner were in charge of giving bonuses for your "performance" at home, how big would this quarter's bonus be?

8. For Junior VPs: Are you practicing your *relationship* skills as diligently as you're practicing your *golf* skills?

9. For CPAs in love: Conduct a cost-benefit analysis of love in your life

10. For engineers in love: Increase your

expression of affection by 23%

11. For job hunters: Create a Relationship Resume that lists your qualifications

12. For company presidents: Are you providing adequate leadership and inspiration at *home*?

13. For CEOs in love: Are you keeping your most important "shareholder" happy?

14. For Big Shot Board Members: Are your daily activities in sync with your "Mission Statement"?

15. For CFOs in love: Review your emotional "investment" in your partner

16. For marketing managers: Identify and meet the Strategic Objectives of your relationship

17. For supervisors in love: Delegate *more*—and get home *earlier*

18. For manufacturing execs: Do you have your suppliers of romantic gifts lined-up?

19. For bankers in love: You don't give

cheap toasters to your most important customers, do you? Well?

20. For sales managers in love: Focus 10% more effort on your most important customer—and watch your "bonus" increase proportionally

21. For computer programmers: Work the "bugs" out of your relationship

22. For quality control execs: Ensure the level of "quality time" spent at home

23. For HR managers in love: Administer to yourself and your mate one of your corporate "Personality Profiles"—Use the results to improve your relationship

24. For entrepreneurs in love: You're creating something new and valuable. Go for it!

25. For workaholics in all fields: It's a cliché, but it's *true*: No one, on his deathbed, *ever* said, "I wish I'd spent *more* time *working*"

5853. Use Morse Code to tap out messages to each other

5854. Use foreign languages to say "I love you"

5855. Use foreign languages to say explicit sexy things!

5856. Use your creativity to be romantic every day

5857. Use your inborn talents to help express your love

5858. Use your time wisely

5859. Call just to say "I love you"

5860. Call from your mobile phone

5861. Call from an airplane phone

5862. Call from work, just to say "Hi"

5863. Call every hour, *on the hour* with reasons why you're in love

5864. Entertain your spouse's friends even if you're not *crazy* about them

---

Favorite Love Songs from 1951

5865. "Because of You," Tony Bennett

5866. "I Get Ideas"

5867. "My Heart Cries for You," Mitch Miller

5868. Write a love letter to your partner—
every day for a month and tell
him/her how you love them

5869. Write a love letter to your partner—
every day for the rest of your life

5870. Take turns writing love letters to
each other

5871. Have a conversation with your
partner—in writing

5872. Write a love note, then fashion it into
an exotic origami shape

5873. "Just one great idea can completely
revolutionize your life."
~ Earl Nightingale

5874. Find *one* great idea in this book and
practice it intensely for one solid
month

5875. Choose a *second* great idea to focus on
during the next month

5876. The "Tea For Two" Coupon: Good
for a quiet afternoon tea, English
style. Served on your best china. No
kids allowed

5877. "There is only one happiness in life, to love and be loved." ~ George Sand

5878. Watch a dramatic thunderstorm together

5879. Give him a Craftsman tool that he

5880. Take your Elvis fan to Graceland: (901) 332-3322

5881. Hire an Elvis impersonator to entertain at a birthday party

5882. Use *only* Elvis postage stamps when mailing love letters

5883. Watch all thirty-three movies that Elvis starred in

5884. Complete your lover's collection of Elvis albums

5885. Believe in the power of love

5886. Note: You need *power* to bring love alive

5887. Read *The Power Is Within You*, by Louise Hay

5888. "Loving, like prayer, is a power as well as a process. It's curative. It is creative." ~ Zona Gale

5889. Read *Unlimited Power*, by Anthony Robbins

5890. "Love Power," by Dionne Warwick & Jeffrey Osborne

5891. Read *The Power of Positive Thinking*, by Norman Vincent Peale

5892. Utilize Flower Power: Order a bouquet (or two)

5893. Read *The Power of Unconditional Love*, by Ken Keyes, Jr.

5894. "The Power of Love," by Huey Lewis & the News

5895. Read *The Inner Lover: Using Passion as a Way to Self-Empowerment*, by Valerie Harms

---

5896. Get the book *InterCourses—An Aphrodisiac Cookbook*, by Martha Hopkins & Randall Lockridge—follow its recipes!

5897. "No one should be allowed to die before he has loved."
    ~ Saint-John Perse

5898. Love Coupon: Entitles you to three full hours of uninterrupted peace and quiet. The coupon-issuer is responsible for the removal of all distractions

5899. Serve champagne in crystal goblets with dinner *tonight*

5900. Give forget-me-nots. Attach a note: "Don't forget me!"

5901. Attend a Tony Robbins seminar together: (619) 535-9900

5902. Pick him up at the airport in a limousine

5903. Have champagne in the limo

5904. Dress provocatively for him

5905. Make love in the back seat on the way home!

5906. Make an effort

5907. Make a homemade greeting card

5908. Make out

5909. Make it work

5910. Make your partner feel *special*

5911. Make the most of your potential

5912. Make love

5913. Make your weekends *special*

5914. Make believe
5915. Make every minute count
5916. Make time
5917. Make up

5918–5927
10 Ways to Turn a C- Relationship into an A+ Relationship

1. Guys: Don't equate *romance* and *sex*
2. Gals: Modernize your concept of "Cupid." (Guys don't relate to naked cherubs)
3. If you tend to be *action*-oriented, try being more *verbal*
4. If you tend to be *verbal*, try being more *action*-oriented
5. Even though "actions speak louder than words," you *still* need to say "I love you" often
6. Unwind together
7. Make a "Commemorative Scroll" to celebrate a special day
8. Create a "Romantic Idea Jar": 100 ideas on slips of paper; choose one each week

9. Read *Romantic Questions: Growing Closer Through Intimate Conversation*, by Gregory J.P. Godek

10. Have an affair—with your wife

5928. Sing a romantic song on your partner's answering machine

5929. Call and make up a song on the spot

5930. Watch the sunrise from a sand dune on Cape Cod

5931. Propose with a message on a scoreboard at a major league ballpark

5932. Read *The G Spot*, by Alice Kahn Ladas

5933. "When love and skill work together, expect a masterpiece." ~ John Ruskin

5934. For nurses in love: Take the "pulse" of your relationship; apply appropriate therapy

5935. Decorate with balloons picturing her favorite cartoon character

5936. Towel her dry after she showers

5937. Gals: Sit in his lap and "make out"

5938. Go out on an extravagant date

5939. Go out on a cheap date
5940. Go out on a limb—express yourself
5941. Go out on a fantasy date
5942. Go out on a dancing date
5943. Go out on a dinner date

5944. Talk, talk, talk
5945. Listen, listen, listen
5946. Read: *The Lost Art of Listening,* by Michael Nichols

5947–5965
19 Different Ways of Viewing Romance

Everyone has a natural inclination: Your easiest inspiration will come from *one*— But interesting surprises will come from the *other*!

1. Gifts vs. Gestures
2. Obligatory vs. Optional
3. Spontaneous vs. Planned
4. Simple vs. Complicated
5. Time Spent vs. Money Spent
6. Micro vs. Macro
7. Public vs. Private
8. Items vs. Experiences

9.   Sexy vs. Lovey
10. Fancy vs. Plain
11. Fun and Light vs. Deep and Meaningful
12. Weekday vs. Weekend
13. Daily vs. Weekly vs. Monthly vs. Yearly
14. Little Passions vs. Big Passions
15. Past-Oriented vs. Now-Oriented vs. Future-Oriented
16. Surprises vs. Expected
17. Quick vs. Time Consuming
18. Practical vs. Frivolous
19. Periodic vs. One-Time

5966. Pay attention when your partner is talking to you
5967. Pay *close* attention to the emotional contents, not merely the words
5968. Pay *really* close attention when your partner is distressed or crying

---

Favorite Love Songs from 1952

5969. "Hold Me, Thrill Me, Kiss Me," Karen Chandler

5970. "How Do You Speak to an Angel"
5971. "Wish You Were Here," Eddie Fisher
5972. "You Belong to Me," Jo Stafford

5973. Send your kids out to the movies with a babysitter—
5974. Spend some uninterrupted time at home alone

5975. Guys: Love her for who she *is*—not for who you wish her to be
5976. Gals: Love him for who he *is*—not for who he used to be

---

5977. Hang a hotel "Do Not Disturb" sign on your bedroom door
5978. Hang in there—through thick and thin
5979. Hang out together—a *lot*

5980. Arrange for your favorite restaurant to play "your song" during dinner
5981. Speak from the heart, but don't leave the head behind
5982. Create a collage of your family photos

5983. Be honest about whatever *rut* your relationship is stuck in—

5984. And take *specific steps* to escape from that rut

5985. Never throw away the Sports Section before your partner has read it

5986. Never throw away the Victoria's Secret catalog without ordering one item from it!

5987. Never throw a temper tantrum

5988–6016
29 Gift Ideas for 23 Different Kinds of Fanatics

1. For Beatles fanatics: Attend a "Beatlefest": Call (888) 9-BEATLES

2. Also, for Beatles fanatics: Take the "Magical Mystery Tour" in Liverpool: Call (44-151) 709-3285

3. For tea lovers: The Tea Club delivers full-leaf teas to your door monthly: (800) 385-5532

4. For baseball card collectors: Rare cards! From Goodwin & Co.: (314) 892-4737

5. For Monty Python aficionados: All forty-five episodes of *Monty Python's Flying Circus*

6. For Barbie Doll collectors: Visit the Barbie Hall of Fame (21,000 Barbies!) in Palo Alto, California: (650) 326-5841

7. For lovers of spicy food: The *Hotter Than Hell* cookbook, by Jane Butel

8. For funny folks: International Clown Hall of Fame. In Milwaukee, Wisconsin: (414) 319-0848

9. For a football fanatic: Get Superbowl tickets

10. For math mavens: The book *The Joy of* π

11. For history buffs: Get original newspapers dating back to 1880. Call The Historic Newspaper Archives at (800) 221-3221

12. For computer fanatics: The "Computer BudVase," with a flexible arm that suctions right to the side of the monitor!

13. For horse lovers: Equitor, for

horseback vacations: (800) 545-0019

14. For horse lovers: A trip to see the Kentucky Derby

15. For garden guys and gals: Jackson & Perkins Roses & Gardens catalog: (800) 292-GROW

16. For your fish aficionado: *Aquarium Fish Magazine:* (714) 855-8822

17. For floating fanatics: Bombard Balloon Adventures: (800) 862-8537

18. For autograph hounds: Call (800) 382-3075 for Autographed Collectibles

19. For Japanese anime enthusiasts: The Right Stuf International: (800) 338-6827

20. For jazz fans: Vacation in New Orleans

21. Also, for jazz fans: Attend the Montreal Jazz Festival, in early July: (800) 361-4595

22. For golf fanatics: Get seats at the U.S. Open

23. Also, for golf fanatics: A new Ping putter

24. For Oprah oglers: Get tickets to be in the audience

25. For classical music fans: All nine Beethoven symphonies

26. Also, for classical music fans: All forty-two Mozart symphonies

27. And more for classical music fans: All ten Haydn symphonies

28. For space nuts: Plan a trip to watch a launch. NASA's home page: www.nasa.gov/

29. For crossword fanatics: The Crosswords Club: (800) 874-8100

6017. Change one bad habit that drives your partner crazy—

6018. In exchange for your partner changing one bad habit that drives *you* up the wall

---

6019–6027

9 Ways to Move from *Practical* to *Elegant*

Add a little spice to your lover's life

1. Replace her cheap pens with a fabulous fountain pen

2. Travel first class instead of coach
3. Replace your plain bed with a classic canopy bed
4. Replace the cookie jar with an antique tin
5. Replace his/her paper bookmarks with *meaningful* markers
6. Give Godiva instead of cheaper chocolate
7. Add a feather bed to your mattress
8. Get her some expensive French lace lingerie
9. Serve breakfast using your best china and crystal

6028. Remember: Romance is *always* about love, but only *sometimes* about sex
6029. Replace the little strips of paper in Hershey's Kisses with your own little love notes

---

6030. Send a love letter that you've cut into jigsaw puzzle pieces
6031. Send the puzzle pieces all at once in a jumble

6032. Leave out one *critical* puzzle piece—
and send it the next day
6033. Send the puzzle pieces one-a-day for
two weeks

6034. Observe "Obligatory Romance Days"
(Valentine's Day, birthdays,
anniversaries)
6035. Focus attention on "Optional
Romance"—every *other* day of the
year!

6036. Remember: Romance is a state of
mind
6037. But: Romance is *also* a state of being

6038. Listen for the feelings between the
words
6039. Listen for the meaning behind the
actions

6040–6050
11 Songs to Help You Express Your
Feelings: *Devotion & Commitment*

1. "Ain't No Mountain High Enough,"

Diana Ross

2. "An Everlasting Love," Andy Gibb
3. "As Long as He Needs Me," Shirley Bassey
4. "Hopelessly Devoted to You," Olivia Newton-John
5. "I Just Want to Be Your Everything," Andy Gibb
6. "I'll Cover You," from the Broadway musical *Rent*
7. "I'll Never Leave You," Harry Nilsson
8. "Love of My Life," Abba
9. "The Right Thing to Do," Carly Simon
10. "Say You'll Be Mine," Christopher Cross
11. "You're My Everything," The Temptations

6051. "Tune-in" to romantic opportunities: They're all around you!
6052. In articles and ads
6053. In newspapers and magazines
6054. On TV and radio
6055. In shop windows and billboards

6056. Share your most vivid dream
6057. Share your recurring dreams
6058. Interpret each other's dreams

6059. Keep your priorities straight: Keep love at the top of your list!
6060. Give 24-karat gold *anything*
6061. Gals: Act out the classic "Sexy Nurse Fantasy"
6062. Give yourself permission to express your emotions
6063. Learn more about the basic, physiological side of sex
6064. Buy your partner *one* share of stock in his/her favorite company!
6065. For singles only: Ask his/her friends for insights into his/her personality
6066. Write a "Declaration of *Interdependence*" based on the Declaration of Independence
6067. For your Romantic Music Library: Suzanne Ciani's *The Velocity of Love*
6068. Give her an umbrella that pictures her favorite flowers

6069–6078
10 Relationship Questions
(For Married Couples Only)

Maintaining an A+ Marriage requires knowing each other *really* well

1. Before anything was "official," how did you *know* you were going to marry each other?
2. Where were you when you proposed (or were proposed to)? *Exactly* what was said?
3. What are your goals as a couple?
4. As you were growing up, what kind of person did you imagine you'd marry?
5. What is the most memorable thing that happened during your wedding?
6. Do you believe that you and your spouse were *destined* to be together?
7. How many children do you want to raise?
8. How do you plan to celebrate your 50th wedding anniversary?
9. Should a husband and wife be each other's best friend?

10. Do you believe that romance can be kept alive between two people for a *lifetime*?

6079. Have a picnic in the nude
6080. Have each piece of your silverware engraved with a different love quote
6081. Give her an box of elegant stationery
6082. "It's kind of fun to do the impossible." ~ Walt Disney
6083. Play "romantic-words-only" Scrabble
6084. An "Old-Fashioned Bowling Date" Coupon: Included: Shoe rental, all bowling fees, soda, and popcorn. Void where prohibited by law
6085. Go lingerie shopping together

6086. Save time by recording *all* your favorite TV shows on video—so you can skip all the commercials
6087. You could easily save fifteen to thirty minutes a day—which you could devote to love

---

6088. Write a list: "33 Reasons I Love You"

6089. Make it into a scroll
6090. Give it to your partner with a red ribbon around it

6091. Hide a small note under the pillow...
6092. Or in the medicine cabinet
6093. Or under a dinner plate
6094. Or in the refrigerator
6095. Or in a pizza box
6096. Or between the pages of a book she's reading

6097. "It is when you give of yourself that you truly give." ~ Pierre Corneille
6098. Give one hour of uninterrupted time to your partner
6099. Use your unique creativity to express your love
6100. Go out of your way, go above and beyond, for your mate

6101–6174
74 Ways to Use the Heart Shape

1. Make a heart-shaped pizza
2. Your initials in a heart—in *skywriting*

3. Cut the kitchen sponges into heart shapes
4. While out at a formal dinner, nonchalantly draw a heart on the back of his hand with a pen
5. Have a heart-shaped pool built
6. Your initials in a heart—on wet cement in a sidewalk
7. Trace a heart-shape in fogged-up windows
8. Your initials in a twenty-foot heart in the snow
9. A quilt with a heart motif
10. Your initials in a heart—etched on a brick in your patio
11. Place the pepperoni in the shape of a heart on the pizza
12. Trace a fifty-foot heart in the sand on a beach
13. Grill burgers in the shape of a heart
14. Heart-shaped sandwiches
15. For math nuts: $r = a(1-\cos A)$
16. Use heart-shaped stickers
17. Band-Aids with heart designs
18. Trace a thirty-foot heart on the ice

when ice skating

19. Heart-shaped place mats
20. A silk tie with hearts on it
21. A heart-shaped chunk of cheese
22. A mug with hearts on it
23. A heart-shaped mug
24. A heart-shaped door mat
25. Socks with heart designs on them
26. Heart-shaped doilies
27. Heart-shaped eyeglasses
28. A front-yard flag with hearts on it
29. Poke holes in the shape of a heart in the crust of a freshly baked pie
30. Make heart-shaped chocolate chip cookies
31. Heart-shaped confetti
32. The classic heart-shaped box of chocolates
33. Individual chocolate treats that are heart-shaped
34. Carve a heart—with your initials in it—in a tree
35. Get a heart-shaped tattoo with her initials in it
36. Greeting cards with heart

37. Fold the dinner napkins into heart shapes
38. Silk boxer shorts with a heart motif
39. Draw hearts on the bathroom mirror with lipstick
40. Use only love stamps with heart shapes on them
41. Find a wine with a heart motif on the label
42. Heart-shaped rubber stamps
43. Heart-shaped cakes
44. Heart designs in icing on a cake
45. Heart-shaped candles
46. Heart-shaped appetizers
47. Heart-shaped picture frames
48. Heart-shaped wreaths
49. Heart-shaped ice cubes
50. A heart-shaped rug
51. Find a heart-shaped Jell-O mold
52. Cut banana slices into heart shapes and put them in Jell-O
53. Shape pancakes into heart shapes
54. Cut toast into heart shapes
55. Cut a heart shape out of toast and fry an egg in the center

56. Heart-shaped Rice Krispy Treats
57. Slice strawberries into heart-shapes
58. A heart-shaped pendant
59. A heart-shaped pin
60. Heart-shaped earrings
61. Heart-shaped pasta
62. Heart-shaped red balloons
63. Heart-shaped cookie cutters
64. Heart-shaped key rings
65. Heart-shaped candy conversation hearts
66. Cut the lawn into the shape of a giant heart
67. Make a heart-shaped kite together!
68. Get a *humongous* heart-shaped box of Valentine candy
69. Heart-shaped shrubbery/topiary
70. A big, heart-shaped ice sculpture
71. Send an envelope filled with heart-shaped glitter
72. While tanning, place a small, heart-shaped piece of cardboard on your body
73. Cut a piece of paper into a heart shape, then write a love letter on it

74. Scrape the ice off his windshield—in the shape of a heart

---

6175. Enemy of Love: Apathy
6176. For couples only: Go out to a singles bar together; talk about how lucky you are to have found each other!

6177. Give her a *variety* of jewelry…
6178. Rings
6179. Bracelets
6180. Necklaces
6181. Earrings
6182. Watches
6183. Pins
6184. Ankle bracelets
6185. Toe rings
6186. Belly button rings

6187. Time yourselves: How *fast* can you make love??
6188. Time yourselves: How *long* can you make sex last??

6189. Lose yourself in a long, lazy evening

of lovemaking
6190. Lose track of time during a long, lazy afternoon together
6191. Lose your (emotional) inhibitions when talking with your partner
6192. Lose your (sexual) inhibitions when making love together

---

6193. Write "I love you" on fifty Post-It notes
6194. Post them all over the house

6195. Learn all the verses to "L Is for the Way You Look at Me"
6196. Sing it to him/her
6197. Make up *additional* verses for the song
6198. Write verses that spell-out your partner's name
6199. On Valentine's Day give her a *real arrow* with a note attached: "To [the two of you], From Cupid"

Favorite Love Songs from 1953
6200. "And This Is My Beloved"
6201. "My Love, My Love"

6202. "No Other Love," Perry Como
6203. "Secret Love"
6204. "That's Amore," Dean Martin
6205. "You, You, You"

6206. Dress in formal wear for a picnic in the park
6207. Dare to express your deepest feelings
6208. Make love on your couch
6209. Don't confuse the size of the sentiment with the size of the price tag
6210. "I've decided to stick with love." ~ Martin Luther King Jr.

6211. Learn all the verses to "Singin' in the Rain"
6212. Rent the romantic movie classic *Singin' in the Rain*
6213. During the next rainstorm: Go for a walk and sing "Singin' in the Rain"
6214. Call your spouse to arrange a "date"
6215. In a love note, tell her: "My *concupiscent* feelings for you can no longer be contained"

6216–6225
10 CDs of Instrumental Music
Hand-Picked for Romantic Evenings

1. *Breakin' Away*, by Al Jarreau
2. *Feels So Good*, by Chuck Mangione
3. *Livin' Inside Your Love*, by George Benson
4. *Suite for Flute & Jazz Piano*, by Jean-Pierre Rampal and Claude Bolling
5. *Touch*, by John Klemmer
6. *Twin Sons of Different Mothers*, by Dan Fogelberg and Tim Weisberg
7. *Silk Road II*, by Kitaro
8. *Solo Flight*, by Markus Allen
9. *Textures*, by Greg Joy
10. *Angel Love*, by Aeoliah

6226. A "Love Code": 1-4-3 means "I love you"

6227. Squeeze your partner's hand, 1-4-3, while out in public

6228. While in adjacent public restrooms, pound 1-4-3 on the wall

6229. Send a postcard, with the message: "1-4-3"

6230. Send one birthday card for each year of his/her age—one-a-day

6231. Send one birthday card for each year of his/her age—all at once!

6232–6242
11 Proverbs of Love from Around the World

1. "If you would understand men, study women." ~ French proverb

2. "The heart that loves is always young." ~ Greek proverb

3. "A man is not where he *lives*, but where he *loves*." ~ Latin proverb

4. "He who is impatient is not in love." ~ Italian proverb

5. "Where love reigns the impossible may be attained." ~ Indian proverb

6. "He gives double who gives unasked." ~ Arab proverb

7. "Try to reason about love and you will lose your reason." ~ French proverb

8. "There is no one luckier than he who

thinks himself so." ~ German proverb
9. "An old man in love is like a flower in winter." ~ Portuguese proverb
10. "Married couples who love each other tell each other a thousand things without talking." ~ Chinese proverb
11. "Not the lover, but his language, wins the lady." ~ Japanese proverb

---

6243. Support your partner *emotionally*
6244. Support your partner *financially*
6245. Support your partner's beliefs and values
6246. Support your partner through a tough time at work
6247. Support your partner through family difficulties
6248. Support your partner *always and forever*

6249–6257
9 "Photo Fantasies" for Lovers
Cameras have inspired many a romantic and/or erotic fantasy
1. He's a *Playboy* photographer, she's a

model: Scene 1: He seduces her
2. He's a *Playboy* photographer, she's a model: Scene 2: *She* seduces *him*
3. Variation: A *sizzling, bold* seduction
4. Variation: A *slow, subtle, flirty* seduction
5. Question: How would you pose for *different* magazines?
6. Variation: She's a *Playgirl* photographer, and *he's* the model
7. Posing for the *Sports Illustrated* "Swimsuit Issue"
8. The "Victoria's Secret catalog photo shoot" fantasy
9. How would you pose *differently* for the "Frederick's of Hollywood" catalog?

6258. Live as lovers
6259. Remember: Medical studies show that people in better relationships live longer, healthier lives!
6260. Live this day as if it were your last
6261. Daily affirmation: "I will be patient with my mate"
6262. "The most important thing a father

can do for his children is to love their
mother." ~ Theodore Hesburgh

6263. Let your children see you kissing and
hugging

6264. Pile onto the couch and cuddle with
the whole family while watching TV

6265. Share stories with your kids about
how the two of you met

6266. Give your *wife* a gift on the *kids'*
birthdays

6267. Gals: Make room for his buddies
(It will take pressure off your
relationship)

6268. Guys: Don't resent her girlfriends (It
will help keep her sane)

6269–6280
12 Questions to Determine
Your "Sex Style"

Very often, a person's "personality style"
doesn't match his/her "sex style"
(Still water runs deep you know!)

1. When it comes to sex, do you stick to
the basics?

2. Do you explore a lot?
3. Are you creative?
4. What are your patterns?
5. Are you spontaneous? Are you habitual?
6. Are you verbal?
7. Do you act out?
8. Are you predictable?
9. Do you adjust your style based on your mood?
10. Do you change your style based on your mate's moods?
11. What are your favorite positions?
12. How important are *setting* and *mood* to you?

6281. Take your movie-loving lover to film-oriented theme parks...
6282. Universal Studios in Orlando, Florida
6283. Universal Studios Hollywood in Universal City, California
6284. Disney-MGM Studios at Walt Disney World in Lake Buena Vista, Florida

6285. Parents: Present a "united front" to your kids

6286. Don't let them play you off one another

6287. "Never cut what you can untie."
~ Joseph Joubert

6288. Most all arguments can be untangled without unraveling the relationship

6289. Hang in there. Have faith. Have hope

6290. Try *everything* to make it work

6291. Pamper him

6292. Give him a foot massage

6293. Wash (and wax) his car

6294. Do his weekend chores for him

6295. Serve his favorite snacks while watching TV

6296. Always be available

6297. Via phone or fax

6298. Via pager or email

6299. Guys: You need to know her dress size

6300. Her shoe size and stocking size
6301. Her blouse size and nightgown size
6302. Her bra size and panty size
6303. Her pants size and coat size
6304. Her finger size (for rings that fit)

6305. Be passionate
6306. Write a book together
6307. Warm up with an electric blanket with "His" and "Hers" controls
6308. Eat dinner at the best Indian restaurant around

6309. Accompany your partner on a business trip
6310. Take an extra day and turn it into a mini-vacation

6311. English: "Hold me"
6312. French: "Prends-moi dans tes bras"
6313. Italian: "Abbracciami"
6314. German: "Halt mich fest"
6315. Spanish: "Abrázame"
6316. Portugese: "Me abrace"

6317. Send a love letter in the mail
6318. Send the kids away for the evening
6319. Send the kids away for the weekend
6320. Send your kids to summer camp
6321. Send a taxi to pick him up at work and drop him off at your favorite restaurant
6322. Send your prayers to your partner
6323. Send away for lots of gift catalogs

6324. Gift & Date Idea: Get the song "Some Enchanted Evening," by Jay & the Americans—
6325. And rent the movie *South Pacific*, featuring the song
6326. Or—surprise your partner with tickets to the musical, live on stage

---

6327. Dare to fondle each other under a blanket at a football game
6328. Splurge on a $1,000 shopping spree in Tiffany's
6329. Enemy of Love: Stinginess with *time*
6330. Put a penny in a jar every time you make love

6331.　Play duets together on the piano

6332–6343
12 Visual Puns to Use in Love Notes

Use actual *items* as part of your love notes

　　1.　"We're quite a (pear)"
　　2.　"You're the (apple) of my eye"
　　3.　"We're a (match) made in heaven"
　　4.　"(Honey), I'm yours"
　　5.　"I'm your biggest (fan)"
　　6.　"Please don't (squash) my hopes"
　　7.　"You're the (toast) of the town!"
　　8.　"Sweetheart, you're a (peach)"
　　9.　"I (wood) do anything for you"
　　10.　"Please go out on a (date) with me!"
　　11.　"(Peas) be mine!"
　　12.　"(Olive) you!"

6344.　Create a weekend of romance with a "theme song"

6345.　Give a copy of the song "Thank God It's Friday," by Love & Kisses—

6346.　And go on a date this Friday to a restaurant you've never visited before

6347.　Give a copy of the song "Saturday in

the Park," by Chicago—
6348. And pack a picnic lunch for a lazy Saturday afternoon together
6349. Give a copy of the song "Sunday Mornin," by Spanky & Our Gang—
6350. And share a romantic Sunday brunch

Favorite Love Songs from 1954

6351. "Answer Me, My Love," Nat King Cole
6352. "If I Give My Heart to You," Doris Day
6353. "Little Things Mean a Lot," Kitty Kallen
6354. "Make Love to Me," Jo Stafford
6355. "Teach Me Tonight," De Castro Sisters

6356. Give her one *beautiful* red rose—
6357. And the song "Roses Are Red (My Love)," by Bobby Vinton

6358. Create a collage of memorabilia from your life together
6359. Don't cramp your partner's style

6360. Gals: *Stop* communicating with him! (Take *action* instead)

6361. Take an inventory of your personal talents, interests, skills, aptitudes, and passions—and use them to generate ideas for expressing your love

6362. Write postcards in code: "I.L.Y." etc.

6363. Create a custom bookmark by laminating a favorite comic strip

6364. Write love notes on 1 dozen eggs

6365. For last minute Broadway seats, call Tickets on Request: (212) 967-5600

6366. Re-define yourself: From "spouse" to "lover"

6367. Go out to a movie

6368. Attend a pro basketball game

6369. Attend a Broadway show

6370. Attend a pro football game

6371. Attend to your partner's needs

6372. Attend to your partner's *wants*

6373. Attend your children's soccer games—*together*

6374. Attend a lecture

6375. Attend an event that you've never

attended before

6376. Attend a pro baseball game
6377. Attend a pro hockey game
6378. Attend to your partner's secret desires
6379. Attend a religious service together
6380. Attend the ballet
6381. Attend a symphony
6382. Attend an opera
6383. Attend a jazz concert
6384. Attend a rock concert
6385. Attend a big band concert

6386. Splurge on a $50 shopping spree in
the Sears Tool Department
6387. "Love is blind." ~ Geoffrey Chaucer

6388–6404
17 Great Books on Marriage

1. *The 7 Marriages of Your Marriage*, by
Mel & Patricia Krantzler
2. *The Book of Marriage*, by Hermann
Von Keyserling
3. *Building a Marriage: Ten Tools for
Creating, Repairing and Maintaining Your
Lives Together*, by Cranor Graves

4.   *Growing a Healthy Marriage,* edited by Mike Yorkey

5.   *Heart Centered Marriage: Fulfilling Our Natural Desire for Sacred Partnership,* by Sue Patton Thoele

6.   *Love Between Equals: How Peer Marriage Really Works,* by Pepper Schwartz

7.   *Marital Myths,* by Arnold Lazarus

8.   *Marriage and Personal Development,* by Rubin & Gertrude Blanck

9.   *Married People,* by Francine Klagsbrun

10. *The Mirages of Marriage,* by William J. Lederer & Don D. Jackson

11. *The Oxford Book of Marriage,* edited by Helge Rubinstein

12. *Speaking of Marriage,* edited by Catherine Glass

13. *'Til Death Do Us Part: How Couples Stay Together,* by Jeanette C. Lauer

14. *The Triumphant Marriage: 100 Extremely Successful Couples Reveal Secrets,* by Neil Clark Warren

15. *The Way of Marriage: A Journal of Spiritual Growth Through Conflict, Love*

and Sex, by Henry James Borys

16. *Training in Marriage Enrichment*, by Don Kinkmeyer & Jon Carlsen

17. *We Can Work It Out: Making Sense of Marital Conflict*, by Clifford I. Notarius

---

6405. An Ice Cream Sundae Coupon: This coupon includes a one hour reprieve from any diets

6406. Fax to him at work: "L.M.L.T." ("Let's Make Love Tonight")

6407. "Life is a flower of which love is the honey." ~ Victor Hugo

6408. Keep one fresh rose in the house *at all times*

6409. Rent matching motorcycles for an afternoon road trip

6410. Share a piece of your wedding cake on your first anniversary

---

6411. Gift & Date Idea: Get the song "Summer Nights," by John Travolta & Olivia Newton-John—And rent the movie *Grease*, featuring the song

6412. Or—surprise your partner with tickets to the musical, live on stage

---

6413. "A man is already halfway in love with any woman who listens to him." ~ Brendan Francis

6414. This reflects the truth that men *do* desire deep communication (not *just* sex!)

6415. Gals: Listen to him with *renewed attention*—and watch him respond

---

6416. Don't buy roses on Valentine's Day! (It's expensive and expected)—

6417. Do buy *different* flowers

6418–6432
15 Ways to Give Money As a Gift in a Creative Way

1. A bouquet of long-stemmed twenty dollar bills

2. A Christmas tree decorated with silver dollar ornaments

3. Origami money

4. A one hundred-dollar-bill single rose

5. A wine bottle filled with cash
6. A great toilet paper roll of dollar bills
7. A twenty pound sack o' quarters
8. A money wreath
9. Streamers made of one dollar bills taped together
10. A cereal box bursting with pennies
11. A large box filled with lots of crumpled-up bills
12. A tiny little box filled with a folded-up one hundred dollar bill
13. A "salad" made of money "greens"
14. An elegantly framed one hundred dollar bill (for emergencies)
15. A giant glass jar filled with cash

6433. Never fake interest in his hobbies—
6434. Be genuine about it or don't bother
6435. Never fake orgasms—It's insulting to him and frustrating for you

---

6436. Your job is to support your partner in his/her changes and challenges—
6437. Not to stand back, point them out, and analyze them

Favorite Love Songs from 1955

6438. "Earth Angel," Penguins
6439. "I Want You to Be My Baby," Lillian Briggs
6440. "I've Got a Woman," Ray Charles
6441. "Love Is a Many-Splendored Thing," Four Aces
6442. "Melody of Love," Billy Vaughn
6443. "Mr. Sandman," Chordettes
6444. "Only You," The Platters
6445. "Pledging My Love," Johnny Ace
6446. "Unchained Melody," Al Hibbler & Les Baxter
6447. "Yellow Rose of Texas," Mitch Miller

6448. Respect each other's privacy…
6449. Don't listen to her phone conversations
6450. Don't go through his wallet

6451. When your partner is feeling low, your job is to lift him/her up
6452. Not to label and analyze the problem

6453. Cater to the kid in her…

6454. Get a copy of her favorite book from childhood

6455. Buy her favorite flavor of bubble gum

6456. Spring a surprise birthday party for her

6457. Respond with love—*regardless* of what your partner says or does

6458. (All negative behaviors are *disguised calls for love*)

6459. Respond to what's *really* going on— not simply to what's on the surface

---

6460. Massage Coupon #1: The Soothing Foot Massage. Administered by the coupon-giver. At least twenty minutes in duration

6461. Massage Coupon #2: The Stress- Releasing Back Massage. Includes scented body lotion and thirty minutes of deep muscle massage.

6462. Massage Coupon #3: The Erotic Massage. Location: Bedroom. Clothing: Optional. Foreplay: Mandatory

6463. Give 100% to your relationship

6464. Don't fall into the trap of "giving 150%"

6465. It's *impossible* to give more than you have; it will just frustrate you and make you feel guilty

---

6466. Hang a flag from the country of his/her ancestors

6467. Get up early—treat yourselves to breakfast at a local diner

6468. Subscribe to *Libido Magazine*—"Erotica for people who like to read"

6469. "Man makes love by braggadocio, and woman makes love by listening." ~ H. L. Mencken

6470. Unlearn your superior attitude about being in touch with your feelings

6471. Toss coins in a wishing well together and share the same wish

6472. Stay young at heart while growing old together

6473. Get a funny or sexy or romantic temporary tattoo

6474–6482
9 Ways to Love a Sagittarius
(23 November–21 December)

1. Sagittarius is a *fire* sign: Cater to his/her passionate, sexual nature
2. Gift tip: Travel-related
3. Travel accessories, maps, travel books
4. Anything—or anywhere—exotic
5. Take an adventurous trekking vacation
6. Carnation; oak trees
7. Nutty flavors, spicy foods
8. The open spaces of Australia
9. Wrap gifts in deep purple for your Sagittarius

6483. Don't complain about your work as soon as you return home

6484. "Shared laughter is erotic too."
~ Margie Percy

6485. Enjoy a lazy Sunday afternoon canoe ride on a beautiful pond

6486. Give him a T-shirt picturing his favorite cartoon character

6487. A song for the engaged: "I Do, I Do, I Do," by ABBA

6488. When playing tennis, refuse to use the word "Love" to mean "Zero"

6489. "Everything belonging to a loved one is precious." ~ P.A.C. de Beaumarchais

6490. For your Romantic Music Library: Acoustic Alchemy's *Reference Point*

6491. Practice your relationship skills as often as you practice your golf swing

6492. Remember: You can fall in love with the same person over and over again!

6493. Write, inscribe, or engrave coded messages on *all* your gifts…

6494. A.T.S.B.O. (And They Shall Be One)

6495. Y.A.M.O.A.O. (You Are My One and Only)

6496. A.A.F. (Always and Forever)

6497. Y.A.M.S. (You Are My Sweetie)

6498. H.D.I.L.T. (How Do I Love Thee)

6499. I.L.Y.M.T.T.Y. (I Love You More Today Than Yesterday)

6500. Y.A.M.A.T.W. (You and Me Against the World)

6501. T.H.B.A.O. (Two Hearts Beating As One)

6502. Y.A.M.—L.F. (You and Me—Lovers Forever)
6503. L.O.M.L. (Love of My Life)
6504. T.L.A. (True Love Always)
6505. M.Y.A. (Miss You Already)
6506. G.M.F.L. (Geese Mate for Life)

6507. Gals: Quit using "feminine wiles" on him—
6508. Be honest and straightforward (Otherwise you'll be forced to wear a mask throughout your entire life together)
6509. Guys: Quit the macho posturing with her—
6510. Be yourself and share yourself (Otherwise you'll have to keep up that macho act throughout your entire life together)

6511. English: "Kiss me"
6512. French: "Embrasse-moi"
6513. Italian: "Baciami"
6514. German: "Küß mich"
6515. Spanish: "Bésame"

6516. Portugese: "Me beija"

6517. Never let jealousy get the better of you

6518. Write "I love you" on his rear-view mirror with lipstick

6519. Choose little tables-for-two at restaurants

6520. Defy superstition: Celebrate your luck in finding each other every Friday the 13th

6521. Visit "Honeymoon Island": Kauai, Hawaii

6522. For engaged couples only: Find a couple happily married for more than fifty years; take them to lunch and learn their secrets

---

6523–6542
20 Romantic Things to Do in Small Spaces

1. Go through revolving doors together
2. Take a road trip in a VW "Love Bug"
3. Have silly pictures of the two of you taken in a photo booth

4. Join her in the dressing room while lingerie shopping

5. Make love in restroom aboard a plane in flight

6. Relax together in a Jacuzzi

7. Make love in a closet at a friend's party

8. Sleep spoon-style in a single bed

9. Squeeze into phone booths together

10. Camp-out in a tent together

11. Make love in the back seat of a car

12. Travel in a train's sleeper car

13. Attend movie theaters that have "loveseats"

14. Sit side-by-side in booths at little diners

15. Make love in an elevator

16. Go on vacation aboard an RV

17. Hold a picnic in a tree fort

18. Make love in the back of a limousine

19. Take a relaxing bubblebath together

20. Make love in a sleeping bag

6543. "Remember that happiness is a way of travel—not a destination."
~ Roy M. Goodman

6544. Read *The Portable Romantic*, by Gregory J.P. Godek
6545. Hike the Grand Canyon
6546. Make love on a deserted beach
6547. Give a gentle massage
6548. Get an original magazine from the year and month of his/her birthday
6549. Share a midnight snack
6550. For your car nut: Have a tiny love note etched in his car's dipstick

---

6551. Compliment her on her sparkling eyes...
6552. "Pretty Blue Eyes," Steve Lawrence
6553. "Brown-Eyed Girl," Van Morrison
6554. "Green-Eyed Lady," Sugarloaf
6555. "Blue Eyes," Elton John
6556. "Sexy Eyes," Dr. Hook

Favorite Love Songs from 1956
6557. "After the Lights Go Down Low," Al Hibbler
6558. "Memories Are Made of This," Dean Martin
6559. "Mr. Wonderful," Peggy Lee

6560. "Since I Met You Baby," Ivory Joe Hunter

6561. "Tonight You Belong to Me," Patience & Prudence

6562. "Why Do Fools Fall in Love," Frankie Lymon & The Teenagers

6563. "You're Sensational"

6564. "Great thoughts come from the heart." ~ Luc de Clapiers

6565. Plan a *great* romantic surprise to take place one month from today

6566. Practice thinking with your *heart*, not just your *head*

6567. Use your heart—instead of your head—to re-evaluate your priorities

---

6568. Explore the unusual, unfamiliar, and unknown

6569. Pursue the extraordinary, exciting, and extravagant

6570. Practice forgiveness, forethought, and foreplay

6571. Pay attention to your intuition, insights, and inquisitiveness

6572–6620
49 States with Romantic and Curious Town Names

Just think of all the romantic possibilities!

Travel cross-country and stay only in "romantic" towns

Target special towns that match the themes in your life

Alabama: Angel, Love Hills

Alaska: Utopia, Wiseman

Arizona: Dateland, Darling, Date, Love, Carefree, Eden, Valentine

Arkansas: Eros, Delight, Heart, Hon, Romance

California: Bridalveil Fall, Happy Camp, Harmony, Newlove, Paradise, Rough and Ready, Tranquility, Truth or Consequences

Colorado: Bridal Veil Falls, Climax, Fairplay, Goodnight, Loveland, Loveland Pass, Mutual, Security

Connecticut: Pleasure Beach

Delaware: Green Acres, Harmony Hills

Florida: Lovedale, Romeo, Kissimmee, Venus, Christmas, Honeymoon

Island, Venus

Georgia: Climax, Ideal, Lovejoy, Sale City, Sparks

Idaho: Bliss, Eden, Star, Sweet

Illinois: Joy, Fidelity, Love, Lovejoy

Indiana: Advance, Hope, Santa Claus, Valentine, Windfall

Iowa: Jewell, Loveland, Lovington, Manly

Kansas: Bloom, Climax, Eureka, Gem, Joy, Lovewell, Paradise, Protection

Kentucky: Beauty, Goody, Lovely, Number One, Ogle, Pleasureville

Louisiana: Eros, Sunset, Valentine

Maine: Friendship, Harmony, Tryon, Union

Maryland: Darlington, Delight, Golden Beach, Halfway, Love Point, Unity, Welcome

Massachusetts: Hopedale, Silver Lake

Michigan: Bliss, Charity Island, Climax, Paradise, Romeo

Minnesota: Climax, Darling, Fertile, Harmony, Welcome

Mississippi: Bond, Darling, Eden, Love, Star

Missouri: Belle, Bliss, Eureka, Fair Play, Neck, Paradise

Montana: Bond, Eureka, Opportunity, Paradise, Valentine

Nebraska: Sparks, Tryon, Valentine

Nevada: Contact, Paradise, Sparks

New Hampshire: Coos

New Jersey: Fellowship, Loveladies

New Mexico: Loving, Climax

New York: Bliss, Climax, Eden, Swan Lake

North Carolina: Climax, Delight, Eden, Lovejoy, Star, Tryon, Welcome, Wise

North Dakota: Bloom, Darling Lake, Heart River, Union

Ohio: Charm, Climax, Loveland, Loveland Park

Oklahoma: Loveland, Loving, Loyal, Sparks

Oregon: Diamond, Bridal Veil, Christmas Lake Valley, Unity

Pennsylvania: Climax, Harmony, Intercourse, Lovejoy, Lover, Paradise, Paris, Venus

Rhode Island: Diamond Hill, Harmony, Hope Valley

South Carolina: Darlington, Eureka, Union

South Dakota: Date, Eden, Eureka, Faith, Ideal, Winner

Tennessee: Bride, Love Joy, Lovetown, Sweet Lips

Texas: Beaukiss, Blessing, Climax, Comfort, Eden, Eureka, Fort Bliss, Groom, Happy, Lovelady, Loving, Paradise, Poetry, Rising Star, Royalty, Star, Utopia, Valentine, Venus

Utah: Eden, Eureka, Paradise, Virgin

Vermont: Blissville, Eden

Virginia: Casanova, Love, Rose Hill, Valentines, Verona, Wise

Washington: Eureka, Loveland, Opportunity, Union

West Virginia: Belle, Romance, Tango

Wisconsin: French Island, Friendship, Luck, Moon, Romance

Wyoming: Diamondville, Eden, Heart Lake, Heart Mountain, Old Faithful, Reliance

---

6621. Gals: Buy a clingy, elegant 1940s-style evening gown—and greet him at the door wearing it

6622. Ice skate

6623. Wear "Eternity" perfume—To show

him that you'll love him for all
eternity

6624. "Between whom there is hearty truth
there is love." ~ Henry David
Thoreau

6625. What's the difference between "truth"
and "*hearty* truth"?

6626. Confide or confess one secret to your
partner today; watch the intimacy
increase

6627. Write a list: "21 of My Favorite
Memories of You"

6628. Create a collage based on this list

6629. Or create a memory album

6630. Start a new list, beginning today

6631. Present your partner with a new list
each time you reach another twenty-one

6632. Hide a small gift in a cereal box...

6633. Or in the glove compartment

6634. Or in his golf bag

6635. Or in her desk drawer

6636. Or in a box of Cracker Jacks

6637. Send a formal, printed invitation to have dinner

6638. Send a formal, printed invitation to have sex

6639. Send a ribboned scroll declaring your neverending love

6640. Send a big box via UPS—with a tiny gift packed in the middle

6641. Send a poem via email—send one line per hour

6642. Create "theme-gifts": Combine similar items and ideas to create fun and meaningful gifts

6643. The poetry book *A Friend Forever*, by Susan Polis Schutz and the CD *Forever Friends*, by Justo Almario

---

6644–6655
The "Dirty Dozen"—12 Relationship Killers to Watch-Out For

1. Apathy
2. Cynicism
3. Immaturity
4. Stereotyped thinking

5. Lack of commitment
6. Poor communication
7. Lack of empathy
8. Poor self-esteem
9. Lack of skills
10. Unresolved resentments
11. Lack of creativity
12. Television

6656. Write a love poem in formal sonnet style
6657. Listen to Gershwin tunes
6658. "Love will make a way out of no way." ~ Lynda Barry
6659. Arrange Sunday brunch at a local fancy restaurant
6660. Spend a wild weekend in Las Vegas together

6661. "At the touch of love, everyone becomes a poet." ~ Plato
6662. Try your hand at writing a love poem
6663. Don't expect your first efforts to be great—but keep at it
6664. Try writing poems for different

occasions in your life

6665. Practice acts of random kindness...
6666. And senseless loving
6667. And daily politeness
6668. And increased sensitivity
6669. And creative romance

6670. Have realistic expectations of your partner
6671. Have realistic expectations of yourself—
6672. But keep striving to do better!

6673. Write a list: "12 Reasons Why We Should Make a Baby Together"
6674. Create a "First Class Weekend" for your mate
6675. A Zen tip: When you're together, *be* together: "Be here now"
6676. "Love that which will never be seen twice." ~ Alfred de Vigny
6677. Single guys: Show your commitment by ritually burning your *Little Black Book*

6678. Attitude Experiment: Imagine that you have just one month to live: How would you treat your partner differently?

6679. Indulge your romantic whims
6680. Indulge your erotic fantasies
6681. Indulge his/her sweet tooth
6682. Indulge yourself
6683. Indulge your partner

6684. Take your time—love deepens over time
6685. Give your time—it's your most precious resource

6686. Spoon
6687. Be his "Boy Toy"
6688. Label a fancy box "Sweet Nothings" and giftwrap it
6689. Slip a love note into her eyeglasses case
6690. "When you get into a tug-of-war, drop the rope." ~ Bart Jarvis
6691. Return to your favorite romantic beach

6692. Enemy of Love: Grudges
6693. Enlarge to poster-size the best photo of the two of you
6694. Make love on the cellar stairs
6695. Have a limousine pick her up at work on her birthday
6696. Get him *an entire library* of books on his favorite hobby
6697. Decorate Christmas cookies together
6698. Live in the moment
6699. Greet her at the airport with two dozen roses
6700. Banish all "negative talk" at meals

6701. Make a habit of taking leisurely walks together
6702. Make a custom tape of "walking music"; make a new tape every two months
6703. "Walkin' My Baby Back Home" (1930)
6704. "Love Walked In," by Kenny Baker (1938)
6705. "Let's Take an Old-Fashioned Walk" (1949)

6706–6718
13 Songs to Help You Express
Your Feelings: *Longing/Yearning*

1. "Against All Odds (Take a Look at Me Now)," Phil Collins
2. "Ain't No Sunshine," Bill Withers
3. "Baby Come to Me," Patti Austin & James Ingram
4. "Closer to Believing," Emerson, Lake & Palmer
5. "How Can I Tell You," Cat Stevens
6. "I Need You," America
7. "If Ever You're in My Arms Again," Peabo Bryson
8. "If I Can't Have You," Yvonne Elliman
9. "Need Her Love," Electric Light Orchestra
10. "Until the Night," Billy Joel
11. "Watching and Waiting," The Moody Blues
12. "When I Need You," Leo Sayer
13. "You Take My Breath Away," Queen

6719. For left-brained, logical folks: Use

your *natural* logical skills in expressing
your love

6720. For right-brained, creative folks: Use
your *natural* creativity in expressing
your love

6721. For left-brained, logical folks: Practice
your *unfamiliar*, creative, wacky side

6722. For right-brained, creative folks:
Practice your *unfamiliar*, logical,
rational side

6723–6729
7 Items for a *Weekly* Romantic Checklist

1. Bring home one small, unexpected
gift or present

2. Share *some* form of physical intimacy

3. Share an *entire* afternoon or evening
together

4. Share two insights you gained this
week

5. Write at least one little love note

6. Mail *something* to your partner

7. Plan something special for the
upcoming weekend

Favorite Love Songs from 1957

6730. "All Shook Up!" Elvis Presley
6731. "An Affair to Remember"
6732. "April Love," Pat Boone
6733. "Come Go with Me," Del-Vikings
6734. "Little Bitty Pretty One," Thurston Harris
6735. "Little Darlin'," Diamonds
6736. "Love Letter in the Sand," Pat Boone
6737. "You Send Me," Sam Cooke
6738. "Young Love," Tab Hunter

6739. Wear matching ski caps
6740. Give your *undivided attention*
6741. Play tourist in your own town
6742. "There is no surprise more wonderful than the surprise of being loved."
~ Charles Morgan
6743. Garden together
6744. For sci-fi fans: Films on video from Science Fiction Continuum: (800) 232-6002
6745. Celebrate a "Final Fling" on the last day of Summer

6746–6795
50 Quotable Quotes on "Love"

1. "Love demands all, and has a right to it." ~ Beethoven

2. "Love does not dominate; it cultivates."
   ~ Johann Wolfgang von Goethe

3. "Love is a verb." ~ Clare Boothe Luce

4. "Love is all we have, the only way that each can help the other."
   ~ Euripides

5. "Love and emptiness in us are like the sea's ebb and flow." ~ Kahlil Gibran

6. "Love and food are equally vital to our sanity and survival." ~ Kuo Tzu

7. "Love conquers all things; let us too surrender to Love." ~ Virgil

8. "Love and the gentle heart are but a single thing." ~ Dante Alighieri

9. "Love begets love. This torment is my joy." ~ Theodore Roethke

10. "Love cannot be commanded."
    ~ Latin proverb

11. "Love comes after the wedding."
    ~ Laplander proverb

12. "Love dies only when growth stops."
    ~ Pearl S. Buck

13. "Love does not—*cannot*—hurt. It is
    the *absence* of love that hurts."
    ~ Gregory J.P. Godek

14. "Love is a fruit in season at all times,
    and within the reach of every hand."
    ~ Mother Teresa

15. "Love is a great beautifier."
    ~ Louisa May Alcott

16. "Love is an act of endless forgiveness,
    a tender look which becomes a
    habit." ~ Peter Ustinov

17. "Love is an energy which exists of
    itself. It is its own value."
    ~ Anonymous

18. "Love is an irresistible desire to be
    irresistibly desired." ~ Robert Frost

19. "Love is being stupid together."
    ~ Paul Valery

20. "Love is blind." ~ Geoffrey Chaucer

21. "Love is blind; that is why he always
    proceeds by the sense of touch."
    ~ French proverb

22. "Love is its own aphrodisiac and is

the main ingredient for lasting sex."
~ Mort Katz

23. "Love is more easily demonstrated than defined." ~ Anonymous

24. "Love is never complete in any person. There is always room for growth." ~ Leo Buscaglia

25. "Love is not love until love's vulnerable." ~ Theodore Roethke

26. "Love is merely an empty concept *unless* you bring it alive through *action*." ~ Gregory J.P. Godek

27. "Love is not only something you feel. It is something you do."
~ David Wilkerson

28. "Love is not ruled by reason." ~ Moliere

29. "Love is patient and kind; love is not jealous or boastful."
~ 1 Corinthians 13:4

30. "Love is staying awake all night with a sick child. Or a very healthy adult."
~ David Frost

31. "Love is supreme and unconditional; like is nice but limited."
~ Duke Ellington

32. "Love is the active concern for the life and growth of that which you love."
~ Erich Fromm

33. "Love is the great asker."
~ D. H. Lawrence

34. "Love is the greatest refreshment in life." ~ Pablo Picasso

35. "Love is the irresistible desire to be desired irresistibly." ~ Louis Ginsberg

36. "Love is the only disease that makes you feel better." ~ Sam Shepard

37. "Love is the only effective counter to death." ~ Maureen Duffy

38. "Love is the only game that is not called on account of darkness."
~ Anonymous

39. "Love is the triumph of imagination over intelligence." ~ H. L. Mencken

40. "Love is trembling happiness."
~ Kahlil Gibran

41. "Love is what you've been through with somebody." ~ James Thurber

42. "Love keeps us hopeful, in all situations, against all evidence."
~ Lewis B. Smedes

43. "Love knoweth no laws."
    ~ Sir John Lyly
44. "Love knows not its depth till the
    hour of separation." ~ Kahlil Gibran
45. "Love stretches your heart and makes
    you big inside." ~ Margaret Walker
46. "Love: the most fun you can have
    without laughing." ~ Anonymous
47. "Love thrives on trivial kindnesses."
    ~ Theodor Fontane
48. "Love wasn't put in your heart to stay,
    Love isn't love till you give it away."
    ~ Anonymous
49. "Love will find a way." ~ Anonymous
50. "Love, you know, seeks to make
    happy rather than to be happy."
    ~ Ralph Connor

6796. One is the loneliest number—so
      spend one whole day together
6797. Tea for two
6798. Three's a crowd, so send the kid away
      for the day!

6799. Highly recommended: *The 7 Habits of*

Highly Effective People, by Stephen Covey

6800. Also, *The 7 Habits of Highly Effective Families*, by Stephen Covey

---

6801. "If living is for loving, and if only Truth is true, Then I dedicate myself to loving you."

6802. From "Wedding Song" by Brit Lay, on the *Illusions & Dreams* CD: Write to Box 127, Barnstable, Massachusetts 02630

6803. Gift & Date Idea: Watch the movie *Titanic* together

6804. Get her a copy of the movie on video

6805. Get her the CD with Celine Dion singing "My Heart Will Go On"

6806. Get a photo taken of the two of you in a "Rose Pose": On a ship's bow, while standing behind her, hold her arms outstretched and enjoy the sunset (All *Titanic* fans will appreciate this)

6807–6819
13 Important Questions for
Engaged Couples

If you want your relationship to last a lifetime, it will help to look at these issues:

1. In what ways do you want your marriage to be like your parents' marriage?

2. In what ways do you want your marriage to be *different* from your parents' marriage?

3. What is the one thing that the opposite gender simply doesn't "get" about your gender?

4. What lessons did you learn from your *previous* love relationships?

5. How much "personal space" do you need?

6. What is your idea of the "perfect wedding"?

7. Where do you want to honeymoon?

8. Under what circumstances would you see a couple's counselor?

9. How frequently would you like to have sex?

10. How many children do you want to have?

11. At what age will you let your children date?

12. If your children are sexually active at the same age that you were, will that be OK with you?

13. Do you fold your underwear or just stuff it in the drawer?

6820. When dining out, sit *next to* each other, instead of *across from* each other

6821. Kiss under water

6822. "Love is love's reward." ~ John Dryden

6823. Greet him at the door wearing a jersey from his favorite football team—*and nothing else*

6824. Build a fire in your fireplace in *August*

6825. The Victorian Inn: (508) 627-4784 (♥♥♥♥ Romantic B&B Rating)

6826. Celebrate with Dom Perignon

America is a *very* romantic place:
Here's how to get vacation info:

6827. Alabama: (800) 252-2262:

www.touralabama.org

6828. Alaska: (907) 465-2010:
www.commerce.state.ak.us/tourism

6829. Arizona: (888) 520-3433:
www.arizonaguide.com

6830. Arkansas: (800) 828-8974:
www.state.ar.us

6831. California: (800) 862-2543:
www.gocalif.ca.gov

6832. Colorado: (800) 265-6723:
www.colorado.com

6833. Connecticut: (800) 282-6863:
www.state.ct.us/tourism/

6834. Delaware: (800) 441-8846:
www.state.de.us

6835. District of Columbia:
(800) 635-6338: www.washington.org

6836. Florida: (888) 735-2872:
www.flausa.com

6837. Georgia: (800) 847-4842:
www.georgia.com

6838. Hawaii: (800) 464-2924:
www.visit.hawaii.org

6839. Idaho: (800) 635-7820:
www.visitid.org

6840. Illinois: (217) 785-6334:
www.enjoyillinois.com

6841. Indiana: (800) 289-6646:
www.ai.org/tourism/

6842. Iowa: (800) 345-4692:
www.state.ia.us/tourism

6843. Kansas: (800) 2KANSAS:
www.kansascommerce.com

6844. Kentucky: (800) 225-8747:
www.kentuckytourism.com

6845. Louisiana: (800) 633-6970:
www.louisianatravel.com

6846. Maine: (207) 287-5710:
www.visitmaine.com

6847. Maryland: (800) 634-7386:
www.mdisfun.org

6848. Massachusetts: (800) 227-6277:
www.mass-vacation.com

6849. Michigan: (800) 78-GREAT:
www.michigan.org

6850. Minnesota: (800) 657-3700:
www.exploreminnesota.com

6851. Mississippi: (800) 927-6378:
www.decd.state.ms.us/tourism.html

6852. Missouri: (800) 877-1234:

www.missouritourism.org

6853. Montana: (800) 847-4868:
www.travel.mt.gov

6854. Nebraska: (800) 228-0774:
www.ded.state.ne.us/tourism/

6855. Nevada: (800) 237-0774:
www.travelelnevada.com

6856. New Hampshire: (603) 271-2343:
www.visitnh.gov

6857. New Jersey: (609) 292-2470:
www.state.nj.us/travel

6858. New Mexico: (800) 545-2040:
www.newmexico.org

6859. New York: (800) I LOVE NY:
www.iloveny.state.ny.us

6860. North Carolina: (800) 847-4862:
www.visitnc.com

6861. North Dakota: (800) 437-2077:
www.ndtourism.com

6862. Ohio: (800) 282-5393:
www.ohiotourism.com

6863. Oklahoma: (405) 521-2409:
www.otrd.state.ok.us

6864. Oregon: (800)547-7842:
www.traveloregon.com

6865. Pennsylvania: (717) 787-5453:
www.state.pa.us

6866. Rhode Island: (800) 556-2484:
www.visitrhode-island.com

6867. South Carolina: (800) 346-3634:
www.travelsc.com

6868. South Dakota: (800) 732-5682:
www.state.sd.us

6869. Tennessee: (800) 836-6200:
www.state.tn.us/tourdev/

6870. Texas: (800) 452-9292:
www.TravelTex.com

6871. Utah: (800) 200-1160:
www.utah.com

6872. Vermont: (800) 837-6668:
www.travel-vermont.com

6873. Virginia: (800) 847-4882:
www.virginia.org

6874. Washington: (800) 544-1800 ext.
800: www.tourism.wa.gov

6875. West Virginia: (800) 225-5982:
www.state.wv.us/tourism/default.htm

6876. Wisconsin: (800) 432-8747:
http://badger.state.wi.us/agencies/
tourism

6877. Wyoming: (800) 225-5996:
www.state.wy.us/state/tourism/
tourism.html

6878. The gift: Seven bottles of scented
bubble bath
6879. The note: "For a week of rest and
relaxation"

6880. Give her a second look
6881. Give him a second chance
6882. Make her second-to-none

6883. Guys: Express your masculinity—
but don't be *trapped* in it
6884. Gals: Glory in your femininity—
but don't be *limited* by it
6885. Guys: Explore your gentle, soft,
sensitive side
6886. Gals: Explore your confident, sexy,
powerful side

6887. Write a "Self-Improvement Plan" for
yourself
6888. Ask for your partner's input

Favorite Love Songs from 1958

6889. "All I Have to Do Is Dream," Everly Brothers
6890. "Devoted to You," Everly Brothers
6891. "Do You Want to Dance," Bobby Freeman
6892. "To Know Him Is to Love Him," Teddy Bears
6893. "Volare," Domenico Mudugno

6894. The gift: Costume jewelry
6895. The note: "The diamond is fake—but the love is real"

6896. Surprise your jazz fan with tickets to the New Orleans Jazz Festival: (504) 522-4786
6897. Or vacation at the Festival International de Jazz de Montréal: (800) 361-4595
6898. And add to the ambiance with "Jazz" cologne
6899. And create a jazzy mood with CDs by Louis Armstrong and Count Basie
6900. And by Fats Waller, Woody Herman,

and Paul Desmond

6901. Peruse the many erotic books by
      Anaïs Nin…*if you dare*
6902. You may want to takes notes, and
      read passages aloud
6903. *Little Birds*
6904. *Delta of Venus*
6905. *Henry and June*
6906. *A Spy in the House of Love*
6907. *A Literate Passion*
6908. *Obnazhennaia Makha*
6909. *Ladders to Fire*
6910. *Paris Revisited*

6911. Gals: Flash him a little cleavage when
      no one else is looking
6912. Attend the Valentine's Day/mid-
      winter carnival in Venice, Italy
6913. Use a love stamp *every time* you mail
      something to your lover
6914. Send a chocolate chip cookie bouquet
6915. For your golf nut: 18 holes at the
      best local course
6916. "Then I saw you through myself, and

found we were identical."
~ Fakhr Iraqi

6917. Sign your love letters: "Your One and Only"

6918. Get fun rubber stamps that reflect his/her hobbies or interests

6919. Give *fragrant* flowers: Daphne, Wisteria, Hyacinth

6920. "There is but one genuine love-potion—consideration." ~ Menander

6921. Cover strategic body parts with whipped cream

6922. Put comics from the *New Yorker* on the refrigerator door

6923. Go on a second honeymoon

6924. Musical lovenote: "Play the CD *Gorilla*, by James Taylor. My message to you is song No. 3"

6925. Divorce. Divorce yourself from your worries—it will make you a better mate

6926. Read *How to Stop Worrying and Start Living*, by Dale Carnegie

6927. Plan a vacation that matches your mate's vacation style:

6928. Romantic: Visit Venice, Italy

6929. Adventurous: Go trekking in Peru

6930. Party: Go to Las Vegas, Nevada

6931. Culinary: Tour the great restaurants of France

6932. Shopping: Cruise Fifth Avenue in NYC

6933. Lazing: Sit on the beach in Maui, Hawaii

6934. Curious: Take a self-improvement seminar

6935. Cultural: Tour the museums of Italy

6936. Spiritual: Visit a monastery or retreat house

6937–6959
23 Romantically *Wet* Things to Do

1. Dance in the rain together and sing "Singin' in the Rain"

2. Be *extravagantly* gallant: Toss your coat over a puddle to keep her dry

3. Go fishing together

4. Go sailing together

5. Swim underneath a waterfall
6. Take a bubble bath together
7. Go skinny dipping (in a neighbor's pool at midnight)
8. Go skinny dipping (at a public beach—remove your suits in the water)
9. Install a hot tub in your back yard
10. Learn to water ski
11. Go jet skiing together
12. Go scuba diving together
13. Pour Cognac on your partner's body—and lick it off
14. Go to the beach together
15. Stroll through the fog in San Francisco
16. Run through a sprinkler together
17. Go snorkeling together
18. Melt an ice cube over your lover's body
19. Go digging for clams
20. Wash your car—and have a hose battle
21. Go river rafting
22. Hold a private Wet T-shirt Contest

(*both* of you must participate!)
23. Learn to surf together

6960. Renew your wedding vows in a *private* ceremony
6961. Gather meaningful music from your first wedding and from the ensuing years
6962. Gather cherished mementos from your years together

6963. Gals: You need to know: His coat size
6964. Shoe size and hat size
6965. Shirt size and pants size
6966. Finger size (for bowling balls that fit)

Favorite Love Songs from 1959

6967. "'Til I Kissed You," Everly Brothers
6968. "Dedicated to the One I Love," Shirelles
6969. "Donna," Ritchie Valens
6970. "Dream Lover," Bobby Darin
6971. "Hawaiian Wedding Song," Andy Williams
6972. "I Only Have Eyes for You," Flamingos

6973. "Put Your Head on My Shoulder," Paul Anka
6974. "Since I Don't Have You," Skyliners
6975. "Venus," Frankie Avalon

6976. Locate a new pattern of stars, and name the new constellation after your lover
6977. Enjoy an autumn hayride together
6978. Get a bumper sticker that reflects her hobby
6979. Ritual: Always say "God bless you" after he/she sneezes

---

6980–6991
12 Love Quotes from Shakespeare

1. "Love's best habit is a soothing tongue."
2. "Now join your hands, and with your hands your hearts."
3. "Speak low if you speak love."
4. "The course of true love never did run smooth."
5. "They do not love that do not show their love."

6. "For stony limits cannot hold
   love out."
7. "Love comforteth like sunshine after
   rain."
8. "Love sought is good, but giv'n
   unsought is better."
9. "If thou dost love, pronounce it
   faithfully."
10. "Doubt thou the stars are fire; Doubt
    that the sun doth move/Doubt truth
    to be a liar/but never doubt I love."
11. "Be thou familiar, but by no means
    vulgar."
12. "Love's gentle spring doth always
    fresh remain."

6992. For police officers in love: Drive your
      squad car to Lover's Lane, scare off
      the teenagers, then stay and make-out
      with your partner!
6993. Start with *subtle* romantic gestures
6994. "Joy is not in things; it is in us."
      ~ Richard Wagner
6995. Fill the glove compartment with
      Hershey's Kisses

6996. Gift & Date Idea: Get the song "Hard to Say I'm Sorry," by Chicago—
6997. And rent the movie *Summer Lovers*, featuring the song

6998. *Living, Loving & Learning*, by Leo Buscaglia
6999. *Personhood*, by Leo Buscaglia
7000. *Born for Love*, by Leo Buscaglia

7001. Make love in the dark
7002. Make love in the dark without speaking a word
7003. Make love in the dark with music on

7004. How would you arouse your partner if you had just ten minutes?
7005. Half an hour? Three hours? All day? All weekend?

7006. The biggest mistake men make in foreplay is that they don't spend enough time doing it!
7007. The biggest mistake women make in

foreplay is that they are too timid and conservative

7008. A framed print of his/her favorite work of art
7009. Create a "Count-Down Calendar" anticipating your next big vacation
7010. Make all of her Holiday gifts "Theme Gifts"
7011. Go on an "Escape from the Kids Date"
7012. Cuddle—caress—curl-up
7013. Replace all the artwork in your bedroom with romantic prints
7014. Daily affirmation: "I am *in love* with my partner"

7015. "How much better is thy love than wine." ~ Song of Solomon 4:10
7016. One guy wrote to his wife, "I love you more than I love the Superbowl."
7017. Write *one simple line* about your love
7018. Stop and take a look at your life: Have superficial things become top priorities? Re-dedicate yourself to love

7019. Promise your lover the moon and the stars…
7020. "Fly Me to the Moon" (1962)
7021. "Blue Moon" (1934)
7022. "In the Chapel in the Moonlight," Ruth Etting (1936)
7023. "By the Light of the Silvery Moon," Ray Noble (1941)
7024. "Stairway to the Stars" (1935)
7025. "You Are My Lucky Star" (1935)
7026. "Love in the Starlight," Dorothy Lamour (1938)
7027. "Don't Let the Stars Get in Your Eyes" (1952)
7028. "Good Morning Starshine," Oliver (1969)
7029. "Stardust" (1940)

7030–7041
12 Questions About Your Beliefs (That Reveal a *Lot* About You)

A+ Couples share more than a fondness for each other; they share a great many of the same "core beliefs"

1. Do you believe that opposites attract?

2. Do you believe that people learn from their mistakes?

3. Do you believe that two people can be soul mates?

4. How does one *recognize* soul mates?

5. Under what circumstances do you believe that therapy is worthwhile?

6. Do you believe in love at first sight?

7. Do you believe in the religion you were raised in?

8. Do you believe in karma?

9. What do you believe is the biggest difference between men and women?

10. Do you believe that things "generally turn out for the best"?

11. Do you believe that "Absence makes the heart grow fonder"?

12. Do you believe that "It's not whether you win or lose, it's how you play the game"?

7042. Learn French together—

7043. And spend two weeks in Paris to get you started!

7044. Invite your animal-lover to the zoo—
7045. With a note inside a box of Animal Crackers—
7046. Follow-up the date with a stuffed animal of his/her favorite animal

---

7047. Give the gift of time (your time)
7048. Give the gift of time (a wristwatch)
7049. Inscribe on a watch: "I'll always have time for you."

Favorite Love Songs from 1960
7050. "Are You Lonesome To-Night," Elvis Presley
7051. "Baby You Got What It Takes," Brook Benton & Dinah Washington
7052. "Georgia on My Mind," Ray Charles
7053. "It's Now or Never," Elvis Presley
7054. "Let It Be Me," The Everly Brothers
7055. "Save the Last Dance for Me," Drifters

7056. Whisper "You're the best" while out at a party
7057. Whisper "I love you" while walking

7058. Whisper her name while making love
7059. Whisper something erotic and suggestive while out in public

---

7060. Hire a wedding consultant to help you plan an extravagant anniversary
7061. Fold up your love notes like you did in high school
7062. If you're basically a shy person, experiment with being sexually demonstrative
7063. Eat dinner at the most elegant restaurant in town

7064–7071
8 Ways to Love a Capricorn
(22 December–20 January)

1. Capricorn is an *earth* sign: Cater to his/her grounded, practical nature
2. Gift tip: Exclusive, quality
3. Fine pens, quality glassware
4. Scented candles, unusual picture frames
5. Pansies; pine trees
6. Elaborate desserts

7. Monumental Moscow
8. Wrap gifts in brown and deep gray

7072. Create a "*perfect* weekend" (your *partner's* definition of perfect)
7073. Toast each other with champagne
7074. Daily affirmation: "I am romantic"
7075. Give greeting cards that are blatantly obscene!
7076. A+ Romance Rating: The musical *Phantom of the Opera*, by Andrew Lloyd Weber

---

7077. Surprise her with a flower for no specific reason
7078. Surprise him at work with a picnic lunch
7079. Surprise her by running a bubble bath
7080. Surprise him by dressing sexy at home

7081. Listen with your ears, mind, and heart
7082. Listen for the message behind the

words your partner says

7083. Balance your head with your heart

7084. Practice feeling your feelings (It's not as easy as it appears to be)

7085. Become familiar with the full range of your feelings

7086. Talk with your partner about your feelings (the good *and* the bad)

7087. "If there is anything better than to be loved, it is loving." ~ Anonymous

7088. Experiment: Is it *really* better to give than to receive? Try it for one month

7089. If you want your partner to be more loving, *you* start the romantic ball rolling

---

7090. Take her on a *Gone with the Wind* tour of Antebellum plantations—Can you arrange to stay in one?

7091. For handymen in love: Install an On-Off switch on your doorbell

7092. Value your mate's opinions

7093–7105
13 Reminders for Wise Lovers

1. The grass is *not* greener on the other side
2. Valentine's Day is *not* the most romantic day of the year!
3. Your love is unique in all the world
4. Love must be *expressed*, otherwise it's just a nice-sounding-but-empty concept
5. Romance is the expression of love
6. Love is a matter of *skills*, not luck
7. Arguing isn't about *winning*, it's about expressing frustration, then re-connecting
8. Romantic gestures have no ulterior motive
9. Relationships involve a lot of compromise
10. Compromise is a two-way street
11. While love is *universal*, your relationship is *unique*
12. Your *relationship* needs as much attention as your *partner* does
13. Time and effort expended are usually

more appreciated than money spent

7106. Dance together at a restaurant, even when there's no music playing!

7107. Gals: A note to him: "Listen to tracks No. 1, No. 8, and No. 12 on Carole King's *Tapestry* CD"

7108. "Never change when love has found its home." ~ Sextus Propertius

7109. Decorate with Waterford crystal

7110. Keep your expectations reasonable

7111. But at the same time, dream big

7112. Hope and pray

7113. And put your whole heart and soul into your relationship

---

7114. Plan a series of weekends that will improve your relationship

7115. Weekend #1: Catch-up on all chores

7116. Weekend #2: Relax

7117. Weekend #3: Re-connect with your partner

7118. Weekend #4: Practice your communication skills

7119. Weekend #5: Explore your sexuality
7120. Weekend #6: Deal with some of your tough issues
7121. Weekend #7: Deepen the intimacy

7122–7128
7 Relationship Myths Masquerading as Truth

Myth #1: Men don't experience love as women do

Truth: Men experience the same longing, passion, and desire that women do

Explanation: It's the *outward expression* of love that often (but not always) differs

Myth #2: Great relationships are 50/50

Truth: Great relationships are really 100/100

Explanation: It's more than meeting your partner halfway; sometimes you have to give a lot more

Myth #3: Men are from Mars, and women are from Venus

Truth: You are not a *stereotype*, but an *individual* unique in all the world

Explanation: Your core personality is not

simply gender-based, but is created
from a mysterious, complex, and
unique mix of spiritual, psychological,
genetic, and social factors

Myth #4: There are "secret rules" that ensure
lasting love

Truth: Nobody has all the answers; *everybody*
is searching, just like you (and me)

Explanation: Poets, philosophers,
psychologists, and scientists search
constantly for rules and formulas to
guide us. *Humans* and *love* simply
aren't reducible to simple rules

Suggestion: Don't despair, but celebrate the
glorious mystery of it all!

Myth #5: Women are better communicators
than men are

Truth: *Some* women—about 60%—*are* better
communicators

Explanation: Be careful of over-
generalizations about the sexes! Many
men are *great* communicators

Note: Don't forget that there are many
different *styles* of communication

Myth #6: It's wise to beware of "The Battle of the Sexes"

Truth: There ain't no such thing

Explanation: While there *is* a "gender gap"— *and* a lot of confusion—there's no "war" between the sexes.

Note: The phrase *itself* sets a dangerous mode of thinking; your thinking creates your reality!

Myth #7: Real men aren't romantic

Truth: Real Men are *human*—not just *male*— and don't follow "rules" set-down in cute books

Explanation: Being a "Real Man" doesn't mean being a Neanderthal

Note: Guys in *groups* act more macho than they really are when you get them one-on-one

7129. Guys: A recommended romantic shopping trip: Buy one item in each of the following stores; giftwrap in individual boxes and give

7130. A bath shop

7131. A lingerie boutique

7132. A card shop
7133. A flower shop
7134. A jewelry store

7135. Express the *spiritual* plane of your love by attending church together
7136. Express the *emotional* aspect of your love by communicating more
7137. Express the *physical* side of your love—well, *you* know

---

7138. Regardless of the gift, thank your partner *enthusiastically*
7139. But if it's really *awful*, tell him/her the truth *the very next day* (You're obligated to tell the truth—but be *gentle* about it)

7140. Share feelings freely with your partner
7141. Let him/her know your likes and dislikes
7142. Help him/her differentiate between your *wants* and *needs*
7143. List your ten favorite restaurants
7144. Post pictures of your dream vacation spots on the refrigerator

7145. Show him/her what you like and dislike in various gift and clothing catalogs

Favorite Love Songs from 1961

7146. "Blue Moon," Marcels
7147. "I Like It Like That," Chris Kenner
7148. "I Want to Be Wanted," Brenda Lee
7149. "Stand by Me," Ben E. King
7150. "Stay," Maurice Williams & Zodiacs
7151. "Tonight My Love, Tonight," Paul Anka
7152. "Will You Love Me Tomorrow," Shirelles

7153. Be child*like*...
7154. But not child*ish*

7155. Dedicate one week to improving your lovemaking skills...
7156. Monday: Get the book *Passion Play*, by Felice Dunas
7157. Tuesday: Talk about your best lovemaking sessions
7158. Wednesday: Talk *specifically* about

what turns you on

7159. Thursday: Talk about specific sexual techniques that work for you

7160. Friday: Practice foreplay for two hours

7161. Saturday: Make love all morning long

7162. Sunday: Make love in a way you've never practiced before

---

7163. Musical lovenote: "Play the CD *Please Please Me*, by The Beatles; my message to you is song No. 11"

7164. Enjoy Dim Sum in San Francisco's Chinatown

7165. Travel to all seven continents during your life together

7166. On a whim, get a discount fare to London for the weekend

7167. Love Enhancer: A good therapist/counselor/pastor

7168. For Teddy Bear lovers: The White Swan Inn in San Francisco: (415) 775-1755

7169. For women only: Take his last name

7170. For men only: Don't make a fuss if she wants to keep her maiden name

---

7171–7177
7 Items for a *Daily* Romantic Checklist

1. Compliment your partner
2. Spend twenty minutes of uninterrupted time together
3. Call on your way home on your mobile phone
4. Perform one small—and *unexpected*—gesture
5. Say "I love you" at least three times
6. Thank your partner for *something*
7. Take one extra minute when kissing good-bye

7178. List the three things you want to change about your relationship habits
7179. Create a very specific two-year plan for enacting those changes
7180. Read three good relationship books to help you
7181. Talk with a good counselor to give you some direction

7182–7241

60 Ways to (Literally) Say "I Love You"

1. English: "I love you"
2. Apache: "Shi ingôlth-a"
3. Arabic: "'Ahebbek"
4. Armenian: "Sírem zk 'ez"
5. Aztec: "Nimitzlaco'tla"
6. Bengali: "Ami tomake bhalo basi"
7. Bulgarian: "Obícom te"
8. Burmese: "Chítte"
9. Cambodian: "Khñoms(r)alañ 'neak"
10. Cantonese: "Kgoh òi nei"
11. Cherokee: "Kykéyu"
12. Cheyenne: "Ne-méhotatse"
13. Chinese: "Wo ài nei"
14. Czech: "Miluji vás"
15. Danish: "Eg elskar dig"
16. Dutch: "It hous van jou"
17. Egyptian: "Anna bahebek"
18. Eskimo: "Nagligivaget"
19. Finnish: "Mínä rákistan sínua"
20. French: "Je t'aime"
21. Gaelic (Irish): "Mo ghradh thú"
22. German: "Ich liebe dich"
23. Greek: "Sàs agapo"

24. Gypsy or Romany: "Mándi komova toot"
25. Hawaiian: "Aloha wau ia oe"
26. Hebrew: "Aní ohev otakh"
27. Hindi: "Mayn toojh ko pyár karta hun"
28. Hungarian: "Szeretlék"
29. Icelandic: "Eg elska pig"
30. Indonesian: "Saja tjinta padamu"
31. Irish: "Thaim in grabh leat"
32. Italian: "Ti amo"
33. Japanese: "Ai shite imasu"
34. Korean: "Na nun tangshinul sarang hamnida"
35. Kurdish: "Asektem"
36. Latin: "Ego Te amo"
37. Mandarin: "Wo ài ni"
38. Mohawk: "Konoronhkwa"
39. Norwegian: "Jeg elsker deg"
40. Persian: "Aseketem"
41. Polish: "Ja cie kocham"
42. Portugese: "Eu te amo"
43. Russian: "Ya lyablyu tyebya"
44. Samoan: "O te alofa ya te oe"
45. Sanskrit: "Aham twan sneham karomi"

46. Sioux: "Techi ´hila"
47. Somali: "Wankudja'alahai"
48. Spanish: "Te amo"
49. Swahili: "Mimi nakupenda"
50. Swedish: "Jag älskar dig"
51. Taiwanese: "Ngùa ai dì"
52. Thai: "Pom rak khun"
53. Tibetan: "Khyod-la cags-so"
54. Turkish: "Seni severim"
55. Ukranian: "Ya vas kikháyu"
56. Vietnamese: "Anh yêu em"
57. Welsh: "Rwy'n dy garu di"
58. Yiddish: "Ich libe dich"
59. Yugoslavian: "Ja te volim"
60. Zulu: "Ngi ya thandela wena"

7242. Fill the cookie jar with love notes
7243. Fill his briefcase with cookies
7244. Browse in a good used clothing shop
7245. "On wings of song, my dearest, I will carry you off." ~ Heine
7246. Buy a top hat and a bowler, and wear them all day
7247. Ask your partner to dress in a way that fulfills a fantasy

7248. Get some funny outfits for Halloween

Favorite Love Songs from 1962

7249. "Can't Help Falling in Love," Elvis Presley
7250. "I Can't Stop Loving You," Ray Charles
7251. "Roses Are Red," Bobby Vinton
7252. "Sherry," Four Seasons
7253. "What Kind of Fool Am I?" Sammy Davis Jr.

7254. Peruse some classic erotic books…
7255. *Lady Chatterley's Lover*, by D.H. Lawrence
7256. *Tropic of Cancer*, by Henry Miller
7257. *Tropic of Capricorn*, by Henry Miller

7258. Most Underutilized Loving Gesture: The *wink*
7259. Wear "Fahrenheit" cologne—And create a night of *hot* sex
7260. A+ Romance Rating: The Raffles Hotel, in Singapore

7261. Give a single red rose on the first day of *every* month

---

7262–7292
31 Customized Gifts for Lovers

1. Get a custom perfume created just for her
2. A monogrammed bathrobe
3. Get a *custom* love song written and recorded: Call (781) 471-8500
4. Create a custom audio tape of romantic music
5. Create a custom audio tape of twelve songs that remind your partner of you
6. Create a custom audio tape of romantic music to have dinner by
7. Create a custom audio tape of "seduction" music
8. Create a custom audio tape of sexy music to make love to
9. Create a custom audio tape to inspire his/her libido
10. Get her a *customized* romance novel! Call (800) 444-3356

11. Monogrammed underwear!
12. Custom-made, monogrammed dress shirts
13. Monogrammed cufflinks
14. Cufflinks with *his* initials on one side, and *your* initials on the other
15. A monogrammed handkerchief
16. Have a favorite photo of the two of you made into a Christmas card
17. To get your poems, lyrics, vows, invitations, etc., rendered in calligraphy: Call (508) 234-6843
18. Custom balloons with your names on them
19. Monogrammed golf balls
20. Give him/her a funny caricature of yourself
21. Insert your *own* messages into Chinese fortune cookies
22. Wine with custom labels: Call (800) 214-9463
23. Get a one-of-a-kind piece of jewelry custom designed for her
24. Monogrammed towels
25. Monogrammed boxer shorts

26. Have her car custom detailed with stripes and designs in her favorite colors

27. Get a custom rubber stamp made with her name on it

28. Have custom jewelry made from *casts of your fingerprints!*

29. An elegant letter opener—engraved with a short love quote

30. Get a book signed by his/her favorite author

31. An oil painting made from your favorite wedding photo

7293. Get her "Safari" perfume

7294. Along with tickets for an African safari

7295. Or just go to the local zoo

7296. Create your own Summer Celebration

7297. Soundtrack: George Winston's *Summer*

7298. Activity: Sleep under the stars together on a warm summer night

7299. Quote: "Shall I compare thee to a summer's day?" ~ William Shakespeare

7300. Remember: *Tiny* changes often produce *major* results

7301. Sports Analogy: It's like changing the grip on your golf club. Try changing your "grip" on your relationship

7302. Cooking Analogy: It's like the importance of one *small*—but *important*—ingredient. *All* the ingredients are important!

7303. Guys: Listen to her. Just *listen*. Listen, listen, listen

7304. Don't problem-solve; don't give advice

7305. Validate her; her feelings; her experience

7306. True listening creates *connection*—and connection keeps love alive

7307. Gals: Send him a letter sealed with a kiss

7308. Use your reddest lipstick

7309. Don't position yourself against his passions

7310. Don't make him choose between you and golf/football/fishing, etc.

7311. Our lives are roomy: There's time enough for sports *and* love

7312. Take the opportunity to develop your *own* passions.

7313. Love Enhancer: Gifts that touch the heart

7314. Slow dance in your bedroom at midnight

7315. "Life is short. Be swift to love! Make haste to be kind!" ~ Henri F. Amiel

7316. Dedicate a song to him/her on the radio

7317. For Web browsers: Answer the FAQs about yourself

7318. Learn what he/she considers *special*

7319. Give three *blue* gifts, wrapped in *blue*, along with a note saying you'll always be "True Blue"

7320. Favorite gifts for women: An item for whatever she collects
7321. Favorite gifts for women: A subscription to her favorite magazine
7322. Favorite gifts for women: A gift certificate for her favorite boutique

---

7323. Honor her with a cherished family heirloom…
7324. A classic family portrait
7325. A relative's favorite piece of jewelry
7326. Your grandmother's engagement ring
7327. An antique music box

7328. For women only: No male bashing!
7329. For men only: Don't tell jokes about your partner
7330. For women only: Gaze at him with *love* in your eyes
7331. For men only: *Always* be gentlemanly toward her in public
7332. For women only: Whisper to him in public, "Let's make love tonight!"
7333. For men only: Whisper to her in public, "You're the *best*."

7334–7341
8 Books *About* Women,
For Women, *By* women

1. *The Cinderella Complex*, by Colette Dowling

2. *The Feminine Mystique*, by Betty Friedan

3. *Moving Beyond Words*, by Gloria Steinem

4. *Reinventing Love: Six Women Talk About Love, Lust, Sex, and Romance*, by Laurie Abraham, et al.

5. *Unfinished Business: Pressure Points in the Lives of Women*, by Maggie Scarf

6. *The Way of Woman: Awakening the Perennial Feminine,* by Helen M. Luke

7. *The Woman's Comfort Book: A Self-Nurturing Guide for Restoring Balance in Your Life,* by Jennifer Louden

8. *A Woman's Worth*, by Marianne Williamson

7342. A resource for the quirky: The book *Offbeat Museums*

7343. Giftwrap that new car with a big red bow
7344. Guys: Perform the classic "Chippendale Dancer Fantasy"
7345. In the spring, hide a love note in the pocket of her winter coat for her to discover next season
7346. Dream (sleeping) together
7347. For your "control freak" partner: Prepare a *detailed itinerary* for a romantic three-day weekend

---

7348–7400
53 Best Romantic Comedies

1. *10* (♥ ♥ ♥ ♥ Romance Movie Rating)
2. *A Midsummers Night's Sex Comedy* (♥ ♥)
3. *A Touch of Class* (♥ ♥)
4. *All of Me* (♥ ♥ ♥)
5. *All Night Long* (♥ ♥ ♥)
6. *Almost You* (♥ ♥)
7. *Annie Hall* (♥ ♥ ♥ ♥)
8. *Arthur* (♥ ♥ ♥ ♥)
9. *Best Friends* (♥ ♥)
10. *Blind Date* (♥ ♥)
11. *Blume in Love* (♥ ♥)

12. *Born Yesterday* (♥ ♥)
13. *Broadcast News* (♥ ♥ ♥)
14. *Cactus Flower* (♥ ♥ ♥)
15. *Continental Divide* (♥ ♥)
16. *Crocodile Dundee* (♥ ♥ ♥)
17. *Cross My Heart* (♥ ♥)
18. *The Cutting Edge* (♥ ♥)
19. *The Electric Horseman* (♥ ♥ ♥)
20. *Father of the Bride* (♥ ♥ ♥)
21. *Frankie and Johnny* (♥ ♥ ♥ ♥ ♥)
22. *The Goodbye Girl* (♥ ♥ ♥ ♥ ♥)
23. *Groundhog Day* (♥ ♥ ♥)
24. *House Calls* (♥ ♥)
25. *Housesitter* (♥ ♥ ♥)
26. *It's My Turn* (♥ ♥)
27. *Manhattan* (♥ ♥ ♥)
28. *Micki and Maude* (♥ ♥ ♥)
29. *Modern Romance* (♥ ♥)
30. *Mr. Jones* (♥ ♥)
31. *Mrs. Doubtfire* (♥ ♥ ♥)
32. *Murphy's Romance* (♥ ♥ ♥)
33. *Night Shift* (♥ ♥)
34. *Overboard* (♥ ♥)
35. *The Owl and the Pussycat* (♥ ♥ ♥ ♥)
36. *Pillow Talk* (♥ ♥ ♥ ♥)

37. *Play It Again, Sam* (♥ ♥ ♥)
38. *The Princess Bride* (♥ ♥ ♥)
39. *Quackser Fortune Has a Cousin in the Bronx* (♥ ♥)
40. *Reuben, Reuben* (♥ ♥)
41. *Risky Business* (♥ ♥ ♥)
42. *Roxanne* (♥ ♥ ♥ ♥ ♥)
43. *Shampoo* (♥ ♥ ♥)
44. *Shirley Valentine* (♥ ♥ ♥)
45. *Silver Streak* (♥ ♥)
46. *So I Married an Axe Murderer* (♥ ♥)
47. *Splash* (♥ ♥ ♥)
48. *Starting Over* (♥ ♥)
49. *The Sure Thing* (♥ ♥)
50. *That Touch of Mink* (♥ ♥)
51. *Tootsie* (♥ ♥ ♥ ♥)
52. *Who Am I This Time?* (♥ ♥)
53. *The Woman in Red* (♥ ♥ ♥)

7401. Set your alarm clock thirty minutes early—enjoy the morning together
7402. Record on videotape his favorite episode of his favorite TV show

---

7403. Always have *some* body part touching

your partner, as you fall asleep

7404. Never open your mate's mail
7405. Always give him/her a phone number where you can be reached when you're traveling
7406. Never argue in public
7407. Always talk to one another with *respect*
7408. Never sulk

7409. Guys: Always, always, *always* treat her like a lady
7410. Never, never, *never* disrespect her
7411. Gals: Always, always, *always* honor his masculinity
7412. Never, never, *never* embarrass him in public

7413. "'Faith' in the language of heaven is 'Love' in the language of men."
     ~ Victor Hugo
7414. Love is a quality that connects the material world with the spiritual world
7415. Light candles to symbolize your love

7416. Attend a church service together

7417–7426
The 10 Commandments
for Loving Couples

1. Thou shalt give 100%
2. Thou shalt treat your partner as the unique individual he/she truly is
3. Thou shalt stay connected through word and deed
4. Thou shalt accept change and support growth in yourself and your mate
5. Thou shalt live your love
6. Thou shalt share: The love and fear, the work and play
7. Thou shalt listen, listen, listen
8. Thou shalt honor the subtle wisdom of the heart and listen to the powerful insights of the mind
9. Thou shalt not be a jerk or a nag
10. Thou shalt integrate the purity of spiritual love with the passion of physical love and the power of emotional love

7427. Write a "Love Warranty" to guarantee your devotion
7428. Attach a small love note to a bunch of balloons
7429. Send a bouquet of your partner's favorite flowers
7430. Hide a little gift so well that he probably won't find it for *months*
7431. Reassure her

Favorite Love Songs from 1963

7432. "Be My Baby," Ronettes
7433. "Candy Girl," Four Seasons
7434. "He's So Fine," The Chiffons
7435. "I Will Follow Him," Little Peggy March
7436. "Love's Gonna Live Here," Buck Owens
7437. "Our Day Will Come," Ruby & Romantics
7438. "Rhythm of the Rain," Cascades
7439. "So Much in Love," Tymes
7440. "Up on the Roof," Drifters
7441. "You've Really Got a Hold on Me," Miracles

7442. Work to *understand* your relationship
7443. But don't *analyze* it to death
7444. Love is an experience to be *cherished*, not scrutinized

---

7445. Get a huge umbrella-built-for-two
7446. Travel to Alaska to watch the Aurora Borealis ("Northern Lights")

7447. Drive up the California coast
7448. Ski down Mount Aspen
7449. Climb up Mount Washington
7450. Raft down the Colorado River
7451. Climb up the Statue of Liberty
7452. Slide down a giant water slide
7453. Rise up in a hot air balloon
7454. Dive down into the Great Barrier Reef
7455. Lift up your spirits
7456. Hike down the Grand Canyon

7457–7464
8 Ways to Love a Aquarius
(21 January–18 February)

1. Aquarius is an *air* sign: Cater to

his/her light, funloving nature
2. Gift tip: Whimsical and unusual
3. Quirky pottery, costume jewelry
4. Almost anything custom-made
5. Orchids; cherry trees
6. Subtle flavors, creamy textures
7. The Taj Mahal, in India
8. Wrap gifts in electric blue and turquoise

7465. Identify *very specific* problem areas in your relationship, *and vow to clear them up*

7466. Come up with a system for balancing the checkbook—*and never argue about it again*

7467. Bring those little sexual frustrations out into the open—before they become *big* problems

7468. Write a household budget—*with enough flexibility built-in*—and stick to it

7469. Divide-up the household chores—*fairly*—and just get on with it

7470. Discuss how you allocate your time—leisure time versus work time

7471. Enemy of Love: Shyness
7472. Turn your anniversary into a *week-long* celebration
7473. Write in tiny letters on a wooden yardstick: Thirty-Six Ways to Measure Your Love for Her
7474. Insert a love note into your mate's morning newspaper
7475. Greet him at the airport with a balloon bouquet

7476. "Make love not war": Well?!
7477. "Love makes the world go round": Do your part to keep it moving!
7478. "Two heads are better than one": Consult one another more often
7479. "It's not *what* you do, but *how* you do it": But you gotta *do* it!
7480. "The way to a man's heart is through his stomach": Cook his favorite meal
7481. "Two steps forward, one step back": This is how we usually make progress in our relationships
7482. "When the going gets tough, the tough get going": Don't give up

7483. To connect your love and spirituality, read *The Road Less Traveled*, by M. Scott Peck

7484. Consider some "less traveled roads" to travel with your lover

7485. Resource: *Off the Beaten Path: A Guide to More Than 1,000 Scenic & Interesting Places Still Uncrowded and Inviting*

7486. Watch together: *Mad About You* (The most romantic show on television)

7487. Charter a luxury yacht for a Caribbean cruise

7488. "Inspiration starts in the home" ~ Alpha English

7489. Have a charm *custom-made* for her charm bracelet

7490. For marrieds only: Inscribe your wedding rings with a romantic verse

7491. Read *Romantic Fantasies: And Other Sexy Ways of Expressing Your Love*, by Gregory J.P. Godek

---

7492. Identify the strengths of your "type" of relationship, and "go with the flow"

7493. Are you a "Two peas in a pod" couple? Or an "Opposites attract" couple?

7494. Are you a "Platonic" couple? Or a "Passionate" couple?

7495. Become more aware of the problems *inherent* in your "type" of relationship, and plan to deal with them

---

7496. Go in search of romantic views...

7497. The Golden Gate Bridge—at sunset

7498. Paris—from the top of the Eiffel Tower

7499. The Grand Canyon—at sunrise

7500. The Pacific Ocean—from a Hawaiian hut

7501. The Caribbean—from the deck of a cruise ship

7502. The New York skyline—from a suite at the Waldorf Astoria

7503. The moon—rising over the Fiji Islands

7504. Niagara Falls—from aboard the Maid of the Mist

7505. Keep your promises
7506. Keep your cool
7507. Keep it up
7508. Keep your big mouth shut (when you're tempted to criticize)

7509. Try a little aromatherapy together
7510. Treat commercials as "Romance Breaks"
7511. Freeze a tiny love note in an ice cube
7512. Record on videotape *every episode* of her favorite TV show
7513. Frame both of your baby photos together
7514. For singles only: Send a copy of your resume with a note: "I want you to get to know me better"

7515. Send twenty stuffed animals to her on her 20th birthday
7516. Send thirty golf balls to him on his 30th birthday
7517. Send forty reasons why you love her on her 40th birthday
7518. Send fifty specially selected love songs to him on his 50th birthday

7519. Send sixty greeting cards to her on her 60th birthday
7520. Send seventy sunflowers to him on his 70th birthday
7521. Send eighty Hershey's Kisses to her on her 80th birthday
7522. Send ninety balloons to him on his 90th birthday
7523. Send one hundred red roses to her on her 100th birthday

---

Favorite Love Songs from 1964

7524. "Chapel of Love," Dixiecups
7525. "Everybody Loves Somebody," Dean Martin
7526. "I Want to Hold Your Hand," The Beatles
7527. "Love Me Do," The Beatles
7528. "My Guy," Mary Wells
7529. "People," Barbra Streisand
7530. "She Loves You," The Beatles
7531. "Under the Boardwalk," Drifters
7532. "Understand Your Man," Johnny Cash

7533. Treat her to a shopping spree at Neiman-Marcus
7534. Tip for How to Buy Gifts for Guys: Look for "Toys-for-Boys" (We never really grow up—our toys just get more expensive)

7535–7570
36 *Kinds* of Gifts to Give Your Guy or Gal

1. The Surprise Gift
2. The Trinket Gift
3. The "Just what I always wanted" Gift
4. The Classically Romantic Gift
5. The Perfume Gift
6. The Sexy Gift
7. The "Oh, you *shouldn't* have!—But I *love* it!" Gift
8. The Obligatory Gift
9. The Optional Gift
10. The Kooky Gift
11. The Keepsake Gift
12. The "How did you *find* it?!" Gift
13. The Homemade Gift
14. The Unbelievably Expensive Gift
15. The Gag Gift

16. The Gift that Keeps on Giving
17. The One Gigantic Item Gift
18. Theme-Gifts
19. Personalized Gifts
20. The Gift of Travel
21. The Gift of Food
22. The Gift in His/Her Favorite Color
23. The Meaningful Gift
24. The Funny Gift
25. The Practical Gift
26. The Frivolous Gift
27. The First Class Gift
28. The Custom Romance Certificate Gift
29. The Gift-Within-a-Gift-Within-a-Gift Gift
30. The Beautifully-Wrapped Gift
31. Birthday Gifts
32. Anniversary Gifts
33. The Gift of Time
34. The Gift of Cash
35. The Gift Certificate
36. The Gift of Yourself

7571. Tie a love note to her dog's collar

7572. Love Enhancer: Good role models
7573. Remember: The most important sex
      organ is the *brain*

7574–7583
10 Questions About Life & Love
(That Reveal a *Lot* About You)

People with A+ Relationships don't *assume* too
much about each other: They *ask!*

1. When do you feel most fully engaged
   in living?
2. What do you do when you feel blue?
3. What makes you angry?
4. What makes you sad?
5. Who is your mentor? Hero? Role
   model?
6. What's the best relationship advice
   you've ever gotten?
7. What one wish do you have for your
   children?
8. What would you like your epitaph to
   read?
9. How did you first learn about sex?
10. What crazy misconceptions did you
    once have about sex?

7584. English: "You make me so happy"
7585. French (spoken to a guy): "Tu me rends très heureux"
7586. French (spoken to a gal): "Tu me rends très heureuse"
7587. Italian: "Tu mi rendi così felice"
7588. German: "Du machst mich sehr glücklich"
7589. Spanish: "Me haces muy feliz"
7590. Portugese: "Você me fax muito feliz"

7591. Gift & Date Idea: Get the song "True Love," by Bing Crosby & Grace Kelly—
7592. And rent the movie *High Society*, featuring the song

7593. Favorite gifts for men: Tools!
7594. Favorite gifts for men: Wristwatches
7595. Favorite gifts for men: Cash!

7596. Be silly
7597. Learn to tie a "Lover's Knot"
7598. Share *everything*: Your secret dreams and desires

7599. "However rare true love is, true
friendship is even rarer."
~ La Rochefoucauld

7600. Teach your parrot to say her name

7601. Don't just *work* at it—*play* at it, too!

7602. Turn to him/her in public and
whisper, "You make life worth
living!"

7603. Take your teddy bear collector to the
Basic Brown Bear Factory, in San
Francisco: (415) 626-0781

7604. Attend a seminar together to build
your relationship skills

7605–7613
The 9 Most Romantic Movie Soundtracks

1. *About Last Night*
2. *Against All Odds*
3. *Bed of Roses*
4. *Casablanca*
5. *Crazy for You*
6. *Dirty Dancing*
7. *Love Affair*
8. *Somewhere in Time*
9. *Titanic*

7614. Buy a new car together
7615. View every anniversary as a new chapter of *The Story of Your Lives Together*
7616. Never, never, *never* say, "I told you so"
7617. Re-design your bedroom with the help of *Beds*, by Diane Von Furstenberg

---

7618. Know *all* of your anniversaries—
7619. And celebrate *several* of them...
7620. The day you first met
7621. Your first date
7622. Your first kiss
7623. The first time you said, "I love you"
7624. The first time you made love
7625. The day you moved-in together
7626. The day you bought your first home
7627. The day you conceived your child

7628. The gift: A four-leaf clover
7629. The note: "I got lucky when I found you."

7630. "Civilized people cannot fully satisfy

their sexual instinct without love."
~ Bertrand Russell

7631. Yes, sexual knowledge and techniques will *enhance* sex—but human sexuality isn't complete without love

7632. If you want to keep your *sex* life active, keep your love—*emotional*—life active!

7633. Splurge on a $100 shopping spree at Radio Shack

7634. Have a drawer-full of Hallmark cards ready to mail

7635. Replace *birth*days with "*mirth*-days"

7636. Perform the classic "Sexy Masseuse Fantasy"

7637. For singles only: Fantasize together about what your wedding might be like

7638. Ritual: Always hand her a towel after her shower

7639. Tape a love note to the center of the rear windshield, and wait for him to see it in the rear view mirror

7640. Give *him* a variety of jewelry…
7641. Cufflinks
7642. Tie tacks
7643. Earrings

7644–7672
29 Gemstones and
Their Symbolic Meanings

Don't give "just jewelry"—give jewelry with *symbolic* and *romantic* meaning!

Write a poem that reflects the symbolic meaning of the gemstone in the jewelry

Find a love song that matches the meaning of the gemstone—and create a theme-gift

1. Agate: *calmness, eloquence, health, virtue, wealth*
2. Amethyst: *deep love, happiness, sincerity*
3. Aquamarine: *happiness & constancy in love, hope, courage*
4. Beryl: *everlasting youth, happiness, hope*
5. Bloodstone: *brilliance, courage, generosity, health*
6. Carbuncle: *energy, self-confidence, strength*
7. Carnelian: *courage, joy, friendship, peace*

8. Cat's Eye: *long life, platonic love*
9. Chrysolite: *wisdom, curiosity*
10. Coral: *attachment, faithfulness*
11. Diamond: *joy, life, love, purity, innocence*
12. Emerald: *spring, hope, peace, tranquillity*
13. Garnet: *faith, loyalty, strength*
14. Hyacinth: *constancy, love, faithfulness*
15. Jade: *intelligence, longevity, strength*
16. Jasper: *courage, joy, wisdom*
17. Lapis Lazuli: *ability, cheerfulness, truth*
18. Moonstone: *pensiveness, intelligence*
19. Onyx: *clearness, dignity*
20. Opal: *confidence, happiness, hope, tender love*
21 Pearl: *beauty, purity, faithfulness, wisdom, wealth*
22. Peridot: *happiness*
23. Ruby: *beauty, dignity, nobility, happiness, love, passion*
24. Sapphire: *calmness, contemplation, hope, purity, truth*
25. Sardonyx: *divine love, joy, marital happiness, vivacity, power*
26. Topaz: *eager love, fidelity, friendship, gentleness*

27. Tourmaline: *courage, generosity, thoughtfulness*
28. Turquoise: *success, depth, understanding*
29. Zircon: *respect, joy*

7673. For your chocoholic: The book *Death by Chocolate*, by Marcel Desaulniers
7674. Find some old Victorian-style greeting cards
7675. Spouses *forever*: Have a "wedding band" tattooed on your ring finger
7676. Remember: You get 1,440 minutes every day. How many do you spend expressing love?
7677. A "Ride in the Country" Coupon: Good for a lazy Sunday afternoon of cruising the countryside. A relaxing day is promised
7678. Don't sweat the small stuff (It's *all* small stuff)

Favorite Love Songs from 1965

7679. "Eight Days a Week," The Beatles
7680. "I Got You Babe," Sonny & Cher
7681. "It's Not Unusual," Tom Jones

7682. "My Girl," Temptations
7683. "Red Roses for a Blue Lady," Vic Dana
7684. "Yes I'm Ready," Barbara Mason
7685. "You Were on My Mind," We Five

7686. For women only: Let your hair grow long, if he desires it
7687. For men only: Shave off your mustache, if she doesn't care for it
7688. For women only: Wear one of his dress shirts—with lingerie underneath
7689. For men only: Wear bikini underwear just for her
7690. For women only: Wear his favorite lingerie under your work outfit today
7691. For men only: Write suggestive notes in the margin of her Victoria's Secret

---

7692–7701
10 Questions We *Dare* You to Discuss With Your Partner!

A+ Couples share all kinds of "secrets" with each other

1. Have you ever had sex in the back seat of a car?

2. What was your most *embarrassing* moment in the presence of a member of the opposite sex?

3. Under what conditions would you consider divorce?

4. How did you lose your virginity?

5. What sexual fantasy would you *love* to enact?

6. What are you afraid of?

7. How are you *just like* your father? Mother?

8. What are your *fondest* childhood memories?

9. What is your *worst* childhood memory?

10. Whose ego is more fragile—yours or your partner's?

7702. Get a copy of *The Kama Sutra*

7703. Read parts of it aloud to each other

7704. Try some of its suggestions

7705. Take your Judy Garland fan to the Judy Garland Museum in Grand Rapids, Minnesota

7706. Wake her at 3 A.M. by gently kissing
her
7707. Get a massage table, and get *serious*
about those backrubs!
7708. Take your mystery lover to visit the
Sherlock Holmes Museum at 221b
Baker Street, London

7709–7734
A to Z Romantic Gifts

Dedicate yourself to finding one romantic
gift for each letter of the alphabet

A is for Artwork, Azaleas, Aretha Franklin
Albums, Antiques, Aphrodisiacs

B is for Balloons, Books, Beatles albums,
Baileys Irish Cream

C is for Chocolate, Candles, Cards, Cookies,
CDs, Cameras, Concerts

D is for Donuts, Dining out, Diamonds,
Dom Perignon

E is for Earrings, Escape weekends,
Engagement rings, Erotica

F is for Films, Flowers, Ferris wheel rides,
Furs, Fishing gear

G is for Gemstones, Gold, Garter belts,

Gourmet Gadgets, Guitars

H is for Hats, Hawaiian vacations, Honeymoons, Hayrides

I is for Ice cream, Italian vacations, Island escapes, Incense

J is for Jewelry, Jacuzzis, Jazz music, Jamaican vacations

K is for Kites, Kinky toys, Kiss coupons, Earl Klugh

L is for Licorice, Lingerie, Luggage, Limousine rides, London

M is for Movie tickets, Magazine subscriptions, Motorcycles, Music

N is for Nightgowns, Necklaces, Nature, Nostalgia, Novels

O is for Opals, Oil lamps, Ornaments, Opera, Off-Broadway

P is for Perfume, Picnic baskets, Popcorn, Poppies, Pianos

Q is for Quilts, Quiet afternoons, Queen Mary cruises

R is for Rings, Roses, Robes, Reggae music

S is for Satin Sheets, Spas, Skates, Silk boxer shorts, Socks

T is for Tickets, Tools, Tents, T-shirts, Time

together, Tea time

U is for Umbrellas, U2 albums,
    Unconditional love

V is for Vacations, Vases, VCRs, Violin
    concertos

W is for Waterfalls, Weekend get-aways,
    Watches, Window shopping

X is for eXtra consideration, eXtravagant
    gifts and gestures

Y is for Yachts, Yukon vacations, Year-of-
    romance

Z is for Zany gifts, Zanzibar vacations, Zorro

7735. And of course, there's always
      romantic music by Yanni…

7736. Selected CDs: *Keys to Imagination;*
      Tribute

7737. *Optimystique; Out of Silence*

7738. *Reflections of Passion; Heart of Midnight*

7739. Mail a lock of your hair to your lover

7740. Encase a special memento (ticket stub,
      wedding invitation, etc.) in acrylic

7741. Get a pendant that honors his/her
      religious beliefs

7742. Enemy of Love: Resentment
7743. Leave the world a better place because you've raised your kids to be loving
7744. Play "sexy-words-only" Scrabble
7745. For plumbers in love: Install a luxurious Jacuzzi in your home
7746. Kidnap your partner for a surprise three-day weekend

7747. When you've got money to spend, *spend it!*
7748. On caviar
7749. Antique fountain pens
7750. Mink teddy bears
7751. Original artwork
7752. 24-karat gold *anything*

7753. Ask your partner to describe his/her "Dream Vacation"
7754. Let your imaginations run wild
7755. Picture this vacation down to the *smallest* detail
7756. Create a long-term plan to make this dream come true

7757. Periodically give gifts that relate to the destination, such as:
7758. Clothes and books
7759. Travel posters and brochures
7760. And finally, make this "Dream Vacation" a reality

7761. English: "You're sweet"
7762. French: "Tu es gentille"
7763. Italian: "Sei dolce"
7764. German: "Du bist süß"
7765. Spanish: "Eres dulce"
7766. Portugese: "Você é gentil"

7767. Turn on the heating blanket before your sweetie gets in bed
7768. Thumbtack a little love note to a beam in the attic—which may not be found for *years*!
7769. Experiment with some love potions (couldn't hurt—might help!)
7770. Get a custom street sign made with her name on it
7771. Surprise her with a briefcase stuffed with Milk Duds

7772. Include a love note in his lunchbox

7773–7788
16 Travel Magazines to Help
You Plan a Romantic Vacation

1. *Adventure Road*—(212) 673-8930
2. *Arizona Highways*—(602) 258-6641
3. *Asia Pacific Travel*—(415) 697-8038
4. *California Highways*—
   (213) 935-3107
5. *Conde Nast Traveler*—(212) 880-2102
6. *Endless Vacation*—(317) 871-9504
7. *Expedition World*—(203) 967-2900
8. *Just Go!*—(415) 255-5951
9. *Leisure Ways*—(416) 595-5007
10. *National Geographic Traveler*—
    (202) 828-5484
11. *Railways*—(818) 500-0542
12. *Relax*—(708) 940-8333
13. *Romantic Traveling*—(415) 731-8239
14. *The Discerning Traveler*—
    (215) 247-5578
15. *Travel & Leisure*—(212) 382-5600
16. *TravelTips*—(718) 939-2400

7789. Stop using lame excuses, like "Real Men aren't romantic"
7790. And "I don't have time"
7791. And "I forgot"
7792. And "Maybe next week"
7793. And "Romance is for teenagers"
7794. And "I don't know what to do"
7795. And "I'm not very creative"
7796. And "I'm too tired"
7797. And "We're *parents* now"
7798. And "I have a career to think about"
7799. And "Romance is going to cost me a fortune"

7800. At a seafood restaurant: Hide a real pearl in an oyster
7801. Increase the frequency of your lovemaking by 33%
7802. Give freely of yourself
7803. Watch the lights of Broadway from the window seats of a restaurant
7804. Eat dinner at the restaurant with the best food at cheap prices
7805. Give one rose for every *day* you've been together!

Favorite Love Songs from 1966

7806. "A Groovy Kind of Love,"
      Mindbenders
7807. "Good Lovin'," Young Rascals
7808. "My Love," Petula Clark
7809. "Strangers in the Night," Frank
      Sinatra
7810. "What Now, My Love," Sonny &
      Cher
7811. "You Are My Soul & Inspiration,"
      Righteous Brothers

7812. Attention guys: You may want to
      check-out: *A Modern Man's Guide to
      Modern Women*, by Dennis Boyles
7813. You'll be relieved to learn about: *The
      Myth of Masculinity*, by Joseph H.
      Pleck
7814. What guys desire *and* fear: *If You
      Could Hear What I Cannot Say*, by
      Nathaniel Branden
7815. Required reading: *The Sensuous Man*,
      by M

7816. "Shared joy is double joy; shared

sorrow is half a sorrow."
~ Swedish proverb

7817. Talk more; spend more time together
7818. Don't keep the hard stuff to yourself:
Two hearts are better than one

7819–7846
28 Bits of Advice from Happy Couples

1. "Do *silly stuff*—like going trick-or-treating together on Halloween."
2. "Celebrate *every single day.*"
3. "Quit being so damn selfish!"
4. "Sometimes a simple hug says more than words possibly can."
5. "Count to ten before expressing anger."
6. "Don't believe the cynics: You *can* keep love alive for a lifetime."
7. "Be the most romantic couple in your neighborhood."
8. "Don't assume you know each other inside out—even after many years together."
9. "Don't follow anybody's 'formula' for love: You gotta live your own love."

10. "Be best friends."
11. "Don't get stuck in your roles."
12. "Hold quarterly 'Relationship Meetings' to discuss what's going on."
13. "Never miss your yearly vacation."
14. "Relationships have cycles—so never despair."
15. "Arguing is God's pressure release valve for couples."
16. "Don't get stuck in a 'Saturday Night Sex Rut.'"
17. "Travel together: It broadens your horizons."
18. "Lots and lots of little surprises."
19. "Most men won't admit it, but *we* like to receive flowers, *too*."
20. "Don't sleep in separate bedrooms, it thwarts intimacy."
21. "Treat your wife like a *girlfriend*, not like a *wife*."
22. "Share a hobby or sport."
23. "Don't keep secrets."
24. "Remember the reasons why you first fell in love with the little devil!"
25. "Love is a journey, not a destination."

26. "A great relationship is a place to 'come home' to."
27. "A relationship is God's gift; it's our job to make the most of it."
28. "I've learned that when you give love, you give from an infinite reservoir."

7847. Music from the romantic crooner himself, Luther Vandross—
7848. Selected CDs: *The Night I Fell in Love*
7849. *Power of Love; I Know*
7850. *Any Love; Never Too Much*

7851. Try making love as *quietly* as you possibly can...the skill may come in handy some day
7852. Try making love as *loudly* as you possibly can...don't hold *anything* back!

Favorite Love Songs from 1967
7853. "All You Need Is Love," The Beatles
7854. "Baby I Love You," Aretha Franklin
7855. "Brown Eyed Girl," Van Morrison
7856. "Daydream Believer," Monkees

7857. "Happy Together," Turtles
7858. "I Never Loved a Man," Aretha Franklin
7859. "I Think We're Alone Now," Tommy James & Shondells
7860. "It Must Be Him," Vikki Carr
7861. "Make Me Yours"
7862. "To Sir with Love," Lulu

7863. Play romantic music on the stereo when he/she comes home from work
7864. Try some Kenny G, Al Jarreau, or Nicholas Gunn

7865. Create your own custom holidays. For example…
7866. Wife Appreciation Day
7867. Redhead Day
7868. A Holiday for Workaholics
7869. Lefthander Day
7870. Beer Lovers of America Day
7871. Create unique rituals for your holiday—and take the day off work to celebrate

7872–7878

7 Best Love Songs by Stevie Wonder

1. "For Once in My Life"
2. "I Just Called to Say I Love You"
3. "I Was Made to Love Her"
4. "Nothing's Too Good for My Baby"
5. "My Cherie Amour"
6. "Signed, Sealed, Delivered I'm Yours"
7. "You Are the Sunshine of My Life"

7879. Play sexy, sultry music when he/she comes home from work
7880. Try some Sade, Enigma, Madonna, or Billie Holiday

7881. Send her a note: "I knead you"— then bake bread together
7882. Collect posters from favorite vacation spots and have them framed
7883. Invite him out by giftwrapping the song "I Wanna Dance with Somebody (Who Loves Me)," by Whitney Houston

---

7884. Favorite gifts for men: Cameras

7885. Favorite gifts for men: Power tools
7886. Favorite gifts for men: Really cool briefcases

7887. When your kids go back-to-school, send *yourselves* "back-to-school" too
7888. Take a relationship seminar together
7889. Or read a good relationship book, like *The Language of Love,* by Gary Smalley & John Trent

---

7890. Gift & Date Idea: Get the song "Can't Help Falling in Love," by UB40—
7891. And rent the movie *Sliver,* featuring the song

7892–7908
17 Things to Thank Your Partner For

Literally write a series of "Thank You" cards to him/her. Some suggestions…

1. "Thank you for falling in love with me"
2. "Thank you for believing in me"
3. "Thank you for your gentle touch"

4. "Thank you for being by my side"
5. "Thank you for putting up with me"
6. "Thank you for being an awesome mom/dad to our children"
7. "Thank you for the chocolate chip cookies"
8. "Thank you for teaching me what love is really all about"
9. "Thank you for hanging in there through thick and thin"
10. "Thank you for that time in bed when you…"
11. "Thank you for getting up at 3 A.M. with the kids"
12. "Thank you for your emotional support"
13. "Thank you for that time when you came to my rescue and…"
14. "Thank you for the hugs"
15. "Thank you for balancing the checkbook"
16. "Thank you for being the best kisser in the world!"
17. "Thank you for the way you hold me"

7909. Read *Romantic Dates: Ways to Woo & Wow the One You Love*, by Gregory J.P. Godek

7910. Special note to the overwhelmed: Remember the 80/20 Rule: "80% of your results come from 20% of your effort." This also works in relationships

7911. Enemy of Love: Patronizing your partner

7912. "I am my beloved's, and his desire is toward me." ~ Song of Solomon 7:10

7913. For engaged couples only: Write your wedding vows together

7914. Expand your Romantic Music Library with Billy Ocean

7915. Remember, gals: When it comes to love, most men believe that "actions speak louder than words"

Favorite Love Songs from 1968

7916. "A Beautiful Morning," Rascals

7917. "Angel of the Morning," Merrilee Rush

7918. "Honey," Bobby Goldsboro

7919. "Light My Fire," Jose Feliciano
7920. "Love Is All Around," Troggs
7921. "Love Is Blue," Paul Mauriat
7922. "Midnight Confessions," The Grass Roots
7923. "The Look of Love," Sergio Mendes & Brazil 66
7924. "This Guy's in Love with You," Herb Alpert & Tijuana Brass

---

7925. Get a copy of *The Joy of Sex*
7926. Mark your favorite pages
7927. Share them with your partner
7928. Reserve an entire weekend to "play"

7929–7938
10 Questions to Spark Your Sex Life

People with A+ sex lives aren't shy about asking—and answering—sexy questions:

1. What is your *secret* sexual fantasy?
2. *Where* would you like to have sex?
3. What kind of *public* clothing do you find sexy?
4. What kind of *bedroom* clothing do you find sexy?

5. Do you know what your partner's favorite foreplay activity is?
6. What is your favorite foreplay activity to *perform*?
7. What is your favorite foreplay activity to *receive*?
8. Do you have a fantasy that turns you on but you'd never actually do?
9. What sexual activity have you never done before and would like to try?
10. What movie scenes do you find sexy?

7939. Write messages using "shoe string licorice"
7940. While in Los Angeles, you may want to drive down Juliet Street or Romeo Canyon Road
7941. Take your tea lover to visit Celestial Seasonings, in Boulder, Colorado: (303) 581-1202
7942. For your golfer: Celebrate Jack Nicklaus' birthday, January 21
7943. In a love note, tell him that you are full of "concupizcence" for him
7944. A+ B&B Rating: The Inn at Long

Lake, in Naples, Maine:
(800) 437-0328

7945. Spend a carefree day at Disney World
together

7946. "A kiss is the shortest distance
between two." ~ Henny Youngman
7947. *Forget* "communicating"; don't *bother*
with "empathy"—just *kiss!*

7948. English: "Sweet dreams"
7949. French: "Fais de beaux rêves"
7950. Italian: "Sogni d'oro"
7951. German: "Träum süß"
7952. Spanish: "¡Que suenos con los
angelitos!"
7953. Portugese: "Durma bem"

7954–7965
12 Creativity Enhancers to Help You

These "creativity enhancers" will enliven your
relationship:

1. A playful attitude
2. Belief that you're creative
3. Ability to handle ambiguity

4. Risk-taking
5. Changing the rules
6. Humor
7. Willingness to consider "dumb" ideas
8. Juxtaposing: Putting things together in odd ways
9. Metaphorical thinking
10. Awareness of your talents and skills
11. In-depth knowledge about your partner
12. Draw, doodle, and make lists

7966. A "Romantic ABC's Coupon": You choose one letter of the alphabet. The Coupon-giver will create a day of romance with gifts and gestures that all begin with that letter
7967. For statisticians: Analyze the number of your sexual encounters as a function of the frequency of your romantic gestures: Is there a correlation?

7968. The gift: A giant jar of nuts
7969. The note: "I'm nuts for you"

7970. If money is no object—go all out!

7971. Rent a Lear Jet for a quick trip

7972. Buy a Jaguar for a joy ride

7973. Fly the Concorde together to Europe

7974. Take a round-the-world trip

7975. Tour the vineyards in Napa Valley, California

7976. Guys: Curb your sarcastic wit with your lover (save it for your buddies)

7977. Rent the movie classic *Tom Jones*. Fast forward to the food foreplay scene. Take notes

7978. Give one rose for every year you've been together

7979. Guys: Perform the classic "Sexy Cowboy Fantasy"

7980. Write him/her a check on something unusual or meaningful

7981. On a brick or lingerie or mattress

7982. "Christen" every room in your house by making love in it

7983. Don't forget to include the stairways and closets

7984. For the adventurous: Include the porches and backyard

7985–7991
7 Best Love Songs by Mariah Carey

1. "Can't Let Go"
2. "Dreamlover"
3. "Emotions"
4. "I'll Be There"
5. "Love Takes Time"
6. "Vision of Love"
7. "Without You/Never Forget You"

7992. "All, everything that I understand, I understand only because I love."
~ Leo Tolstoy

7993. Like education, love is a major doorway to understanding and wisdom

7994. Calculate how many years you spent in school, becoming "educated." Now plan to spend the same amount of time learning love

Favorite Love Songs from 1969

7995. "Baby I Love You," Andy Kim
7996. "Love (Can Make You Happy),"
Mercy
7997. "Love Theme from *Romeo & Juliet*,"
Henry Mancini
7998. "My Cherie Amour," Stevie Wonder
7999. "Put a Little Love in Your Heart,"
Jackie DeShannon
8000. "Sugar, Sugar," Archies
8001. "Too Busy Thinking 'Bout My
Baby," Marvin Gaye
8002. "Yester-Me, Yester-You, Yesterday,"
Stevie Wonder
8003. "You Make Me So Very Happy,"
Blood, Sweat & Tears

8004. Visit local coffeehouses
8005. Visit restaurants featuring live music
8006. Visit bars with live bands

8007. Go ice skating together
8008. For marrieds only: Treat him/her like
you did while dating
8009. "A simple enough pleasure, surely, to

have breakfast alone with one's husband, but how seldom married people in the midst of life achieve it."
~ Anne Morrow Lindbergh

8010–8016
7 "Couple Questions" to Discuss with Your Partner

People with A+ Relationships don't avoid the tough questions…

1. What do the two of you argue about most often?
2. What is your "style" of arguing? (Logical, emotional, heated, calm)
3. How do you balance *your* needs with your *partner's* needs?
4. How do you balance kids and spouse? Work and home?
5. Can a person be "too much" in love?
6. What made you fall in love?
7. What are the three *best* things about him/her?

8017. Wear "Escape" perfume—The perfect accompaniment to a vacation

8018. Give a gift based on a favorite TV show
8019. "It doesn't matter who you love or
      how you love, but that you love."
      ~ Rod McKuen
8020. When traveling, write a love letter—
      one paragraph per day—and give it
      to him/her when you return home

8021. Find your passion in life, and create
      your career around it
8022. Your satisfaction will make you a
      better partner/lover/friend

8023. Guys: *Triple* your time spent on
      foreplay—she'll adore you for it!
8024. Gals: Occasionally initiate a
      "quickie"—he'll adore you for it!

8025. Become a *magnet* for romantic ideas
8026. Look at the world through romance-
      colored glasses
8027. And ideas will *leap* out at you from
      newspapers, magazines, TV, etc.

8028. For waiters/waitresses in love: Don

your apron and serve your partner
dinner at home, and provide
extraordinary service

8029. Erotic Book Alert! *Forbidden Flowers*,
by Nancy Friday

8030. Make fresh-squeezed orange juice
tomorrow morning

8031. A note: "Thank you for being the
father of our children."

8032. Memorize your wedding vows

8033–8050
18 Things About You That
Your Partner Would *Love* to Know

You'll build intimacy by sharing more of
yourself with your partner

1. What was the single most significant
turning point in your life?

2. When/why/how do you lose your
temper?

3. How do you see your life in five
years? ten years? twenty years?

4. If you're so smart, why aren't you a
millionaire?

5. What feeling do you have the most

difficulty controlling?

6. What feeling do you have the most difficulty expressing?

7. What are your pet peeves?

8. How consistent are your actions with your beliefs?

9. How do you handle your own inconsistencies?

10. What two accomplishments are you most proud of?

11. Are you indecisive—or are you always *certain* that you're right?

12. How do you handle being lost when you're driving?

13. What movie or TV scene last brought tears to your eyes?

14. Is it possible for a man and a woman to have a truly platonic relationship?

15. What would you like most to change about yourself?

16. What *really* makes you laugh?

17. What makes you jealous?

18. Have you ever had a broken heart? (Who? When? Why?)

8051. "How bold one gets when one is sure of being loved." ~ Sigmund Freud

8052. Slow down and think about how empowered you feel when you feel the love from your partner

8053. Love *literally* gives us strength and confidence; it's *not* just a metaphor

8054. Assure your partner of your love; leave no doubt about it—and watch him/her *flourish*

8055. Gift & Date Idea: Get the song "How Deep Is Your Love," by the Bee Gees—

8056. And rent the movie *Saturday Night Fever*, featuring the song

8057. And then go out dancing on Saturday

8058. Turn your *house* (an architectural structure) into a *home* (a place where love lives)

8059. Eat in New Orleans' most romantic restaurant: The Grill Room

8060. Avoid pushing your partner's "Hot Buttons"

8061. English: "My love"
8062. French: "Mon amour"
8063. Italian: "Amore moi"
8064. German (spoken to a guy): "Mein lieber"
8065. German (spoken to a gal): "Meine liebe"
8066. Spanish: "Mi amor"
8067. Portugese: "Meu amor"

8068–8132
Her Name in a Song:
65 Hits Named for Gals

1. "Amanda," Boston
2. "Angelia," Richard Marx
3. "Angie," The Rolling Stones
4. "Annie's Song," John Denver
5. "Beth," Kiss
6. "Bernadette," The Four Tops
7. "Cecilia," Simon & Garfunkel
8. "Cindy, Oh Cindy," Eddie Fisher
9. "Clair," Gilbert O'Sullivan
10. "Come on Eileen," Dexy's Midnight Runners
11. "C'mon Marianne," The Four Tops

12. "Cracklin' Rosie," Neil Diamond
13. "Delta Dawn," Helen Reddy
14. "Diana," Paul Anka
15. "Donna," Ritchie Valens
16. "Georgia" (1922)
17. "Georgia on My Mind," Ray Charles
18. "Georgy Girl," The Seekers
19. "Hello Mary Lou," Ricky Nelson
20. "Hello, Dolly!" Louis Armstrong
21. "Help Me, Rhonda," The Beach Boys
22. "Hey Paula," Paul and Paula
23. "Holly Holy," Neil Diamond
24. "I Saw Linda Yesterday," Dickey Lee
25. "Jenny, Jenny," Little Richard
26. "867-5309 Jenny," Tommy Tutone
27. "Joanna," Kool & the Gang
28. "Julie, Do Ya Love Me," Bobby Sherman
29. "Laura" (1945)
30. "Lay Down Sally," Eric Clapton
31. "Little Jeannie," Elton John
32. "Long Tall Sally," Little Richard
33. "Louise," Human League
34. "Love Grows (Where My Rosemary Goes)," Edison Lighthouse

35. "Lucille," Kenny Rogers
36. "Maggie May," Rod Stewart
37. "Mandy," Barry Manilow
38. "Maria," from *West Side Story*
39. "Marianne," Terry Gilkyson & The Easy Riders
40. "Maybellene," Chuck Berry
41. "Michelle," The Beatles
42. "My Maria," B.W. Stevenson
43. "Oh Julie," The Crescendos
44. "Oh Sheila," Ready for the World
45. "Oh Sherrie," Steve Perry
46. "Oh! Carol," Neil Sedaka
47. "Patricia," Perez Prado
48. "Peggy Sue," Buddy Holly
49. "Proud Mary," Creedence Clearwater Revival
50. "Rosanna," Toto
51. "Ruby Tuesday," The Rolling Stones
52. "Sara," Fleetwood Mac
53. "Sara," Starship
54. "Sara Smile," Daryl Hall and John Oates
55. "Sheila," Tommy Roe
56. "Sherry," The Four Seasons

57. "Sunny," Bobby Hebb
58. "Susie Darlin'," Robin Luke
59. "Sweet Caroline," Neil Diamond
60. "Tammy," Debbie Reynolds
61. "Think of Laura," Christopher Cross
62. "Tracy," The Archies
63. "Trudie," Joe 'Mr. Piano' Henderson
64. "Wake Up Little Susie," Everly Brothers
65. "Walk Away Renee," The Four Tops

8133. Buy three new lingerie outfits
8134. Model them for him
8135. Select sexy music to perform to
8136. Arrange the lighting just right

8137–8146
10 Ways to Love a Pisces
(19 February–19 March)

1. Pisces is a *water* sign: Cater to his/her dreamy, romantic nature
2. Gift tip: Sensuous
3. Silk, velvet, soft
4. Scarves and lingerie
5. Feather beds and lots of pillows

6. Sometimes shy, so enjoy couple-only activities
7. Viburnum; willow trees
8. Anything sweet, chocolate
9. An island in the Mediterranean
10. Wrap gifts in sea green

Favorite Love Songs from 1970

8147. "ABC," Jackson Five
8148. "Close to You," Carpenters
8149. "Everything Is Beautiful," Ray Stevens
8150. "Green Eyed Lady," Sugarloaf
8151. "I Think I Love You," Partridge Family
8152. "I'll Be There," Jackson Five
8153. "Signed, Sealed, Delivered," Stevie Wonder

8154. Write a list: "25 Clues That Tell Me We're Soul Mates"
8155. Along with the book *SoulMates: Honoring the Mysteries of Love and Relationship,* by Thomas Moore
8156. Create a "soulmates" certificate for the two of you

8157. Create a "soulmates" license to carry in your wallet

8158–8167
10 Technological Tools
for Saying in Touch

1. Email
2. Mobile phones
3. Faxes
4. Pagers
5. Palm-held computers
6. Walkie-talkies
7. Airphones
8. Private Web sites
9. Laptop computers
10. Videophones

8168. Splurge on a $100 shopping spree at Victoria's Secret
8169. Surf www.homefilmfestival.com: For foreign and independent films
8170. Enemy of Love: Nagging
8171. Surprise her with stuffed animals from a favorite fairly tale

8172. Create a "Lingerie Fantasy" for him…
8173. You're a lingerie model
8174. He's a retail buyer
8175. Put on a private fashion show
8176. Use your imagination!

8177–8194
18 Ways to Put the *Sizzle* Back into Your Relationship

1. Take a sauna together
2. Make love three nights in a row—in three different places!
3. Vacation in the Australian outback
4. Barbecue a couple of juicy steaks on the grill
5. Plan a surprise vacation to the French Riviera
6. Go on a caravan in the Egyptian desert
7. Share some of your "naughty" thoughts with your partner
8. Frolic on a Hawaiian beach together
9. Cook a hot, spicy meal
10. Check-out the *Some Like It Hot* cookbook, by Robin Robertson

11. Make love in a semi-public place
12. Guys: Spend a *solid hour* performing foreplay
13. Visit Casablanca, Morocco
14. Visit a nude beach
15. Take a cruise in the Southern Pacific
16. Go on an African safari
17. Dance the Tango together
18. Make love to the tune of "Principles of Lust," by Enigma

8195. Ask him to pick a number between one and fifty; reward him with that number of kisses
8196. "The opposite of love is indifference." ~ Rollo May
8197. Go to an *inexpensive* vacation spot— and get the *most expensive* accommodations
8198. Write one hundred love poems in haiku style
8199. For your spontaneous spouse: Go on an "open-ended" weekend: Hop in the car with no plans and no destination in mind

8200. Visit the Egyptian pyramids
8201. Gals: Never, never, *never* withhold sex to punish him

8202. The gift: A cactus
8203. The note: "I'm stuck on you."
8204. (Alternate gift): The song "Stuck on You," by Lionel Richie

---

8205. Name your child after her
8206. Celebrate the Winter Solstice (the longest night of the year) by spending it in *bed* together!
8207. Visit Aspen off-season, and stay at The Little Nell
8208. Love Coupon: This coupon entitles you to an *entire* week of romance! What's your pleasure?? The issuer of this coupon will grant your every wish! (Aladdin never had it so good!)

Favorite Love Songs from 1971
8209. "All I Ever Need Is You," Sonny & Cher
8210. "If You Could Read My Mind," Gordon Lightfoot

8211. "Never Can Say Goodbye,"
Jackson Five
8212. "Temptation Eyes," Grass Roots
8213. "That's the Way I've Always Heard It
Should Be," Carly Simon
8214. "Treat Her Like a Lady," Cornelius
Brothers & Sister Rose

8215. "Happiness is a present attitude—not
a future condition." ~ Hugh Prather
8216. Now! Right now! Don't wait! Not
tomorrow, not in an hour—now!
This very minute!
8217. Pick up the phone and call!
8218. Pick up a pen and write a love letter
8219. Take him/her in your arms and whirl
around in circles
8220. Take him/her by the hand and take a
carefree walk in the park

8221–8225
5 Songs to Help You Express Your
Feelings: *Friendship & Appreciation*

1. "Bridge over Troubled Water," Simon
and Garfunkel

2. "Stand by Me," Ben E. King
3. "Thank You for Being a Friend,"
   Andrew Gold
4. "That's What Friends Are For,"
   Dionne & Friends
5. "You've Got a Friend," James Taylor

8226. Take a walk together on the first day
of spring—and talk about your hopes
and dreams for the future

8227. Take a walk together on the first day
of summer—and talk specifically
about your relationship

8228. Take a walk together on the first day
of autumn—and talk about your best
memories

8229. Take a walk together on the first day
of winter—and talk about everything
you have to be thankful for

8230. Explore aphrodisiacs together: Read
Aphrodite: A Memoir of the Senses, by
Isabel Allende, which combines
recipes with eroticism

8231. Dedicate your book to your partner

8232. If she always misplaces her keys, get her *twelve* extra sets

8233. Buy ten extra pillows to make your bed more luxurious

8234. A+ B&B Rating: The Don Gaspar Compound, in New Mexico: (505) 986-8664

8235–8262
28 Greatest Love Songs from Broadway Musicals

1. "Almost Like Being in Love," from *Brigadoon*

2. "Can't Help Loving Dat Man," from *Showboat*

3. "Do I Love You Because You're Beautiful," from *Cinderella*

4. "Embraceable You," from *Crazy for You*

5. "I Could Be Happy with You," from *The Boyfriend*

6. "I Could Have Danced All Night," from *My Fair Lady*

7. "I Have Dreamed," from *The King and I*

8. "I Wanna Be Loved By You," from
   Good Boy
9. "I'm in Love with a Wonderful Guy,"
   from *South Pacific*
10. "I've Never Been in Love Before,"
    from *Guys & Dolls*
11. "If I Loved You," from *Carousel*
12. "Just in Time," from *Bells Are Ringing*
13. "Love Song," from *Pippin*
14. "Me & My Girl," from *Me & My Girl*
15. "My Heart Is So Full of You," from
    The Most Happy Fella
16. "On the Street Where You Live,"
    from *My Fair Lady*
17. "People," from *Funny Girl*
18. "People Will Say We're in Love,"
    from *Oklahoma*
19. "She Loves Me," from *She Loves Me*
20. "So in Love," from *Kiss Me Kate*
21. "They Say It's Wonderful," from
    Annie Get Your Gun
22. "This Can't Be Love," from *The Boys
    from Syracuse*
23. "Til There Was You," the *The
    Music Man*

24. "Too Much in Love to Care," from
    Sunset Boulevard
25. "Try to Remember," from
    The Fantastics
26. "What I Did for Love," from
    A Chorus Line
27. "Wonderful Guy," from *South Pacific*
28. "You're the Top," from *Anything Goes*

8263. For a Beatles fan: Get collector's
      original singles of all their No. 1 hits
8264. Share a park bench on a sunny
      afternoon
8265. "Love eagerly believes everything it
      wants to." ~ Jean Racine
8266. Never buy cars with bucket seats
8267. The Ultimate Gift for Audiophiles: A
      stereo system from Bang & Olufsen:
      (800) 323-0499

Favorite Love Songs from 1972

8268. "Happiest Girl in the Whole USA,"
      Donna Fargo
8269. "Lean on Me," Bill Withers
8270. "Let's Stay Together," Al Green

8271. "Nice to Be with You," Gallery
8272. "Precious & Few," Climax
8273. "Without You," Harry Nilsson

8274. Gift: A set of white satin sheets
8275. Presentation: Along with the song "Nights in White Satin," by The Moody Blues
8276. Activity: Make sweet love

8277–8282
6 Items for a *Monthly* Romantic Checklist

1. Plan one romantic *surprise*
2. Re-stock your stash of greeting cards
3. Go out to dinner once or twice
4. Rent at least *two* romantic movies
5. Make plans for a romantic weekend sometime soon
6. Plan one romantic event with a *seasonal* theme

8283. Read *The Lovers' Bedside Companion*, by Gregory J.P. Godek
8284. Snuggle in flannel sheets during the winter months

8285. Use the song "I Can't Give You Anything but Love" as the theme for a low-budget date

8286. Wake him gently at 3 A.M. by fondling him

8287. Wear "Dreamer" cologne—Give him something to dream about

8288. Take a stroll in the swirling snow

8289–8295

If You Read Only Seven Books to Improve Your Relationship, Read These Seven

1. *The Soul's Code: In Search of Character and Calling,* by James Hillman

2. *The Art of Loving,* by Erich Fromm

3. *Emotional Intelligence: Why It Can Matter More Than IQ,* by Daniel Goleman

4. *The Prophet,* by Kahlil Gibran

5. *You Just Don't Understand—Women and Men in Conversation,* by Deborah Tannen

6. *Iron John,* by Robert Bly

7. *Love—The Course They Forgot To Teach You In School,* by Gregory J.P. Godek

8296. Gals: Do something *for* him that you hate to do

8297. It only counts as a loving gesture if you do it cheerfully and without complaint

8298. Iron his shirts, wash his car, cut the lawn

8299. English: "My honey"

8300. French: "Mon chou"

8301. Italian: "Mia dolcezza"

8302. German: "Mein schatz"

8303. Spanish: "Mi cariatz"

8304. Portugese: "Meu bem"

8305. "A great flame follows a little spark." ~ Dante Alighieri

8306. Little Spark #1: Write a little note: "My fondest memory of you is…"

8307. Little Spark #2: Make gentle, gentle love together

8308. Little Spark #3: Turn off the TV tonight and *just be together*

8309. Most loving gestures are little, inexpensive, and easy

8310. Love, once ignited, rarely goes out altogether; it usually smolders quietly, waiting for something to fan the flames

---

8311–8330
20 Creative Ways to "Pop the Question"

1. Send her a telegram that says: "W.Y.M.M.?"
2. Apply for the job of "Husband"
3. Write an "Engagement Resume"— listing your qualifications!
4. Hide a diamond ring in a rose bud— and wait for it to bloom!
5. Return to the place where you first met
6. Pop the question in the middle of a lovemaking session
7. Gals: Don't wait for *him*—*you* do the asking!
8. Get her the most perfect diamond your budget will allow
9. Be *different:* Get a ruby, emerald, or sapphire engagement ring

10. Be Old Fashioned: Ask her father for his permission to marry her
11. Hide the ring in a box of Cracker Jacks
12. Choose the exact time based on specific astrological forecasts
13. Ask her to marry you on a local radio show
14. Place the ring in the bottom of a glass of champagne
15. The outrageous skywriting proposal
16. The insistent sky banner proposal
17. The custom jigsaw puzzle proposal
18. The really big billboard proposal
19. The lucky Chinese fortune cookie proposal
20. The classic get-on-one-knee-and-ask-her proposal

8331. Gift & Date Idea: Get the song "Love Me Tender," by Elvis Presley—
8332. And rent the movie *Love Me Tender*, featuring the song
8333. (Then spend a night of tender lovemaking)

Favorite Love Songs from 1973

8334. "Behind Closed Doors," Charlie Rich
8335. "Dancing in the Moonlight," King Harvest
8336. "I'm Gonna Love You Just a Little More," Barry White
8337. "Pillow Talk," Sylvia

8338. For romantic campers: *The Complete Guide to America's National Parks*, from the National Park Foundation
8339. Color Easter eggs together
8340. Discuss your family finances together
8341. "Great is the man who has not lost his child-like heart." ~ Mencius
8342. Get him a book on his favorite hobby

8343. For Christmas, give ten music CDs
8344. Then hang them on the tree like ornaments

8345. Learn the elegant art of Bonsai
8346. Grow and design two Bonsai trees together

8347. Watch the final scenes of the movies
Michael and *All of Me*

8348. Allow yourselves to be inspired, and
create a joyful dance of your own!

8349. For guys: A gift certificate from
Radio Shack

8350. Or Sears

8351. Or The Sharper Image

8352. Or the local stereo shop

8353. Or the local auto parts store

8354. Or his favorite hardware store

8355–8375
21 *More* Relationship Do's and Don'ts

1. Don't go out on New Year's Eve—

2. Do stay home and cozy-up to your
lover near the fireplace

3. Don't buy roses for Valentine's Day—

4. Do buy flowers that begin with the
first letter of her name

5. Don't go to the beach on crowded
weekends—

6. Do go mid-week

7. Don't go to popular vacation spots during their busy seasons—

8. Do go right before or after the busy season

9. Do make some sacrifices for each other—

10. But don't turn yourself into a martyr

11. Don't read the newspaper at the breakfast table—

12. Do talk with one another over breakfast

13. Don't give him a birthday present—

14. Do give him seven gifts, one for each day of his birthday week

15. Don't be afraid to share your feelings

16. Don't leave lovemaking until just before sleeping

17. Do schedule more time for foreplay

18. Don't make love the same way every time

19. Do eliminate distractions for two to three hours

20. Don't try to change your partner

21. Don't act your age

8376. Once every five years, do something incredible, outrageous, and truly memorable

8377. Daily affirmation: "I will make the most of my abilities"

8378. Visit a spiritually meaningful place, like Sedona

8379. As part of foreplay, read aloud a passage from *Little Birds*, by Anaïs Nin

---

8380–8385
6 Songs to Help You Express Your Feelings: *Love & Joy*

1. "How Sweet It Is (To Be Loved By You)," James Taylor
2. "It Had to Be You," Harry Connick, Jr.
3. "Let's Hang On," The Four Seasons
4. "Love Me Do," The Beatles
5. "The Way You Do the Things You Do," Temptations
6. "What a Wonderful World," Louis Armstrong

8386. Collect prints of paintings by the

great artists of the Romantic Period

8387. William Blake, Jean Baptiste Camille, John Robert Cozens

8388. Jacques Louis David, Eugene Delacroix, Francisco Goya

8389. Samuel Palmer, Johan Anton Alban Ramboux

Favorite Love Songs from 1974

8390. "A Very Special Love Song," Charlie Rich

8391. "The Best Thing That Ever Happened," Gladys Knight & Pips

8392. "Feel Like Makin' Love," Roberta Flack

8393. "Hooked on a Feeling," Blue Swede

8394. "I Will Always Love You," Dolly Parton

8395. "If You Love Me," Olivia Newton-John

8396. "Let Me Be There," Olivia Newton-John

8397. "Love's Theme," Love Unlimited Orchestra

8398. "Then Came You," Dionne Warwick

8399. "You Make Me Feel Brand New,"
Stylistics

8400. Create your own Winter Celebration
8401. Soundtrack: Windham Hill's *Winter Solstice I*
8402. Activity: Take a sleigh ride in the snow
8403. Quote: "One kind word can warm three winter months." ~ Japanese saying

---

8404. Find a local "romantic hideaway"—like a quiet aisle at the public library
8405. Nibble on her ear
8406. Take out a full-page ad in your local newspaper, declaring your love for your mate

---

8407–8429
23 Romantic Resources on the Internet

1. The "CandyBouquet":
www.franchise1.com/comp/cndybok1.html
2. To locate classical music events:

rec.music.classical.performing

3. For tickets to rock concerts:
   www.mindspring.com/~acetix/concerts
   .html
4. To locate film festivals worldwide:
   filmfestivals.com/
5. Beatle-related items, trivia and travel
   info:
   www.eecis.udel.edu/~markowsk/Beatles/
6. For opera lovers: rec.music.opera
7. The ultimate Shakespeare site: the-
   tech.mit.edu/Shakespeare/works.html
8. A bed & breakfast resource:
   www.infinityquest.com/absolute.html
9. Another B&B resource:
   www.virtualcities.com/ons/
   0onsadex.htm
10. To get info on festivals, carnivals,
    etc.: www.eventseeker.com/
11. A tea-lover's resource:
    www.teatraders.com
12. A movie-lover's resource:
    www.hollywood.com
13. A wine-lover's resource:
    www.princetonol.com/biz/wine

14. A book-lover's resource: amazon.com
15. A Napa Valley Virtual Visit:
    www.freerun.com/cgi-bin/home.o
16. London Theatre Guide:
    www.londontheatre.co.uk/online/
17. For animal lovers, info on every zoo
    in the world:
    www.mindspring.com/~zoonet/
18. A great music resource: N2K.com
19. For Broadway and Off-Broadway
    info: piano.symgrp.com/playbill/
20. For acoustic and New Age music:
    www.windham.com
21. A resource for sports collectables:
    www.sportscardsplus.com
22. The Erotic Print Society:
    www.eps.org.uk
23. For reviews and previews of current
    films: www.movielink.com

8430. Delight your mate with origami
    creations (Learn on the Internet, via
    ccwf.cc.utexas.edu/~vbeatty/origami)
8431. "I wonder, by my troth, what you and
    I did, till we lov'd." ~ John Donne

8432. For engaged folks only: Write a letter to your future in-laws, promising to love and care for their son/daughter

---

8433–8438
6 Songs to Help You Express Your Feelings: *Gentle & Sweet*

1. "All Right," Christopher Cross
2. "Hearing Your Voice," Moody Blues
3. "My Love," Paul McCartney & Wings
4. "Strange Magic," Electric Light Orchestra
5. "Summer Soft," Stevie Wonder
6. "(They Long to Be) Close to You," The Carpenters

8439. Gift & Date Idea: Get the song "Can You Feel the Love Tonight," by Elton John—

8440. And rent the movie *The Lion King*, featuring the song

8441. For his "second childhood," get him a Corvette!

8442. And the song "Little Red Corvette," by Prince

8443. Read *The Art of Kissing*, by William Cane
8444. Slow down your kissing
8445. Kiss with concentration
8446. Spend 10% as much time kissing as you spend watching TV every day

---

8447. For being romantic in NYC, read *The Best Places to Kiss in New York City: A Romantic Travel Guide*, by Paula Begoun
8448. There are also editions for *Los Angeles, San Francisco, Southern California,* the *Northwest,* and the *Northeast*!

8449–8478
30 Years of Celebrity Birth-Years
Celebrate the celebrities that match your partner's age...

1941　Ann-Margret, Joan Baez, Beau Bridges, Chubby Checker, David Crosby, Faye Dunaway, Bob Dylan

1942 Barbra Streisand, Paul McCartney, Paul
Simon, Aretha Franklin, Harrison Ford,
Linda Evans

1943 Julio Iglesias, Mick Jagger, George
Harrison, Chevy Chase, Robert DeNiro,
Penny Marshall, Joni Mitchell

1944 Danny DeVito, Timothy Dalton, Roger
Daltry, Gladys Knight, Patti LaBelle

1945 Mia Farrow, Goldie Hawn, Tom Selleck,
Rod Stewart, Priscilla Presley, Rob Reiner

1946 Candice Bergen, Sally Field, Diane
Keaton, David Lynch, Liza Minelli, Ozzy
Osbourne, Dolly Parton, Linda
Ronstadt, Susan Sarandon, Sylvester
Stallone, Robert Urich

1947 Arnold Schwarzenegger, Elton John,
David Bowie, Glenn Close, Billy Crystal,
Ted Danson, Farrah Fawcett, Kevin
Kline, David Letterman, Olivia Newton-
John, Steven Spielberg

1948 Mikhail Baryshnikov, James Taylor,
Barbara Hershey, Jeremy Irons, Kate
Jackson, Perry King, Stevie Nicks,
Donna Summer, Steve Winwood

1949 Whoopi Goldberg, Billy Joel, Bruce

Springsteen, Meryl Streep, Sigourney Weaver, Jeff Bridges, Richard Gere, Don Johnson, Jessica Lange

1950 Stevie Wonder, Cybill Shepherd, Tony Danza, John Candy, Peter Gabriel, William Hurt, Bill Murray, Randy Quaid

1951 Phil Collins, Sting, Timothy Bottoms, John Mellencamp, Elvira, Mark Hamill, Harry Hamlin, Mark Harmon, Michael Keaton, Joe Piscopo, Kurt Russell, Jane Seymour

1952 Robin Williams, Mr. T, Dan Aykroyd, Roseanne, David Byrne, Nora Dunn, Pee-Wee Herman, Grace Jones, Isabella Rossellini

1953 Kim Basinger, Jeff Goldblum, John Goodman, Cyndi Lauper, John Malkovich, Tom Petty

1954 Patrick Swayze, John Travolta, Ellen Barkin, Corbin Bernsen, Ron Howard, David Keith, Dennis Quaid

1955 Kevin Costner, Kirstie Alley, Jeff Daniels, Billy Idol, David Lee Roth, Bruce Willis, Debra Winger

1956 Mel Gibson, Tom Hanks, Larry Bird, Delta Burke, Carrie Fisher, Eric Roberts, Mickey Rourke, Joe Montana, Dale Murphy, Martina Navratilova

1957 Michelle Pfeiffer, Theresa Russell, Vanna White, Geena Davis, Spike Lee, Donny Osmond, Melanie Griffith

1958 Madonna, Prince, Michael Jackson, Arsenio Hall, Steve Guttenberg, Wade Boggs, Jamie Lee Curtis

1959 Judd Nelson, Rosanna Arquette, Sheena Easton, Holly Hunter, Victoria Jackson, Marie Osmond, Martha Quinn, Randy Travis

1960 Valerie Bertinelli, Eric Dickerson, Joan Jett, Nastassja Kinski, Apollonia Kotero, Sean Penn, Tracey Ullman

1961 Eddie Murphy, Jon Bon Jovi, Boy George, Rae Dawn Chong, Amy Grant, Wayne Gretzky, Daryl Hannah, Timothy Hutton, Don Mattingly

1962 Tom Cruise, Matthew Broderick, Emilio Estevez, Jodie Foster, Demi Moore, Meg Ryan, Ally Sheedy

1963 Whitney Houston, Michael Jordan,

Julian Lennon, Andrew McCarthy,
George Michael

1964 Tracy Chapman, Jose Canseco, Phoebe
Cates, Melissa Gilbert, Robin Givens,
Rob Lowe, Matt Dillon

1965 Brooke Shields, Nicolas Cage, Ronnie
Gant, Mario Lemieux, Paulina
Porizkova, Katarina Witt

1966 Justine Bateman, Tom Glavine, Janet
Jackson, Dave Justice, Charlie Sheen

1967 Julia Roberts, Boris Becker, Lisa Bonet,
John Cusak, Deion Sanders

1968 Mary Lou Retton, Molly Ringwald,
Jonathan Knight

1969 Andrea Elson, Steffi Graf, Donnie
Wahlberg, Danny Wood

1970 Kirk Cameron, Debbie Gibson, Jordan
Knight, Emily Lloyd, Malcolm-Jamal
Warner

8479. Recognize the Yin and Yang aspects
of your relationship...

8480. Yin: Celebrate your differences—

8481. Yang: Take comfort in your
similarities ☯

8482. Yin: Actions speak louder than words (Talk is cheap!)—

8483. Yang: Communication is the cornerstone of a good relationship ☉

8484. Yin: Live in the present—

8485. Yang: Keep your memories alive ☉

8486. Yin: Read books (They contain great wisdom and inspiration)—

8487. Yang: Throw the books away! (Listen to your Inner Voice) ☉

8488. Yin: Say what you feel when you feel it—

8489. Yang: Choose your words carefully ☉

8490. Yin: Treat her like your best friend (You'll build intimacy)—

8491. Yang: Treat her like your girlfriend (You'll build passion) ☉

8492. Yin: Lighten up! (Have more fun)—

8493. Yang: Get serious! (Relationships are hard work) ☉

8494. Yin: Travel inspires romance (Exotic locales, adventure!)—

8495. Yang: Home is where the heart is (Cozy, comfortable) ☉

8496. Yin: Shake-up your life! (Do

something different and exciting!)—

8497. Yang: Slow down your life (Meditate, find your center) ☯

8498. Rent a horse and suit of armor—and surprise the *heck* out of her!

8499. Watch classic cartoons together on Saturday morning

8500. Make a ritual of taking a stroll after dinner every evening

8501. Paint her toenails (bright red)

8502. "What greater thing is there for two human souls than to find that they are joined for life." ~ George Eliot

8503. Make love on a bearskin rug in front of a fire

8504. Collect jokes all month, and share them on the last day of each month

8505. For your frequent flyer: Get an inflatable neck pillow

8506. *Never* take off your wedding ring

8507. Hide her favorite stuffed animal in unexpected places around the house

8508. Take a mud bath together at a spa

8509. Get matching cashmere sweaters

8510. A+ Relationships are built equally of passion, commitment and intimacy
8511. Passion alone is just a fling
8512. Commitment alone is a hopeless, aching relationship
8513. Intimacy alone is too fragile to last
8514. Passion and commitment without intimacy is a shallow relationship
8515. Commitment and intimacy without passion is flat and unexciting
8516. Passion and intimacy without commitment is short-lived

8517. Engrave a Cross pen with both of your names
8518. Install a mirror on your bedroom ceiling
8519. Make Tuesday "Game Night": Play board games instead of watching TV
8520. Send "audio taped letters" instead of written letters
8521. Lover's Ritual: Hold hands and say a prayer of thanks at every meal
8522. Call (800) COOKIES for Mrs. Fields!
8523. Volunteer together

8524. Go for a midnight swim in the ocean
8525. Take a stroll on a foggy evening
8526. Make *s'mores* over a campfire in your backyard
8527. "Stroll" and "saunter"—it's more romantic than simply "walking"
8528. Host a formal "prom" for your friends
8529. Double-date with your *grandparents*
8530. Enjoy a "progressive dinner" by stopping at a series of street vendors

---

8531. Take her on a "Neiman-Marcus Shopping Spree"
8532. Take him on a "Radio Shack Shopping Spree"
8533. Take each other on a "Victoria's Secret Shopping Spree"

8534. Whisper "sweet nothings" in her ear
8535. Throw a birthday party for his/her favorite movie star
8536. Spend an afternoon on horseback
8537. Stuff his mailbox *full* of lovenotes
8538. Count your blessings; assign dollar values to them; add them up!

8539. Sleep in the buff
8540. Build sandcastles on the beach together
8541. Name a new mixed drink after her; serve it at your next party
8542. Play "Name That Tune" while taking a long road trip together
8543. Hide a love note in a sea shell and place it on the beach where she will find it
8544. "Women fall in love through their ears, men fall in love through their eyes." ~ Woodrow Wyatt
8545. Spray paint "Welcome Home" on an old sheet; hang it on a tree

---

8546. Imagine it's twenty-five years in the future: List your five favorite memories with your lover
8547. List the great places you've visited together
8548. List the great gifts you've given and received
8549. List your favorite holiday memories you've shared

8550. List the high points of your family life
8551. Now—start working to make this future come true

8552. Create two cartoon characters based on the two of you
8553. Have a local artist draw them for you
8554. Create a series of comic adventures that parallels your life
8555. Occasionally paste them onto the newspaper comic page
8556. After twenty-five years, collect them into a book

8557. Chase rainbows—
8558. Literally: Following a storm
8559. Figuratively: Follow your dreams together

8560. A themed "Dinner-and-a-Movie: Rent *Like Water for Chocolate*
8561. Serve tacos and burritos
8562. Drink margaritas
8563. Then take a siesta together

8564. Hold a "ribbon-cutting" to celebrate your new home
8565. Attend a stress management seminar together
8566. Accompany your partner to the airline gate—don't just drop him/her off at the curb
8567. Get some motivational tapes from Nightengale-Conant: (800) 323-3938
8568. Find a special shady spot under a tree
8569. Pull taffy together
8570. Wade in a public fountain together
8571. Go horseback riding at dusk on a deserted beach
8572. Host a surprise birthday party for his/her dog/cat
8573. Take simultaneous sabbaticals from your jobs
8574. Watch holiday cartoon specials together
8575. Get him/her snacks during the commercials
8576. Go on a charity walk-a-thon together
8577. Make-out "under the boardwalk" at a beach

8578. A lifetime goal: Dine at every five-star restaurant in the world!

8579. Don't just "meet"—have a "*rendezvous*"

8580. Wear the sexiest swimsuit that you dare

8581. On a hot summer afternoon have a water balloon fight

8582. Help her with her Christmas shopping

8583. Speak in a fake French accent throughout an entire date

8584. Create a snow sculpture together

8585. Offer your shoulder to cry on

8586. Offer your lap to sit on

8587. Give a hand

8588. Lend an ear

8589. Open your heart

8590. Whisper this: "You mean the world to me."

8591. Focus on being your lover's best friend

8592. Play footsie with your sweetheart

8593. Hang out at the local donut shop

8594. Vow to be more romantic in the 21st Century than you were in the 20th Century

8595. While watching *Titanic*, whisper to her: "I'd go down with the *Titanic* to save you"

8596. Watch Jay Leno's monologue together

8597. Get him a knick-knack, a tchochke, a bric-a-brac, and a doo-dad

---

8598. There's no cure for an incurable romantic

8599. But there is hope for the romantically impaired

8600. Give one Christmas gift that's "naughty"

8601. And one that's "nice"

8602. Attend the taping of a favorite TV show together

8603. Do some star gazing at Mann's Chinese Theater in Los Angeles

8604. Crash a wedding reception at a local hotel

8605. Write a letter to your unborn child together

8606. Go on a "backwards date": Kiss goodnight, then eat dessert, then eat dinner, etc.

8607. Stroll through a farmers market together

8608. Accompany your partner to his/her doctor appointments

8609. Find a cool jazz bar

8610. Make a custom, gourmet, homemade pizza together

8611. Rent a houseboat for a mini-vacation

8612. Serve a couple of pina coladas

8613. Take your sailor to view the America's Cup race

8614. Collect fresh rain water and wash her hair with it

8615. Attend a blue grass music festival

8616. Visit a garden maze in England

8617. "One word frees us of all the weight and pain of life: that word is love."
~ Sophocles

8618. Give her a diamond for *every* birthday

8619. Even if they're sometimes very, very small
8620. Or really, really imperfect

8621. For your book lover: A personalized embosser
8622. Shampoo her dog for her
8623. Wear matching running shoes
8624. Nibble on his ear
8625. Do her taxes for her
8626. Get your sweetheart a membership in a fan club
8627. Go on "Spring Break"—even if you're not in school!
8628. Spend all day watching the ocean waves
8629. Hang out at a piano bar together
8630. Squeeze fresh orange juice for your lover

8631. Look through your high school and college yearbooks together
8632. And share stories of your best times
8633. And personal stories of heartbreak, too

8634. Get a proof set of coins from the year you married

8635. Brew your own beer together

8636. Get a special "Hearts on Fire" cut diamond

8637. Put together a giant jigsaw puzzle— even if it takes a year!

8638. Over a weekend: Write, star-in, and videotape your own 10-minute movie

8639. Teach your partner about the one topic you're an expert in

8640. Get each other 3 Swatch Watches that match your personalities

8641. Take your race fan to the Indianapolis 500

8642. Visit the French Quarter of New Orleans

8643. Whisper this: "I'm lucky I found you."

8644. Watch again the very first movie you saw together

8645. Memorize the balcony scene from *Romeo and Juliet*

8646. And act it out together

8647. Date concept: Watch movies back-to-back:

8648. A good combination: *You've Got Mail* and *The Shop Around the Corner*

8649. Go to a fortune teller together

8650. Newlywed gift: A return address stamper with both of your names on it

8651. Knit, crochet or needlepoint a gift for your partner

8652. Organize his closet for him

8653. Flip a coin: Heads you have sex—tails you go out to dinner

8654. Heads you watch TV—tails you watch the sunset

8655. Heads, *he* cooks dinner—tails, *she* cooks dinner

8656. Heads you go to a movie theater—tails you rent a movie

8657. Heads, *he* chooses the rental movie—tails, *she* chooses

8658. Heads it's take-out *pizza*—tails it's take-out *Chinese*

8659. Heads, *he* gives a backrub—tails, *she*

gives a backrub

8660. Heads it's an exciting night out—tails it's a quiet night in

8661. Heads it's red wine—tails it's white wine

8662. Heads it's Mozart—tails it's The Beatles

8663. Heads, *she* gets a "day off"—tails, *he* gets a "day off"

8664. Touch in many different ways—

8665. Softly, innocently, teasingly, sexually, quietly, daily, insistently, persuasively, sensually, lightly, secretly

---

Favorite Love Songs from 1975

8666. "Best of My Love," Eagles

8667. "Falling in Love," Hamilton, Joe Frank & Reynolds

8668. "Love Will Keep Us Together," Captain & Tennille

8669. "Some Kind of Wonderful," Grand Funk

8670. "You're the First, the Last, My Everything," Barry White

8671. Prepare a plate of luscious fruits and chocolates, and feed them to each other

8672. Give a *lifetime* subscription to his/her favorite magazine

8673. Create *incredible* giftwrappings: Get the book *Creative Gift Packaging,* by Yoko Kondo

8674. Honor his/her individuality

8675. Go beachcombing together

8676. Get a cardboard crown at Burger King: Crown him King-for-a-Day

---

8677. Collect CDs of romantic acoustic music...

8678. *She Describes Infinity,* by Scott Cossu

8679. *Openings,* by William Ellwood

8680. *Down to the Moon,* by Andreas Vollenweider

8681. *A Winter's Solstice,* by various Windham Hill artists

8682. *Childhood and Memory,* by William Ackerman

8683. *Barefoot Ballet,* by John Klemmer

8684–8695
12 Creativity Blockers to Beware Of

Creativity is a spark that keeps relationships exciting. Beware of these "creativity blockers":

1. Following the rules
2. Looking for one right answer
3. Logical thinking
4. Fear of failure
5. Giving in to peer pressure
6. A narrow point-of-view
7. Giving-up too soon
8. Fear of embarrassment
9. Belief that you're not creative
10. Lack of self-confidence
11. Being overly practical
12. Concern over cost

8696. Write a list: "50 Reasons I Married You"

8697. Express each of those reasons with a small gift

8698. Renew your wedding vows, and include these reasons

8699. Keep this list handy when you've had an argument

8700–8709
10 Qualities That 5,000 Women
Dislike Most in Husbands

1. Messy
2. Insensitive sexually
3. Dogmatic
4. Overworked
5. Sulking/The "quiet treatment"
6. Macho attitudes
7. Stubborn
8. Self-centered
9. Uncooperative
10. Dresses poorly

8710. "As long as one can admire and love,
then one is young forever."
~ Pablo Casals

8711. Forget exercise, vitamins and
meditating: The *real* secret to staying
young is *love*

8712. What do you *admire* about your
partner? *Tell* him/her

8713. Create one *daily* ritual—to honor
your spirituality

8714. Create one *weekly* ritual—to keep the two of you connected

8715. Create one *monthly* ritual—centered around turning the calendar page

8716. Create one *yearly* ritual—to mark the passage of time

8717–8728
12 Toll-Free Numbers for Romantic Gifts/Ideas/Inspirations

1. (800) 367-7765: Critics Choice video catalog

2. (800) 466-8437: Movies Unlimited: Huge video catalog

3. (800) 645-4727: PBS Home Video: Free catalog!

4. (800) 742-2403: Suzanne's Mail Order Muffins

5. (800) 634-9088: The Lladro collection of figurines

6. (800) USA-24HR: Black Tie Roses

7. (800) 528-STAR: Name a star after your partner, via the Federal Star Registration

8. (800) SEND-FTD: Flowers

9. (800) 84-LEX-KY: Visit beautiful Lexington, Kentucky
10. (800) FLA-KEYS: Vacation in the Florida Keys
11. (800) 34-SPRINGS: Enjoy Palm Springs
12. (800) 8888-TEX: Visit Texas

8729. For one week, give up 10%of your TV time, and give it to your partner
8730. Gals: Be outrageous: "Flash" him when you're out in public together

---

8731–8737
7 Best Love Songs by Rod Stewart

1. "All for Love" (with Bryan Adams & Sting)
2. "Have I Told You Lately"
3. "Infatuation"
4. "Love Touch"
5. "Stay with Me"
6. "Tonight's the Night (Gonna Be Alright)"
7. "You're in My Heart (The Final Acclaim)"

8738. Don't forget the basics, when it comes to sex!
8739. Read several books by Dr. Ruth
8740. (And share them with your lover)
8741. *The Art of Arousal*
8742. *Dr. Ruth's Guide to Good Sex*
8743. *Dr. Ruth's Guide for Married Lovers*
8744. *Dr. Ruth's Encyclopedia of Sex*

Favorite Love Songs from 1976

8745. "Afternoon Delight," Starland Vocal Band
8746. "Let Your Love Flow," Bellamy Brothers
8747. "Love Hangover," Diana Ross

Favorite Love Songs from 1977

8748. "Best of My Love," The Emotions
8749. "Handy Man," James Taylor
8750. "Feels Like the First Time," Foreigner
8751. "So in to You," Atlanta Rhythm Section
8752. "You're My World," Helen Reddy

8753. Build your partner's self-esteem—it will benefit *both of you*

8754. Get him a T-shirt with a Superman logo on it

8755. Create a *totally nonsensical* reason to go out and celebrate

8756. "Pains of love be sweeter far, than all other pleasures are." ~ John Dryden

---

8757. English: "I'll miss you"

8758. French: "Tu vas me manquer"

8759. Italian: "Mi mancherai"

8760. German: "Ich werde dich"

8761. Spanish: "Te echaré de menos"

8762. Portugese: "Eu vou sentir saudade sua"

8763. "I have found that if you love life, life will love you back." ~ Arthur Rubinstein

8764. The people with the best *attitudes* have the best *lives*

8765. Embrace life, embrace your mate

8766–8777
12 Months' Notes from a Romantic's Planning Calendar

January   Make one *romantic* resolution

February	Plan your *summer* vacation
March	Begin your Christmas shopping
April	Plan a "Springtime Get Away"
May	Begin looking for *next* year's Valentine gift
June	Meet with your travel agent: Research exotic locations for a *major* vacation
July	Plan to make your *own* "fireworks"
August	Celebrate "Romance Awareness Month"
September	Start making plans for this coming New Year's Eve
October	Plan a ski weekend for the upcoming winter
November	Make reservations at a bed & breakfast for Valentine's Day
December	Get schedules for local theaters and symphonies

8778. The gift, part 1: A classy beer mug engraved with his initials

8779. The gift, part 2: A six-pack of his favorite brew

8780. The gift, part 3: A custom Romance
Coupon for a six-pack-a-month

8781. Consciously "change gears" at the end
of the day: From work-mode to
home-mode
8782. Having rituals can help you get back
in touch with your self—*and* your
partner
8783. Meditate for half an hour
8784. Exercise till ya sweat
8785. Play with the kids (A great way to
re-connect with your *own* fun-loving
nature)

8786–8801
16 Naughty Books for
Adventurous Couples

1. *Erotic Tales of the Victorian Era*, from
   Prometheus Books
2. *Erotica*, edited by Margaret Reynolds
3. *Fantasex,* by Rolf Milonas
4. *Fever: Sensual Stories by Women
   Writers*, another collection from
   M. Slung

5. *Forbidden Journeys: Fairy Tales & Fantasies by Victorian Women Writers,* edited Nina Auerbach
6. *Gates of Paradise*, by Alberto Manguel
7. *Good Sex: Stories from Real People*, by Julia Hutton
8. *Intimate Play: Playful Secrets for Falling and Staying in Love,* by William Betcher
9. *My Secret Garden,* by Nancy Friday
10. *Pleasures—Erotica for Women by Women*, edited by Lonnie Barbach
11. *Slow Hand: Women Writing Erotica*, edited by Michele Slung
12. *The Doctor Is In*, by Charlotte Rose
13. *The Erotic Mind*, by Jack Morin
14. *Women on Top*, by Nancy Friday
15. *Yellow Silk: Erotic Arts and Letters* (the book), edited by Lily Pond & Richard Russo
16. *Yellow Silk: Journal of the Erotic Arts* (the magazine)

8802. Guys: Have a new print made of the best photo of *her* from your wedding

8803. Wrap it up, and give it to *yourself* for your birthday or Christmas

---

8804. "And now these three remain: faith, hope, and love." ~ 1 Corinthians 13:13

8805. From the Bible to rock 'n roll, the core message remains the same!

8806. Demonstrate your *faith*: Get a gift that symbolizes your partner's faith

8807. Express your *hope*: Write down three of your deepest hopes for your relationship

8808. Live your *love*: Consciously decide to make "love" your Number One Priority

---

Favorite Love Songs from 1978

8809. "I Go Crazy," Paul Davis

8810. "Our Love," Natalie Cole

8811. "You Needed Me," Anne Murray

8812. Create a custom soundtrack to accompany a Saturday evening date

8813. Greet her at the airport wearing a

tuxedo, and carrying two dozen roses

8814. "The Ultimate Bubblebath" Coupon: One luxurious bubblebath complete with scented bath oils, soft music, champagne and candles. Plus, one sensual toweling-off by the coupon-issuer

8815. Guys: A recommended romantic shopping trip: Get all these items in coordinated fragrances:

8816. Body lotion and hand lotion

8817. Shampoo and conditioner

8818. Perfumed soap and bath gel

8819. Fragranced candle and dusting powder

8820. Remember: Love is a *feeling*. You feel love—you don't *do* love

8821. Remember: *Romance* is what you *do*. Romance is the expression of love

8822. Get some really cool "His" and "Hers" sunglasses

8823. Formally ask her to be your Valentine

8824. Get a copy of *People Magazine's* "Top People of the Year" issue: Paste-up photos of your partner and write a fun article

---

8825. Gals: Let the poor guy watch his favorite sports team in peace

8826. Guys: But it's unfair to claim that *every* team is your favorite team

---

8827–8843
The 17 Best Love Songs of All Time

1. "Colour My World," Chicago
2. "Coming Around Again," Carly Simon
3. "Crazy for You," Madonna
4. "Endless Love," Diana Ross & Lionel Richie
5. "(Everything I Do) I Do It for You," Bryan Adams
6. "In Your Eyes," Peter Gabriel
7. "(I've Had) the Time of My Life," Bill Medley & Jennifer Warnes
8. "I Won't Last a Day Without You," Paul Williams

9. "Just the Way You Are," Billy Joel
10. "Lady," Kenny Rogers
11. "Lara's Theme," from *Doctor Zhivago*
12. "The Rose," Bette Midler
13. "Something," The Beatles
14. "Unchained Melody," Righteous Brothers
15. "You Are So Beautiful (To Me)," Joe Cocker
16. "You Light Up My Life," Debbie Boone
17. "You're My Home," Billy Joel

8844. English: "Take me"
8845. French: "Prends-moi"
8846. Italian: "Prendimi"
8847. German: "Nimm mich"
8848. Spanish: "Me prendes"
8849. Portugese: "Me come"

8850. You can never go wrong with music from the fabulous Ms. Barbra Streisand...
8851. Selected CDs: *Memories; One Voice*
8852. *Songbird; Emotion; Till I Loved You*
8853. *The Way We Were; Higher Ground*

8854–8860

7 Romance Coupons for a Week of Love

1. The "Sexy Saturday" Coupon: The coupon-giver will create a day of eroticism, sexiness, hedonism, delight, and loving for you

2. The "Spiritual Sunday" Coupon: A day devoted to spiritual growth and deeper understanding of your relationship

3. The "Mellow Monday" Coupon: The coupon-giver is responsible for making Monday evening mellow and relaxing (with music and massage?)

4. The "Togetherness Tuesday" Coupon: Do *everything* together, e.g., shower, prepare meals, do chores, make love

5. The "Wonderful Wednesday" Coupon: *You* define "wonderful"— and your *partner* fulfills that definition this Wednesday

6. The "Thankful Thursday" Coupon: Your partner expresses his or her thanks for you—with little gifts and gestures all day

7. The "Funny Friday" Coupon: Your partner is responsible for making you laugh—with jokes, movies, and crazy antics

8861. A+ Rating, Romantic Music Artist: Grover Washington, Jr.
8862. *Always* give her the seat in a bus, train, or subway
8863. Whisper softly while making love
8864. Help her create the wedding of her dreams
8865. Appreciate his quirks
8866. Go on a "Travel Date"

Favorite Love Songs from 1979
8867. "A Little More Love," Olivia Newtown-John
8868. "Babe," Styx
8869. "Reunited," Peaches & Herb

8870. "Love has the patience to endure the fault it sees but cannot cure."
~ Edgar Guest
8871. Paste *this* quote on your refrigerator!

8872. Practice patience, understanding, and forgiveness

8873. Create your own Spring Celebration
8874. Soundtrack: George Winston's *Winter Into Spring*
8875. Activity: Plant a flower garden together
8876. Quote: "In the Spring a young man's fancy lightly turns to thoughts of love." ~ Alfred Lord Tennyson

---

8877–8886
10 Underwater Wonders of the World in Range of Snorkelers

1. Crystal River, Florida: Swim side-by-side with manatees
2. Providenciales Island, Turks and Caicos: Reefs like bonsai gardens
3. Heron Island, Australia: A microcosm of the Great Barrier Reef
4. Sting Ray City, Grand Cayman: Swim with sting rays
5. The Red Sea's Gulf of Aqaba: Incredibly colorful coral reefs
6. Qamea Island, Fiji: Some of the

world's best soft corals
7. Madang, Papua New Guinea: Vibrant with oceanic activity
8. Yap, Micronesia: If you like manta rays
9. Delos, Greece: Sunken ruins: Temple columns and mosaics
10. La Paz, Mexico, in the Sea of Cortez: Consort with playful sea lions

---

8887. Write a list: "15 Reasons Why You're the Sexiest Thing Alive"
8888. Gals: Print the list on a pair of silk panties—
8889. Gals: Let him read the list while you're *wearing* them
8890. Guys: Print the list on fine parchment—
8891. Guys: Wrap it with a gift of elegant lingerie

8892. Train your subconscious mind to recognize romantic ideas when they pass your way
8893. Train your heart to speak loudly to your head

8894. Train your mind to be open
8895. Train your inner eye to "read between the lines" when your partner communicates with you

---

8896. Experiment: Gals, wear really nice lingerie every day for a week
8897. Does he notice? How does he react? Is it worth it?

8898–8911
14 "Either-Or" Questions
(That Reveal a *Lot* About You)

Some questions are deceptively simple, yet reveal a lot about your character

1. Are you a peace-keeper or a trouble-maker?
2. Do you tend to see things as black-and-white, or as shades of gray?
3. Are you open or secretive?
4. Are you more or less sensitive than most people?
5. Do you live to work—or work to live?
6. Are you more or less thoughtful than

7.   most people?
7.   Are you a cat-person or a dog-person?
8.   Is it "love" or "money" that makes the world go 'round?
9.   Are you humble or arrogant?
10.   Are you an outdoors person or a homebody?
11.   Are you good or bad with money?
12.   Are you more or less intelligent than most people?
13.   Are you more or less competitive than most people?
14.   Do you evaluate things in terms of *time* or *money*?

8912.   Guys: Stuck for gift ideas? Ask her *mother*
8913.   Give one kiss for every day you've been a couple
8914.   Float a laminated love note in a punch bowl
8915.   "No disguise can mask love, nor feign it for long." ~ La Rochefoucauld
8916.   A+ Romantic Music Rating: Walter Beasley's *Intimacy* CD

8917. Add to her collection of porcelain angels
8918. The only acceptable prenuptial agreement: "Everything I have is yours"

8919. Celebrate your similarities
8920. Honor your differences
8921. Practice your talents
8922. Cherish your uniqueness

8923–8932
10 Ways to Love an Aries
(20 March–20 April)

1. Aries is a *fire* sign: Cater to his/her passionate, sexual nature
2. Gift tip: Intellectual, puzzling
3. As the head is ruled by Aries, give books and educational classes
4. Elegant hair brushes and hair ornaments are great gifts
5. Hats! (Sometimes gaudy)
6. Aries likes brightly-colored clothes
7. Honeysuckle; thistles
8. Spicy and exotic foods

9. The romance and history of Florence
10. Wrap gifts in bright red

8933. Compromise over the little things
8934. (Choose your battles wisely)
8935. You'll be appreciated for your flexibility on the little things
8936. And you'll be respected for holding your ground on the big things

---

Favorite Love Songs from 1980
8937. "(Just Like) Starting Over," John Lennon
8938. "Magic," Olivia Newton-John
8939. "Sailing," Christopher Cross

8940. Give him/her a homemade timeline of your lives together, highlighting your lives together with world events
8941. Draw it on poster paper
8942. Or have a calligrapher design it

8943. "'Tis not love that hurt my days, but that it went in little ways."
~ Edna St. Vincent Millay

8944. Beware of love slipping away while your attention is focused elsewhere

8945. Make love a habit

8946. For three weeks, be 25% more creative in your relationship

8947. Establish "your" table at a favorite restaurant

8948. Bana-gram: A love note on a banana

8949. Enemy of Love: "Humoring her"— Not really engaging your partner

8950. Re-create your wedding cake exactly for your 20th anniversary

8951. Tell your lover that he is the "crème de la crème"

8952. Visit the amazing Flower Fields at Carlsbad Ranch, California

---

8953. Gift & Date Idea: Get the song "Tonight," by Ferrante & Teicher—

8954. And rent the movie *West Side Story*, featuring the song

8955. Or—surprise your partner with tickets to the musical, live on stage

8956. Drop hints

8957. Drop-in unexpectedly
8958. Don't drop the ball

8959. And, of course, there's always
romantic music by Al Jarreau—
8960. Selected CDs: *L Is for Lover; Glow*
8961. *Heart's Horizon; Tenderness*

8962–8966
5 Songs to Help You Express
Your Feelings: *Falling in Love*

1. "Could It Be I'm Falling in Love?"
The Spinners
2. "Could It Be Magic," Barry Manilow
3. "Fallin' in Love," Hamilton, Joe
Frank & Reymolds
4. "If I Fell," The Beatles
5. "Knocks Me off My Feet," Stevie
Wonder

8967. Get her "Unforgettable" perfume
8968. And a copy of "Unforgettable" sung
by Natalie Cole
8969. And write a poem about how she's so
unforgettable

8970. Gals: What every guy *wants* you to know: *203 Ways to Drive a Man Wild in Bed*, by Olivia St. Claire

8971. Gals: Something you *need* to know: *How Men Feel*, by Anthony Astrachan

8972. Gals: Required reading: *The Sensuous Woman*, by J

8973. Gals: You may want to explore: *The Male Ego*, by Willard Gaylin

8974. Gals: More of what you ought to know: *What Every Woman Should Know About Men*, by Dr. Joyce Brothers

---

8975–8989
15 Ways to Learn More About Your Lover

1. Have a three-session "Relationship Check-Up" with a relationship counselor

2. Review your photo albums together

3. Listen to your partner more closely and more often

4. Review the list of "Favorite Things You Should Know About Your Lover" elsewhere in this book

5. Have astrological readings done for

the two of you
6. Be Bridge partners on a regular basis
7. Talk about your religious beliefs
8. Attend a relationship seminar together
9. See if numerology has any insights to offer
10. Take a "Psychological Profile" test together
11. Join a Marriage Encounter group
12. Analyze your "personal styles" by reading *Please Understand Me: Character & Temperament Types,* by David Keirsey & Marilyn Bates
13. Spend an "all-nighter" together: Talk and make love all night long
14. Talk about your childhoods
15. Do the "Relationship Report Card" exercise in the book *Love—The Course They Forgot To Teach You In School*

Favorite Love Songs from 1981
8990. "Celebration," Kool & the Gang
8991. "Keep on Loving You," REO Speedwagon

8992. "The One That You Love," Air Supply

8993. Send her on a "Blank Check Shopping Spree"—on Rodeo Drive in Beverly Hills

8994. Get her a replica of Rose's "Romantic Heart Necklace" as seen in *Titanic*

8995. "In the coldest February, as in every other month in every other year, the best thing to hold on to in the world is each other." ~ Linda Ellerbee

8896. A+ Rated acoustic music from Eric Tingstad & Nancuy Rumbel: *Homeland; Give and Take; In the Garden*

8997. Peruse a book of "toasts" for some inspiration

8998. Clip newspaper and magazine articles you know will amuse and interest your mate

8999. Turn to your partner in public and whisper, "There's no one I'd rather be with!"

9000. Try to set the record for the world's longest kiss

9001–9006
6 Songs to Help You Express
Your Feelings: Adoration

1. "Cherish," The Association
2. "Heaven Must Be Missing an Angel," Tavares
3. "I Just Want to Be Your Everything," Andy Gibb
4. "My Eyes Adored You," Frankie Valli
5. "My Love," Paul McCartney & Wings
6. "Wind Beneath My Wings," Bette Midler

9007. Buy her a reproduction of the sculpture "The Kiss" by Auguste Rodin

9008. Give him a poster of the painting "The Kiss" by Gustav Klimt

---

9009. Write your own wedding vows for your ceremony

9010. If your partner was formerly in the military, give him/her a "Lover's Medal of Honor," "Survivor in the

Battle of the Sexes," "Bravery in the Face of Parenthood," etc.

9011. For Married Folks: Think like a single person: *Date* your spouse

9012. Save some sand in a jar from each of your beach vacations

---

9013. "We don't remember the days; we remember the moments."
~ Cesare Pavese

9014. Forget about *extravagant* romantic gestures—focus on individual *moments*

9015. Stop. Hold her face in your hands. Gaze into her eyes. Tell her you love her. And really, really, really mean it

9016. Create a special moment of intimacy—not sexuality—in bed tonight

9017. Find a copy of "This Magic Moment," the 1960 hit by The Drifters

---

9018. Guys: Don't demean her by saying to your kids, "Oh, you know how your mother is"

9019. Gals: Don't make him the bad guy by threatening your kids with "Wait until your father gets home!"

9020–9062
43 Reasons to Be Romantic

1. You'll be happier
2. Your *partner* will be happier
3. You'll have sex more often
4. You'll enjoy sex more
5. You'll keep your love alive
6. You'll experience the spark of infatuation again
7. You'll reduce the chance your partner might cheat on you
8. You'll increase the probability that you'll stay married
9. You'll add depth and meaning to your relationship
10. You will create a safe haven where you can really be yourself
11. You will be truly heard and deeply understood by one other human being

12. You'll save money by expressing your love in lots of little, creative ways
13. Exercising your creativity will benefit you in other areas of your life
14. You'll probably live longer
15. You'll be better parents
16. You'll be great role models for your children
17. You'll be great role models for friends and neighbors
18. Your children will understand love better than most kids
19. Your children will experience what love is really all about
20. Your children will have a better chance of choosing partners wisely
21. Your children will be better able to create healthy love relationships
22. You'll make the world a better place
23. You'll come to appreciate your own uniqueness
24. You'll come to appreciate your partner's uniqueness
25. You'll reduce or eliminate therapy bills!

26. You'll get more of what you want out of life
27. You'll strengthen your self-esteem and self-confidence
28. You'll never have to write to Dear Abby for love advice
29. You'll be better able to live your faith (love is central to every religion)
30. You will have the quiet confidence that you've achieved something that few people accomplish
31. You'll create a truly mature relationship
32. You'll move beyond treating your partner like a stereotype
33. You'll have more energy and focus for your career
34. You'll surprise your skeptical in-laws!
35. You'll deepen your understanding of the opposite sex
36. You'll re-connect with your creative, impulsive, spontaneous, childlike nature
37. You'll live up to your true potential in life

38. You'll never again be panic stricken on Valentine's Day
39. You'll never again have to feel guilty for having forgotten a birthday or anniversary
40. You'll stay young-at-heart
41. Love makes the world go 'round
42. Your partner *wants* you to be romantic—What more reason do you *need*?
43. Why *not*??

9063. For cat lovers, visit the Feline Info Page: www.best.com/~sirlou/cat.shtml
9064. For you dog lovers: ftp://rtfm.mit.edu/pub/usenet/news.answers/dogs.faq
9065. For horse lovers: www.spyder.net/horseadvice/
9066. For butterfly fans: mgfx.com/butterfly/
9067. And for *exotic* pet lovers: dca.net:80/exoticpets/

Favorite Love Songs from 1982

9068. "One Hundred Ways," Quincy Jones & James Ingram

9069. "Turn Your Love Around," George Benson

9070. "Up Where We Belong," Joe Cocker & Jennifer Warnes

9071. "Why Do Fools Fall in Love," Diana Ross

9072. Use the three most powerful words in the world: "I love you"

9073. (The *second* most powerful three words: "Let's eat out")

9074. Set your alarm clock thirty minutes early—make love as the sun rises

9075. Discuss your core values and beliefs

9076. "Love is...an endless mystery, for it has nothing else to explain it." ~ Rabindranath Tagore

9077. For your Judy Garland fan: *Judy*—a four-CD retrospective

9078. Enemy of Love: Stereotyping

9079. Spend a week at a spa together:

The Spa at Cordillera, in Colorado: (800) 548-2721

9080. Give her a hand massage

9081–9088
8 Breathtaking-But-Smaller Waterfalls in America

"Bigger" is not necessarily better:

1. Amicalola Falls State Park, Georgia
2. Cumberland Falls State Resort Park, Kentucky
3. DeSoto Falls, DeSoto State Park, Alabama
4. Gorman Falls, Colorado Bend State Park, Texas
5. Issaqueena Falls, Stumphouse Tunnel Park, South Carolina
6. The Kaanapali area on Maui, Hawaii
7. Linville Falls, Brue Ridge Parkway, North Carolina
8. Turner Falls Park, Oklahoma

9089. "We kiss. And it feels like we have just shrugged off the world."
~ Jim Shahin

9090. Tender kisses communicate caring to your partner

9091. Passionate kisses connect emotional love with physical sexuality

9092. Long, lingering kisses slow you down

9093. Deep kisses connect you— on *several* levels

9094. Quick kisses keep you connected

9095. Guys: Sure lingerie is great—but approach the subject with her *gently*

9096. Don't: Start by giving her a peek-a-boo bra

9097. Do: Attach a one hundred dollar bill to a Victoria's Secret catalog along with a note saying, "You choose"

9098. "Don't hate. It's too big a burden to bear." ~ Martin Luther King Jr.

9099. "Don't look for love; give love—and you will find love looking for you." ~ Beth Black

9100. "I don't want to live. I want to love first, and live incidentally." ~ Zelda Fitzgerald

9101. "Don't Go Breaking My Heart,"
Elton John & Kiki Dee

9102. "Don't Fall in Love with a Dreamer,"
Kenny Rogers & Kim Carnes

9103. "Don't Let the Sun Go Down on
Me," George Michael & Elton John

9104. "Don't Ever Leave Me," Helen Morgan

9105. "Don't Sit Under the Apple Tree,"
The Andrews Sisters

9106. "Don't Get Around Much Anymore"

9107. "You Don't Know What Love Is"

9108. "Why Don't You Do Right?" Peggy
Lee

9109. "You Don't Have to Be a Star,"
Marilyn McCoo & Billy Davis Jr.

9110. "Baby Don't Go," Sonny & Cher

9111. Remember: Love *begins* all by itself. It
requires no effort to *fall* in love

9112. But *staying* in love requires two
things: 1) Conscious decision, and
2) consistent action

9113. Soundtrack for a summer celebration:
Paul Winter's CD *Sun Singer*

9114. Write a love note on a rock, then toss it into the deep end of your pool

9115. An "Adult Ed" Coupon: The coupon-giver will pay for and accompany you to an adult education class of your choosing

---

9116–9211
7 Items for a *Yearly* Romantic Checklist

1. Make a New Year's Resolution to be more loving next year
2. Make plans for your next anniversary
3. Think of an *unusual* way to celebrate your partner's birthday
4. Review your plans for your next vacation
5. Create a "Romance" category in your household budget
6. Make plans for Valentine's Day at least six months in advance
7. Write "Relationship Goals" for the next five years

9123. Watch the snow from a cozy cabin window

9124. Love and learn: Read *You're Not What I Expected: Learning to Love the Opposite Sex,* by Polly Young-Eisendrath

9125. Spend your entire Christmas gift budget on lottery tickets—You may just win enough for some *great* gifts

9126. "How vast a memory has love." ~ Alexander Pope

9127. For your ice cream lover: Tour Ben & Jerry's factory: (802) 244-TOUR9128. Be her chauffeur during busy times; provide "extra" services

9129. Have a poem delivered to your table at a restaurant

9130. Rent a beach bungalow on Cape Cod for a sandy vacation

Favorite Love Songs from 1983

9131. "All Night Long (All Night)," Lionel Richie

9132. "Baby, Come to Me," Patti Austin & James Ingram

9133. "Heart to Heart," Kenny Loggins

9134. "Straight from the Heart," Bryan Adams

9135. "Total Eclipse of the Heart," Bonnie Tyler

9136. "You Are," Lionel Richie

9137. Gift & Date Idea: Get the song "Call Me," by Blondie—

9138. And rent the movie *American Gigolo*, featuring the song

9139. And there's always Wynton Marsalis for some jazzy romantic music…

9140. Selected CDs: *Intimacy Calling*

9141. *Carnival; Jump Start and Jazz*

9142. *The Majesty of the Blues*

9143–9146
4 Aspects of Love—Based on the Ancient 4 Elements

A well-rounded relationship incorporates aspects of all four elements. Where are your strengths and weaknesses? Do you have an over-abundance—or a lack—in another area?

Earth: Grounded, solid, dependable, strong

Air: Light, free flowing, flexible

Fire: Passionate, powerful, sexual

Water: Soothing, filling, comforting

9147. English: "Will you marry me?"
9148. French (spoken to a gal): "Tu veux être ma femme?"
9149. French (spoken to a guy): "Tu veux être mon mari?"
9150. Italian: "Vuoi sposarmi?"
9151. German: "Heiratest du mich?"
9152. Spanish: "¿Te casarías conmigo?"
9153. Portugese: "Você quer casar comigo?"

9154. "A loving heart is the truest wisdom." ~ Charles Dickens
9155. What a mistake we make when we believe that wisdom comes from the *head*
9156. Trust your heart. Listen for that Inner Voice. Pay attention to the spirit speaking to you

---

9157. Get a stone Cupid to place in her garden
9158. Remember: 5 = 1 (5 minutes devoted to love equals 1 day of harmony)
9159. Go whitewater rafting on the Gauley River, in West Virginia

9160. See a couple's counselor: Not because you've got problems, but simply to help you deepen your relationship

9161. A luscious surprise: Ice cream made from flowers! Call Out of a Flower at (800) 743-4696

9162. "Any time that is not spent on love is wasted." ~ Torquato Tasso

9163. Discuss with your partner: Is this an overstatement, or the truth?

9164. Experiment: For the next thirty days, spend thirty additional minutes per day being loving

---

9165–9174
Top 10 Public Golf Courses

For your golf nut: Plan vacations where the golfing is *great*

1. Bethpage, Farmingdale, New York
2. Blackwolf Run (River Course), Kohler, Wisconsin
3. Cog Hill (Number 4), Lemont, Illinois
4. Pebble Beach, Pebble Beach, California

5. Pinehurst (Number 2), Pinehurst, North Carolina
6. Pumpkin Ridge (Ghost Creek), Cornelius, Oregon
7. Spyglass Hill, Pebble Beach, California
8. TPC at Sawgrass (Stadium), Ponte Vedra Beach, Florida
9. Troon North (Monument), Scottsdale, Arizona
10. World Woods (Pine Barrens), Brooksville, Florida

9175. Turn to him in public and whisper, "I'm not wearing any panties."
9176. Enemy of Love: Emotional withdrawal
9177. A+ Romance Rating: *Kiss Under the Moon*, Warren Hill's jazzy, romantic music
9178. Nurture your partner in as many ways as possible
9179. Carve your Halloween pumpkin with *hearts*
9180. After you've talked on the phone for

a long time, call back in three
minutes to say you miss her

9181. Remember: Romance isn't just a
weekend sport!

9182. Spend an afternoon at MOMA in
NYC

Favorite Love Songs from 1984

9183. "Almost Paradise," Mike Reno &
Ann Wilson

9184. "Hello," Lionel Richie

9185. "Leave a Tender Moment Alone,"
Billy Joel

9186. "Let's Go Crazy," Prince

9187. "Missing You," John Waite

9188. "Time After Time," Cyndi Lauper

9189. Gift & Date Idea: Get the song
"April Love," by Pat Boone—

9190. And rent the movie *April Love*,
featuring the song

9191. Send a bouquet of *mistletoe*!

9192. Kiss in at least five different countries
over the next ten years

9193. Turn to her in public and whisper, "I wouldn't trade you for *anything.*"

9194. Take an inn-to-inn hike through the Grand Canyon: (800) 417-2453

9195. Hire a celebrity look-alike of his/her favorite actor to entertain at a party

9196. Anticipate her desires

9197–9202
6 Songs to Help You Express Your Feelings: *Forgive Me/Don't Leave Me!*

1. "Baby Come Back," Player
2. "Don't Give Up on Us," David Soul
3. "Hard to Say I'm Sorry," Chicago
4. "If You Leave Me Now," Chicago
5. "One More Night," Phil Collins
6. "Sorry Seems to Be the Hardest Word," Elton John

9203. Guys: On your wedding anniversary, re-create her wedding bouquet

9204. Show a wedding photo to your florist

9205. Present her with the photo and bouquet together

9206. "As we think in our hearts, so we are." ~ Proverbs 23:7

9207. This Biblical quote elegantly unites the *heart* (emotions) and the *head* (thinking)

9208. The popular notion that the head and heart are *separate* is just plain *wrong*

9209. It is not true that "being in love" is *entirely* a matter of the heart

9210. True love involves a *dynamic balance* of the head and heart

9211. Clarification: *Infatuation* is about heart and sex—and ignoring the head

9212. Note: Boredom and cynicism result when the head leaves the heart behind

---

9213. Always have one set of tickets to an upcoming event tacked to your bulletin board

9214. "May you live all the days of your life." ~ Jonathan Swift

9215. Set up a large screen TV and VCR in your garage and create your own "Drive-In"

9216. Get him Box Seats for the local pro baseball team

9217. Put a tiny love note inside a walnut; seal it back up

9218. Hang a world map on the wall, and place little flags on spots you want to visit

9219. "Life is a paradise for those who love many things with passion."
~ Leo Buscaglia

9220. Wear matching Hawaiian shirts

9221. Do something just plain *ZaNy*

9222. Take your rock fan to the Rock & Roll Hall of Fame, in Cleveland

9223. Make flags from toothpicks and tiny squares of paper; write tiny love notes on them and stick them in pancakes, rolls, etc.

Favorite Love Songs from 1985

9224. "Can't Fight This Feeling," REO Speedwagon

9225. "Everytime You Go Away," Paul Young

9226. "Method of Modern Love," Daryl

Hall & John Oates

9227. "Saving All My Love for You,"
Whitney Houston

9228. "And I will make thee beds of roses
And a thousand fragrant posies."
~ Christopher Marlowe

9229. You want romantic inspiration? Read
some poetry!

9230. In poetic form, this is the classic
romantic strategy of "overdoing
something"

9231. Start *literally*: Cover your bed with
roses…

9232. Or *fill a room* with posies for your
partner

9233. Or bring home a bouquet of flowers
every day for a month

9234. Or every Friday for the rest of your
life!

9235–9245
11 Ways for Women to
Get Men to Be Romantic

1. Appeal to his competitive nature:

Hold a "Who Can Be More Romantic" contest

2. Get a buddy of his (who "gets it" when it comes to relationships) to have a talk with him

3. Stop using the word "romance" altogether—And replace it with the word "fun"

4. Be a good role model—*You* be romantic first

5. Give him this book—with your favorite items circled

6. Give him a list of all your "favorite things"

7. Ask him for a list of *his* "favorite things"

8. Give him three "Romance Coupons" for things you want him to do for you

9. Schedule one lunch "meeting" a month for the two of you

10. You be romantic *first*, then take turns every other week

11. *Barter* with him for romantic favors

9246. Visit America's West Coast Romantic Hideaway Island: Catalina
9247. Live your wedding vows
9248. For anyone in or into the performing arts: The Music Stand Catalog: (802) 295-7044
9249. The Red-Hot "Kiss" Coupon: Redeemable for one hour of "making-out"
9250. "I love thee with the breath, smiles, tears, of all my life" ~ Elizabeth Barrett Browning
9251. Romantic piano by Peter Kater: The *Two Hearts* CD
9252. Place a single red rose in his/her briefcase
9253. Make a ten-foot-tall greeting card
9254. Attend a live production of *Romeo and Juliet*
9255. Do something that's sexy to the point of being illegal

9256–9263
8 Sexy Ways to Celebrate the Holidays
1. Christmas: Wrap yourself in a red

bow and wait underneath the
Christmas tree

2. Independence Day: Wrap yourself in
a flag—and see if he salutes!

3. Halloween: Dress-up as favorite
fantasy characters

4. Thanksgiving: Give thanks for your
relationship by giving sexual favors

5. Groundhog Day: Go "underground":
Skip work and stay in bed all day
together

6. Memorial Day: Create a sexual
encounter that will be truly *memorable*

7. Valentine's Day: Treat your partner
(and yourself) to edible massage
lotion!

8. St. Patrick's Day: Wear green
underwear

9264. Musical lovenote: "Play the CD *Mud
Slide Slim and the Blue Horizon*, by
James Taylor. My message to you is
song No. 2"

9265. Tour the French countryside

9266. Remember: Romance isn't about

"giving in" to your partner

9267. Use romantic gestures to create a bridge between the two of you

9268. Mood music: Create a peaceful, thoughtful mood with the *Canon in D* by Johann Pachelbel

9269. Create your own Autumn Celebration

9270. Soundtrack: George Winston's *Autumn*

9271. Activity: Watch the blazing colors of the trees in Maine

9272. Quote: "Autumn's flaming colors inspire passion in lovers' hearts." ~ Anonymous

---

9273. When apart, think about one another for one minute at a pre-determined time

9274. Cartoon lovers celebrate Bullwinkle's birthday on January 20

9275. Eat in the most romantic inn in Edinburgh: Prestonfield House

9276. Add a bottle to his wine cellar

9277. Write a detailed "Job Description" for your role as husband or wife

9278.   Leave brief love poems on the
        exterior of his/her car with "Magnetic
        Poetry: Bumper Sticker Edition"

9279–9287
9 Books *About* Men, *For* Men, *By* Men

1.   *American Manhood: Transformations
     in Masculinity from the Revolution to
     the Modern Era*, by E. Anthony
     Rotundo
2.   *Boys Will Be Men: Masculinity in
     Troubled Times*, by Richard Hawley
3.   *The End of Manhood: A Book for Men
     of Conscience*, by John Stoltenberg
4.   *In the Company of Men: Freeing the
     Masculine Heart*, by Marvin Allen &
     Jo Robinson
5.   *The Lover Within: Accessing the Lover
     in the Male Psyche*, by Robert Moore
6.   *Men Talk*, by Alvin Baraff
7.   *Myths of Masculinity*, by William
     Doty
8.   *Secrets Men Keep*, by Ken Druck
9.   *Sexual Peace: Beyond the Dominator
     Virus*, by Michael Sky

9288. Name your boat after her
9289. Never, never, *never:* Teach your partner to drive a car
9290. Gift resource for wine enthusiasts: The Wine Enthusiast Catalog: (800) 231-0100
9291. Adopt his/her kids from a previous marriage

9292–9295
4 *Poignant* Love Songs

1. "Do You Love Me?" from *Fiddler on the Roof*
2. "One More Night," Phil Collins
3. "Truly," Lionel Richie
4. "Without You," from the Broadway musical *Rent*

9296. Kidnap him from work on a Friday afternoon
9297. Visit a spiritually meaningful place, like Mecca
9298. Create your own "Romance Game" using an old Monopoly Game
9299. Unlearn the attitude "Give her an

inch and she'll take a mile."

9300. Erotic Book & Movie Alert! *The Unbearable Lightness of Being*

9301. "Motivation is what gets you started. Habit is what keeps you going." ~ Jim Ryun

9302. Romantic piano concerto: Beethoven's Piano Concerto No. 5 in E flat

9303. Tuck a love note in the finger of his baseball glove

9304. Hold a "His" and "Hers" Weekend: On Saturday you both do whatever *she* wants to do and on Sunday, you both do whatever *he* wants to do

9305. Believe that the best is yet to come

Favorite Love Songs from 1986

9306. "Addicted to Love," Robert Palmer

9307. "Burning Heart," Survivor

9308. "Glory of Love," Peter Cetera

9309. "Take My Breath Away," Berlin

9310. "This Could Be the Night," Loverboy

9311. "True Colors," Cyndi Lauper

9312. "It's the thought that counts"
9313. Pay attention to the details, the little extra touches
9314. Be 10% more thoughtful/considerate
9315. Remember how you thought about your mate when you first met
9316. Put your thoughts on paper: Write a love note

9317. Enemy of Love: Fear of rejection
9318. Give a subscription to *Sports Illustrated*
9319. Tell your mate you think he/she is "pulchritudinous"
9320. Press some flowers that you've received
9321. Share *everything:* Your ice cream cones and snack foods
9322. Get a professional massage table

9323–9332
10 "Love Codes" for Lovers

1. SWAK—Sealed With A Kiss
2. X's stand for kisses; O's stand for hugs (Often used to sign letters)
3. *Red* roses symbolize love and passion

4. *Pink* roses symbolize friendship
5. *Yellow* roses symbolize respect
6. *White* roses symbolize purity
7. Point to your eye; then point to your heart; then point to your partner
8. Learn the sign language gesture for "I love you"
9. Three soft taps on the shoulder mean "I love you"
10. Three soft taps on the thigh mean "Let's make love"

9333. Gift & Date Idea: Get the song "Baby I Love Your Way," by Big Mountain—
9334. And rent the movie *Reality Bites*, featuring the song

9335. Soundtrack for a winter celebration: Paul Winter's CD *Wintersong*
9336. Have mimosas with breakfast
9337. A little follow-up gift to a night of great lovemaking: A copy of "You Make Lovin' Fun," by Fleetwood Mac

9338. Call when you're running late
9339. Enemy of Love: Thoughtlessness
9340. Give her Chanel No. 5
9341. Enemy of Love: Short-term thinking
9342. Stay at the fanciest hotel in Rome: Sole al Pantheon
9343. Gift & Date Idea: Get the song "(Everything I Do) I Do It for You," by Bryan Adams—
9344. And rent the movie *Robin Hood: Prince of Thieves*, featuring the song

---

9345–9351
7 Best Love Songs by The Four Tops

1. "Ain't No Woman (Like the One I've Got)"
2. "Baby I Need Your Loving"
3. "I Can't Help Myself (Sugar Pie, Honey Bunch)"
4. "Reach Out I'll Be There"
5. "River Deep—Mountain High" (with The Supremes)
6. "Something About You"
7. "Sweet Understanding Love"

9352. A "Happy Anniversary!" Coupon:
Choose *one* of the following:
1) Dinner for two, 2) A romantic
movie date, 3) An awesome backrub,
or 4) A sexy lovemaking session

9353. Love Coupon: This coupon entitles
the holder to . . . flowers! Your
choice: One dozen of any kind of
flower. Flowers to be delivered within
three days of issuance of Coupon

9354. For sports fans: Birthday cakes in the
shape of footballs, basketballs, etc.

9355. Say "I love you" in Morse Code:
.. / ._.. ___ ..._ . /
_.__ ___ .._

9356. Carry a lock of her hair in your wallet

9357. Be frugal all year so you can *live it up*
on vacation

9358. If you're talkative by nature, talk 20%
less, and listen 20% more

9359. Keep handy left-handed scissors, etc.,
for your southpaw spouse

9360. A note: "Time and time again you
amaze me because . . ."

Favorite Love Songs from 1987

9361. "Lean on Me," Club Nouveau
9362. "Nothing's Gonna Change My Love for You," Glenn Medeiros
9363. "Nothing's Gonna Stop Us Now," Starship
9364. "Somebody," Depeche Mode
9365. "Somewhere Out There," Linda Ronstadt and James Ingram

9366. "As soon as you cannot keep anything from a woman, you love her."
    ~ Paul Geraldy
9367. Lovers don't keep secrets from each other
9368. Picture the two of you as the *center* of a series of concentric circles that comprise your life

---

9369. Help her study for a class she's taking
9370. Sing duets in the shower together
9371. Send a mysterious "Treasure Map" to lead her to a secret rendezvous
9372. If he's a former Boy Scout: Award him with some custom "Merit

Badges"—for "Loving Skills," "20
Years of Loyal Service," etc.

9373. Write an entire love letter on the
surface of a balloon, with a magic
marker

9374. FYI: Arguments between A+ Couples
end with *two* winners

9375. Go "Garage Sale Hopping" and buy
$25 of junk for each other

9376. Prepare an Easter basket with plastic
eggs filled with love notes and tiny
gifts

9377. Expand your Romantic Music
Library with Anita Baker

9378. Experiment: For two weeks, set aside
one hour every evening to do
"romantic homework"; your partner
gets to choose the "assignment"

9379. Create a "Count-Down Calendar"
anticipating your 10th anniversary

9380. Give your partner permission to play

9381. Love Enhancer: Listening with your
heart

9382. Write to your congressperson

requesting that Valentine's Day be
made a federal holiday

9383. Attach a note to his calculator: "You
can count on me"

9384. Get your space nut a piece of jewelry
that incorporates a meteorite

9385. A+ Rating, Romantic Music Artist:
Tom Scott

9386. Diamond astrological pins (with
diamonds for each star of the
constellation): (800) 341-0788

9387–9396
10 Songs to Help You Express
Your Feelings: *Hot Passion*

1. "All I Wanna Do Is Make Love to
You," Heart
2. "Deeper and Deeper," Madonna
3. "Do You Wanna Make Love," Peter
McCann
4. "Hot Stuff," Donna Summer
5. "I Do What I Do" (Theme for
9 1/2 Weeks), John Taylor
6. "I'm Your Baby Tonight," Whitney
Houston

7. "Kiss You All Over," Exile
8. "Light My Fire," The Doors
9. "Make Me Lose Control," Eric Carmen
10. "Touch Me (I Want Your Body)," Samantha Sang

9397. Attend a Renaissance Fair together
9398. Visit America's East Coast Romantic Hideaway Island: Martha's Vineyard
9399. If you both play piano, play Mozart's *Sonata in F*—a piece for *4 hands*
9400. Plant one rose bush for every anniversary (Plan ahead for a 75-bush garden!)
9401. "If it is not erotic, it is not interesting." ~ Fernando Arrabal
9402. Attach a note to a bottle of Tabasco Sauce: "You're *hot stuff!*"
9403. Create a romantic screen-saver for his computer
9404. Share *everything:* Your meals and desserts, when dining out
9405. Bring home one pint of Häagen-Dazs Rum Raisin

9406. A "Classic Romance" Coupon: You will be treated to a weekend of champagne, romantic movies, dinner, and dancing

9407. Stay at the fanciest hotel in Monte Carlo: Hôtel de Paris

9408. Trek through the Himalayas together

9409. Use Alpha-Bits cereal to spell-out love messages

9410. Hold a "Romantic Idea Brainstorming Party" with ten friends

---

9411–9417
7 Best Love Songs by Marvin Gaye

1. "Ain't Nothing Like the Real Thing" (with Tammi Terrell)
2. "How Sweet It Is to Be Loved by You"
3. "If I Could Build My Whole World Around You"
4. "Let's Get It On"
5. "Too Busy Thinking About My Baby"
6. "You're a Special Part of Me" (with Diana Ross)

7. "You're All I Need to Get By" (with Tammi Terrel)

9418. Go in search of little-known vacation spots

9419. Roll-up a little love note and insert it in a tube of her lipstick

9420. Kiss at the top of the Eiffel Tower

9421. Watch the tide go out on a Jamaican beach

9422. Have a trophy made: "World's Best Wife"

9423. Hang a fancy, Victorian Christmas stocking, filled to the brim with goodies

9424. Order a 14K gold pin of two geese (symbolizing "Geese Mate for Life"): From Cross Jewelers: (800) 433-2988

9425. Paint "I love my wife" in two-foot letters on the side of your pick-up truck

9426. For tea lovers: Share afternoon tea, like the British do

9427. Give a case of wine from the country of his/her ancestors

9428. Have the face of his wristwatch engraved with "Time for love"

9429. Don't just buy her *perfume*, get her a "fragrance wardrobe"

9430. Keep extra batteries hidden away for his electronic gizmos

---

Favorite Love Songs from 1988

9431. "Groovy Kind of Love," Phil Collins

9432. "Hungry Eyes," Eric Carmen

9433. "I Get Weak," Belinda Carlisle

9434. "I'm Gonna Be," The Proclaimers

9435. "Lost in You," Rod Stewart

9436. "Waiting for a Star to Fall," Boy Meets Girl

9437. And, of course, there's always romantic music by Kenny G...

9438. Selected CDs: *Silhouette; Kenny G*

9439. *G-Force; Duotones*

9440. Enemy of Love: Speed (modern life's fast pace)

9441. Try a different *position* the next time you make love

9442. Put quarters in her parking meter
9443. Present your partner with a movie poster signed by his/her favorite star
9444. Make love on top of the washer/dryer (while it's running)
9445. Remember: Romance is the language of love
9446. "Nothing is worth more than this day." ~ Johann Wolfgang Von Goethe
9447. Expand your Romantic Music Library with Mike Howard CDs
9448. Spray your "signature" perfume in his car
9449. When traveling for a week, leave behind seven wrapped boxes filled with trinket gifts labeled with the days of the week
9450. Watch the sunset from an Italian villa
9451. Take her off the pedestal and place her by your side
9452. Musical lovenote: "Play the CD *To Our Children's Children's Children*, by The Moody Blues. My message to you is song No. 13"
9453. Get great clothing for him/her from

the J. Peterman Catalog:
(800) 231-7341

9454. For Christmas, wrap seven *shoe boxes* for her: Each box contains a gift certificate for a new pair of shoes

---

9455. Make fun "deals" with your lover:
9456. She'll accompany him to a topless beach—
9457. If he'll buy her diamond earrings
9458. He'll treat her to a shopping spree at Saks Fifth Avenue—
9459. If she'll buy him a wide screen TV
9460. She'll give him a backrub—
9461. If he'll do the week's grocery shopping
9462. He'll forego his Sunday golf game—
9463. If she'll serve him breakfast in bed

9464. Send an "S.O.S." message ("Sex On Saturday"); send S.O.S. emails
9465. Is he a Blue Ribbon lover? Give him one!
9466. Love Enhancer: Appreciation for *life*
9467. Secretly pass a love note to her

9468. Perfume his pillow as a signal that you want to make love tonight

9469. The Romantic "Cuddle Coupon": You are entitled to one solid hour of cozy cuddling with the coupon-issuer, in any location you choose

9470. Spend two weeks together at a quaint French villa

9471. Stop the elevator between floors to make-out (beware of surveillance cameras!)

9472. Sign her up for the Panty-of-the-Month Club: (800) 935-5937

9473. Get her a little gold Cupid pin

9474. Take a paddle boat down the Mississippi River

9475. Prepare a perfumed milk bath for her

9476. "Perseverance is not a long race; it is many short races one after another." ~ Walter Elliott

9477. Attend the Grand Opening of a new restaurant in town

9478. Turn to your partner in public and whisper, "You look *wonderful* tonight!"

9479. "The more I wonder...the more I love." ~ Alice Walker
9480. Spoil her
9481. Romantic piano concerto: Schumann's Concerto in A Minor for Piano & Orchestra
9482. Learn some little magic tricks to amuse her
9483. Enemy of Love: Inattentiveness
9484. Eat in the most romantic restaurant in Amsterdam: De Goudsbloem
9485. Work together to complete the *New York Times* Sunday Crossword Puzzle
9486. Share a good laugh together

Favorite Love Songs from 1989

9487. "Don't Know Much," Linda Ronstadt & Aaron Neville
9488. "Everlasting Love," Howard Jones
9489. "I'll Be There for You," Bon Jovi
9490. "Right Here Waiting," Richard Marx
9491. "She Drives Me Crazy," Fine Young Cannibals
9492. "When I See You Smile," Bad English

9493. Photograph all the stages of her pregnancy
9494. Don't let a single day go by without telling her how beautiful she is

---

9495. "Re-frame" your relationship
9496. She's not your wife—she's your *lover*
9497. He's not your husband—he's that handsome devil you flipped for

---

9498. A "Day of "Kissin'-an'-a-Lovin'" Coupon: If you need directions for this one, you need more help than a mere coupon can provide!
9499. For your gourmet: A kitchen gadget he's been lusting after
9500. For electricians in love: Install dimmer switches in your bedroom
9501. Gals: Don't use "feminine wiles" on him: It's deceitful
9502. Give yourself permission to be sexy
9503. Note: If love is really your top priority, then you never really "sacrifice" for it
9504. Come down with a serious case of

"Spring Fever"; the cure is to spend all day in bed with your mate

9505. If you're quiet by nature, open up and talk 20% more

9506. Eat in the most romantic restaurant in Budapest: Paradiso

9507. Create a "Romance Credit Card": Establish two types of credit—time and money—and establish your credit limits quarterly; chart your expenditures

9508. Get a shower head built-for-two

9509. Celebrate the Spring Equinox by watching a sunrise together

9510. Celebrate the Summer Solstice by taking a stroll together

9511. Celebrate the Autumn Equinox by watching a sunset together

9512. Celebrate the Winter Solstice by cuddling in front of a fire together

---

9513. To help you celebrate: The Celebration Fantastic Catalog: (800) 527-6566

9514. Write a love note in French/German/Swedish/etc.—and wait for her to translate it!

9515. Get your pianist partner a Steinway baby grand

9516. Listen to Frank Sinatra's *Songs for Young Lovers*: Widely acknowledged as the best of all his albums

9517. Eat in Boston's most romantic restaurant: The Hungry i

9518. "There's more to love than love, when it's right." ~ John O'Hara

9519. While at parties and dinners, share one glass all evening

9520. Love Enhancer: Time—*Quantity* of time

9521. In a love note, describe your lover as "sui generis"

9522. Create a "Count-Down Calendar" anticipating your wedding

9523. For two weeks, compliment your partner 50% more than usual

9524. Make a wish on the first star that appears at night

9525. Eat in the most romantic restaurant

in Venice: Da Fiore

9526. Send a telegram. Call Western Union: (800) 325-6000

9527. Enemy of Love: Poor time management

9528. Write down your excuses for not being romantic, put a big red "X" through them, and give the list to your partner

---

Favorite Love Songs from 1990

9529. "I'll Be Your Everything," Tommy Page

9530. "Love Will Never Do Without You," Janet Jackson

9531. "Nothing Compares 2 U," Sinead O'Connor

9532. "The Way You Do the Things You Do," UB40

9533. "If you love somebody, tell them." ~ Rod McKuen

9534. We often need to be reminded of the basics, the ABCs, of love

9535. No one ever tires of hearing the

words "I love you"

9536. Tell your partner you love him/her with just a look

9537. Tell your partner you adore him/her with just a touch

9538. Tell your partner you're crazy about him/her with a little gesture

---

9539. Musical lovenote: "Play the CD *A Hard Day's Night*, by The Beatles. My message to you is song No. 2"

9540. Erotic Book Alert! *Tart Tales: Elegant Erotic Stories*, by Carolyn Banks

9541. Before vacationing in Venice, watch the movie *Summertime* together

9542. For four weeks, be 20% more communicative with your partner

9543. Use a business Dictaphone for making "audio greeting cards"

9544. "It is a beautiful necessity of our nature to love something."
~ Douglas William Jerrold

9545. Provide "turn-down service" for her at home: Place little chocolates on her pillow

9546. Play valet, and lay out your partner's night clothes on the bed

9547. Send a series of postcards picturing romantic movie couples

9548. For two weeks, be 10% more considerate to your partner

9549. Brush her hair for her

9550. Make this a regular nightly ritual

9551. Use this as a time to slow down and re-connect

9552. Buy her an antique silver plated hair brush

9553. Wednesday is "Hump Day": Celebrate as you see fit

9554. Guys: Never, never, *never* give her the "silent treatment"

9555. Visit the best bar for watching sunsets in Italy: The Casina Valadier, on Pincio Hill in the Villa Borghese Gardens

9556. Love Enhancer: Time—*Quality* time

9557. Stop trying to change your partner

9558. "Soul meets soul on lovers lips."
~ Percy Bysshe Shelley

9559. English: "You're so beautiful"
9560. French: "Tu es très belle"
9561. Italian: "Sei molto bella"
9562. German: "Du bist sehr schön"
9563. Spanish: "Eres preciosa"
9564. Portugese: "Você é muito bonita"

9565. The "Ultimate, Fantastic, Delicious Pizza" Coupon: Good for one date at the best pizza joint in town
9566. Gals: When in his presence, wear *only* his favorite perfume
9567. Some people prefer gifts over gestures. What does *your* partner prefer?
9568. Make love, have sex, do it, make it, sleep together, be romantic
9569. For traveling lovers: *Bed and Breakfast U.S.A.*, by Betty Rundback
9570. Write ten romantic ideas on a board game "spinner": Take a romantic spin once-a-week
9571. Place a custom "parking ticket" under the windshield wiper: A coupon for going "parking" together!

9572. Buy raffle tickets together
9573. Create a collage of photos of the two of you

9574. Give your Texas gal one huge yellow rose
9575. And the song "The Yellow Rose of Texas," by Johnny Desmond

---

9576. Plant a flower garden consisting *entirely* of flowers in her favorite color
9577. Have a plaque made: "Lover of the Year Award"
9578. Go in search of her G-Spot
9579. Attach a note to the TV remote control: "Turn *me* on instead!"
9580. If she's a former Girl Scout: Award her with some custom "Merit Badges"—for "Friendship," "Communication Skills," etc.

Favorite Love Songs from 1991
9581. "All the Man That I Need," Whitney Houston
9582. "I'll Be There," The Escape Club

9583. "That's What Love Is For," Amy Grant
9584. "When a Man Loves a Woman," Michael Bolton

9585. Create your own rituals around bubblebaths
9586. Enemy of Love: Blaming—Refusing to take responsibility for your part
9587. Give an "Expand Your Sexual Horizons" Coupon: You get to ask the coupon-issuer to participate in a sexual activity that is slightly outrageous and/or positively scandalous
9588. Fly through the clouds together in a chartered private plane
9589. "None is so near the gods as he who shows kindness." ~ Seneca
9590. Make his favorite cookies
9591. Use red spray paint to write a message in the snow
9592. Read *Hug Therapy*, by Kathleen Keating—a fun little book
9593. Enemy of Love: Feelings of powerlessness

9594. Renew your wedding vows in a public ceremony

9595. Write your own "Updated Marriage Vows" reflecting on what you've learned from the experiences since your first ceremony

9596. Create an altar of meaningful symbols

9597. Invite *everyone* you'd invited to your first ceremony—plus new friends

9598. Eat in the most romantic restaurant in Rome: Girone VI

9599. Remember this: Love is simple, but *people* are complicated

9600. Hold a "Spring Fling" on the first day of Spring

9601. Engrave Cupid on the back of his watch (so only he'll know!)

9602. Be a good sport: Attend your partner's high school/college reunions

---

Favorite Love Songs from 1992

9603. "Achy Breaky Heart," Billy Ray Cyrus

9604. "I'd Die Without You," PM Dawn

9605. "I Will Always Love You," Whitney Houston

9606. "Save the Best for Last," Vanessa Williams

9607. Stay in romantic splendor in Paris: La Tremoille

9608. Save sea shells from your beach vacations and display them at home

9609. Gals: Get an engagement ring for *him*

9610. Call each other by private "pet names"

9611. Take your "Parrot-Head" to a Jimmy Buffett concert

9612. Insert three lottery tickets into her birthday card

9613. Enemy of Love: Stinginess with *money*

9614. Don't play "relationship games" with each other

9615. Stay at the Ritz

9616. For married men: Ask her to marry you—*again*

9617. And *this* time, give her a *huge* diamond engagement ring

9618. (But buy smart! Read *How to Buy a Diamond*, by Fred Cuellar)

9619. Wallpaper a room with greeting cards you've exchanged

9620. "Let your hair down" with each other: No games, no masks

9621. Make love in a purely physical, passionate manner

9622. Frame a travel poster from your honeymoon location

9623. "I have enjoyed the happiness of the world; I have lived and loved."
~ Johann von Schiller

9624. For one week, listen to your partner with 20% more attentiveness

9625. Love Enhancer: Respect for your partner

9626. Love Coupon: An evening of "Classic Romance." Included: The movie *Casablanca*; music by Glenn Miller, candlelight, and champagne

9627. Read her favorite book to get to know her better—Surprise her by asking to discuss it!

9628. Gals: Treat him as if he were your Prince Charming

9629. Guys: Treat her as if she were your Princess

9630. Visit a secret romantic garden: El Capricho Park, in Madrid, Spain

9631. Wish her "Good Luck" before a big presentation

9632. Familiarity often leads to laziness about personal habits; be a little more polite, like when you were dating

9633. "'Tis better to have loved and lost, than to never have loved at all."
~ Alfred Lord Tennyson

9634. Thought Experiment: Imagine having *everything*—wealth, power, prestige, comfort, talent—*except* love. What good would it do you?

9635. Create a homemade Hawaiian lei

9636. Gotta get her a Gund (stuffed animal)

9637. Wrap her gently in your arms

9638. In addition to considering color, space, and style when designing your home, use "romance" as a design element

9639. Make more time for your lover: *Read How to Put Ten Hours in an Eight Hour Day*, by Kay Johnson

9640. Enemy of Love: Modern life's complexity

9641. Love Enhancer: Presents that *symbolize* your love

9642. Spend a week at a spa together: Saybrook Point Inn, in Connecticut: (860) 395-2000

9643. The Ultimate Chocoholic's Coupon: Redeemable for five pounds of your all-time favorite chocolate treats

9644. Stay in a Baroque palace in Vienna: Romischer Kaiser

9645. Thank your love for being patient with you

9646. Thank your love for being there for you

9647. Thank your love for all the good times

9648. Thank your love for being a *friend*

9649. Thank your love for caring for you

9650. Thank your love for persevering through the bad times

9651. Thank your love for *being* your love

9652. Learn to barbecue burgers *exactly* the way she likes them

9653. Musical lovenote: "Play the CD *Angel Clare*, by Art Garfunkel. My message to you is song No. 6"

9654. Stay at the fanciest hotel in Milan: The Grand Hotel Et de Milan

9655. Make love in the most romantic setting and in the most romantic manner you can imagine

9656. "There is more pleasure in loving than in being loved."
~ Thomas Fuller

9657. Write an article describing your love; format it to look like a *Wall Street Journal* article; paste it into his paper

9658. Send a bouquet made of little love notes fashioned into flowers

9659. Kiss at the top of the Empire State Building

9660. "In order to love simply, it is

necessary to know how to show love."
~ Fyodor Dostoevsky

9661. Make love without using your hands
9662. Increase the *quality* of your lovemaking by 21%
9663. Make love using a silk scarf
9664. Watch your wedding video on your anniversary
9665. Roll out a real red carpet to welcome him/her home

Favorite Love Songs from 1993

9666. "Breathe Again," Toni Braxton
9667. "Dreamlover," Mariah Carey
9668. "(I Can't Help) Falling in Love with You," UB40
9669. "Have I Told You Lately," Rod Stewart

9670. "Absence makes the heart grow fonder." ~ Sextus Propertius
9671. "Absence sharpens love, presence strengthens it." ~ Thomas Fuller

9672. Build a "Rube Goldberg" device for

presenting an engagement ring to her

9673. Enemy of Love: Macho attitudes

9674. Can't get him to write a love letter? Create a *fill-in-the-blanks* love letter for his use

9675. Get a 50th anniversary card from the President! (Mail request to: White House Greetings Dept., Executive Office Building No. 39, Washington, D.C. 20500)

9676. Wrap yourself around your partner like a pretzel in bed tonight

9677. Celebrate the moment you fell in love

9678. Have a birthday cake delivered to her at work by a courier

9679. A+ Romance Rating: The Hotel Hassler, in Rome, Italy

9680. Favorite gifts for men: High-powered stereo equipment

9681. Favorite gifts for men: Silk boxers

9682. Favorite gifts for men: Tickets to sporting events

9683. Note: Little white lies in the service

of creating romantic surprises don't really count as lies

9684. A Theme-Gift: Give her one pink rose, a pink lingerie outfit, and a bottle of pink champagne

9685. Give him chili peppers with a note: "I'm hot for you!"

9686. Enemy of Love: Superior attitudes

9687. Give her a Lladro figurine that reflects her personality

9688. Get off the "career treadmill" and lead a more balanced, loving life

9689. Write "I love you" on a cake with icing

9690. For two weeks, be 15% less inhibited in your lovemaking

9691. Travel on the fabled Orient Express

9692. Stencil a cryptic love message on your driveway

9693. Stay at the fanciest hotel in Tokyo: The Imperial Hotel

9694. Winner, Enticing Book Title Award, 1998: *Dip Me in Chocolate*, by Aaron Maree

9695. Make love with the only goal being to help your partner achieve orgasm

9696. Enemy of Love: Condescending attitudes

9697. Tape a love note to the inside of her bedroom closet door

---

9698. Gals: Do something *with* him that you hate to do

9699. It only counts as a loving gesture if you do it cheerfully and without complaint

9700. Go fishing, bowling, bird-watching, hiking, or camping with him

---

9701. A "Happy Anniversary!" Coupon: You are entitled to a day of True Togetherness. This means a day just for the two of you; no kids, no job, no responsibilities, no chores

9702. Perform the classic "Doctor-Patient Fantasy"

9703. "Keep me as the apple of the eye, hide me under the shadow of thy wings." ~ Psalms 17:8

9704. Romantic piano concerto: Mozart's Piano Concerto No. 21 in C

9705. Send a birthday greeting via telegram

9706. FYI: Outrageous behavior is contagious

9707. Romantic piano: Grieg's Concerto in A Minor for Piano & Orchestra

9708. Slow down: Take the scenic route

9709. Enemy of Love: Fear of intimacy

9710. Get your partner a cardboard standup of his/her favorite celebrity

9711. Make him a custom gingerbread man for Christmas

9712. During a winter walk, surprise him with a thermos full of hot cocoa

9713. Share a milkshake

9714. Eat in San Francisco's most romantic restaurant: Masa's

9715. Buy throw-away cameras; spend an afternoon on a "Photo Safari"

9716. Have two photos of her mounted together in one frame: A photo of her as a baby, and a current photo of her

9717. Give it to her along with a recording of "You Must Have Been a Beautiful Baby ('Cause Baby Look at You Now!)"

9718. When he's traveling, give him a sexy wake-up call at 6 A.M.

9719. Wear "Obsession" perfume—To help you express your infatuation

9720. Give her a face massage

9721. Create a "Romantic Weekend-on-a-Budget" together

9722. Create a custom ritual: Give a little gift *every* Wednesday

9723. Go whitewater rafting on the Salmon River, in Idaho

9724. Change one of your habits that really bugs your partner

Favorite Love Songs from 1994

9725. "All for Love," Bryan Adams & Rod Stewart & Sting

9726. "I'll Make Love to You," Boyz II Men

9727. "When Can I See You," Babyface

9728. "You Mean the World to Me," Toni Braxton

9729. A+ Rating, Romantic Music Artist: Stan Getz

9730. Musical lovenote: "Play the CD *Beatles*

'65; my message to you is song No. 8"

9731. Ask a "Magic 8 Ball" questions about your relationship

9732. Learn the hand gesture for "Live long and prosper" (from *Star Trek*)

9733. Spend a lazy Saturday afternoon in a hammock together

9734. Clip and mail relationship cartoons from *The New Yorker* magazine

9735. A great music resource: cdnow.com

9736. Eat in the most romantic hotel in Zurich: Ermitage

9737. Enemy of Love: Escalating *discussions* into *arguments*

9738. Love your partner *unconditionally*—

9739. When you slip, love *yourself* unconditionally

9740. Charter a luxury yacht for an evening cruise

9741. Learn how to make his favorite mixed drink *perfectly*

9742. Hum "your song" together when walking hand-in-hand

9743. Hire an organizational consultant to straighten-up his out-of-control office

9744. When traveling for a week, leave behind seven greeting cards, labeled with the days of the week

9745. Place friendly $5 bets when you disagree over factual trivia

9746. Love Enhancer: Playful attitude

9747. Never, never, *never* return his car with an empty gas tank

9748. Gals: Let him keep his macho facade in public—as long as he lets you see the "real him" when you're alone together

---

9749. Have a graphic designer create a logo out of her name

9750. And have custom stationery made: letterhead, thank you cards, etc.

9751. Enemy of Love: Assuming a *parental* role in your relationship

9752. Kiss on a chairlift

9753. For Married Folks: Think like a single person: *Flirt* with your spouse

9754. Go to an *expensive* vacation spot—and get the *least expensive* accommodations

9755. Never watch TV during dinner!

9756. "Lips only sing when they cannot kiss." ~ James Thomson

9757. Pack yourself into a big box and have yourself delivered to her porch

9758. Use scented oil while giving a massage

9759. A "Formal Dinner" Coupon: You both dress in formal attire. Your partner will prepare and serve an elegant dinner-for-two at home

9760. "We two form a multitude." ~ Ovid

9761. Don't let your chores be divided strictly along gender lines

9762. Share in the grocery shopping

9763. Share in the lawn care

9764. Share in the housework

9765. Share in the auto maintenance

9766. Help with the cooking

9767. Help with the snow shoveling

9768. Do the laundry together

9769. Pay the bills together

9770. A+ Rated romantic music: *The Sacred Fire*, by Nicholas Gunn
9771. Guys: Yes, there's a "fine line" between being *tenderhearted* and being a *wimp*, but women *love* tenderhearted guys
9772. Compliment him

Favorite Love Songs from 1995

9773. "Have You Ever Really Loved a Woman?" Bryan Adams
9774. "I Can Love You Like That," All-4-One
9775. "On the Verge," Colin Raye
9776. "Only Wanna Be with You," Hootie & the Blowfish

9777. Love Enhancer: Eye contact
9778. Help him conduct research for a big work project
9779. Guys: Watch *The Full Monty* as inspiration—and then perform a private show for her!
9780. Garnish a special dinner with *edible flowers*: Nasturtiums, calendulas, pineapple sage, or rose geraniums

9781. Gift & Date Idea: Get the song "Love Theme from Romeo and Juliet," by Henry Mancini—

9782. And rent the movie *Romeo and Juliet*, featuring the song

9783. Or—surprise your partner with tickets to the musical, live on stage

---

9784. Create romantic gestures based on "Eight Days a Week" by The Beatles

9785. Share comfort food

9786. New Gizmo Alert: The Wristwatch Remote Control, from Casio

9787. Topics to be avoided during romantic interludes: Work, money, parents, kids

9788. Dribble a liqueur on your body; invite your partner to lick it off

9789. Enjoy a campfire in your own backyard

9790. For a fan of rock and classical music: A cool CD called *What If Mozart Wrote "Born to Be Wild"*

9791. The "Instant Celebration" Coupon: *At any time* you may demand that

your partner create an *instant*,
romantic celebration

9792. Keep a journal of your life together
9793. Keep a journal of your best memories
9794. Keep a "Joint Journal," in which you
both write

9795. For your gourmet: A bottle of
fine wine
9796. Use your typing skills to help speed
along his/her weekend work
9797. Stay at the fanciest hotel in Hong
Kong: The Peninsula
9798. Make her proud of you at family
reunions
9799. Single gals: The first Saturday in
November is Sadie Hawkins Day—
Tradition says *you* can propose
9800. "Kissing is the most pleasant way of
spreading germs yet devised."
- Anonymous
9801. Hold a truly magical wedding at
Disney World
9802. Put your partner's phone number in

the No. 1 place on your "speed dial"

9803. Shop for costume jewelry

9804. Be her sex slave

9805. Serve dinner amid billowing clouds, created by dry ice in water

9806. See your relationship as a safe place to stretch yourself

9807. Get classy gifts from the catalog of the Museum of Fine Arts, Boston: (800) 225-5592

9808. English: "Take your clothes off"

9809. French: "Déshabille-toi"

9810. Italian: "Spogliati"

9811. German: "Zieh dich aus"

9812. Spanish: "Desnúdate"

9813. Portugese: "Tire sua roupa"

9814. A+ Rating, Cool Gift Resource: The Parkleigh, in Rochester, New York— or via www.parkleigh.com

9815. Send him a pair of oven mitts in the mail, with this note attached: "I'm going to be *too hot to handle* tonight, so wear these!"

9816. Note for a love letter: Describe your relationship as "the *quintessential* love affair"

9817. Dinner-and-a-movie tip: Always see the movie *first*. This way you won't have to rush through dinner

9818. Bring home her favorite style of bagel

9819. Go on a "New Activity Date"

9820. Buy *anything* from Tiffany's

9821. Make love to the rhythm of your background music

9822. Make dried flower arrangements from bouquets you've received

9823. Turn to your partner in public and whisper, "I can't wait to be alone with you!"

9824. Keep candles at your bedside at all times

9825. Make love as Rhett Butler and Scarlett O'Hara

9826. Learn to say what's on your mind

9827. Learn to say what's in your heart

9828. Learn to say "I'm sorry"

9829. A great "undiscovered" love song: "Chagall Duet," by Jon Anderson & Sandrine Piau, on *Change We Must*

9830. Help him find things, instead of complaining about his forgetfulness

9831. Create a "Count-Down Calendar" anticipating your baby's birth

9832. Wear matching sweatshirts when you work out

9833. Hire a barbershop quartet to sing "Happy Birthday" to her

Favorite Love Songs from 1996

9834. "If You Could Only See," Tonic

9835. "(I Love You) Always Forever," Donna Lewis

9836. "One Sweet Day," Mariah Carey & Boyz II Men

9837. Practice "emotional generosity"

9838. Give an antique bottle with a special love note in it based on Jim Croce's song "Time in a Bottle"

9839. A+ Rating, Romantic Music Artist: David Benoit

9840. Shout your love into a valley and listen for the echo

9841. Flash a love message on a ballpark's scoreboard

9842. Favorite gifts for men: Fishing rods
9843. Favorite gifts for men: Golf clubs
9844. Favorite gifts for men: Bowling balls

9845. Love Coupon: This coupon entitles you to one evening of "stimulation." You define what *kind* of stimulation you want, and the coupon-giver will supply it. (You may choose *intellectual* stimulation—or the physical kind!)

9846. Sensual Music Alert: The CD *Embrya*, by Maxwell

9847. A+ Rated loving lyrics: In "State of Independence," on *The Friends of Mr. Cairo* CD by Jon Anderson

9848. "Love unreciprocated is like a question without an answer."
~ Kathryn Maye

9849. Make love by the light of a full moon

9850. Read Paul Reiser's hilarious book

Couplehood—then write a chapter
about *your* relationship!

9851. Learn the art of S-L-O-W-L-Y
undressing your lover

9852. Copy some of your body parts on a
Xerox machine and mail the pages
to her

9853. Great resource: *Honeymoon Magazine*:
(888) 994-4494

9854. Go on a "Surprise Week-Night Date"

9855. Make love to him *the way he wants to
be made love to*

9856. Get a tourist guidebook for your
state: Visit someplace new

9857. You used to carry her *books*—Now
carry the *groceries*

9858. If you have the same argument over
and over and over again, dedicate
yourselves *once-and-for-all* to get to the
bottom of it!

9859. Read books, talk more, try different
approaches…

9860. Talk to a counselor, minister,
therapist

9861. Give yourselves plenty of time (several years!) but stay focused and dedicated

---

9862. Eat in the most romantic restaurant in Stockholm: Min Lilla Tradgard

9863. Talk with your partner openly and honestly about sex

9864. Give her a tiara

9865. Surprise him with an antique desk for his home office

9866. A great "undiscovered" love song: "Lend Your Love to Me," by Emerson Lake & Palmer, on *Works II*

9867. Translate your pet name for her into French, Italian, or Japanese

9868. Give *fragrant* flowers: Stock, Roses, Gardenias

9869. Go to a drive-in movie together and make out in the back seat

---

9870–9879
10 Qualities that 5,000 Men Want *Most* in Wives

1. Loving/Demonstrative

2. Attentive
3. Sexiness
4. Confident
5. Caring
6. Independent
7. Intelligent
8. Beauty
9. Romantic
10. Sense of humor

9880. For tea lovers: Get a special tea pot
9881. "Breakfast-in-Bed" Coupon: Redeemable sometime within a year
9882. When it's raining, place a love note inside a Zip-Lock bag, and place it under her windshield wiper of her car
9883. Charter a small plane to fly you to the nearest major city for dinner
9884. Order room service
9885. Consciously say "Yes" to your relationship every morning
9886. Bring her a stack of her favorite magazines when she's home sick
9887. Save the decorative metal cap from the top of a special bottle of

champagne, and have it made into a jewelry pin

9888. Make love in a pool
9889. Always stop whatever else you're doing to greet your mate
9890. Order a huge *wedding cake* for a special *birthday*

9891. Honor him with a cherished family heirloom…
9892. An oriental rug
9893. An antique pocket watch
9894. A grandfather clock

9895. Sing a lovesong duet at a Karaoke bar
9896. Brainstorm romantic ideas with your partner
9897. Musical lovenote: "Play the CD *Coming Around Again*, by Carly Simon. My messages to you are songs No. 2 and No. 4"
9898. Share many private jokes
9899. Give her a written bill for repairing her car: "Oil change: Four kisses. Check battery: Two hugs. Tighten

belts: One backrub"

9900. Hold an extravagant surprise party—
for her *beloved pet*

9901. Design an Old West "Wanted" poster
that describes why you *want* him/her

9902. Stay a week in Buenos Aires

9903. Spend all day at a giant flea market
together

9904. Feed her grapes on a lazy Saturday

9905. Create a personal holiday based on
her most charming quirk

9906. Buy greeting cards in foreign
languages

9907. Buy your partner clothes that flatter
his/her shape

Favorite Love Songs from 1997

9908. "How Do I Live," Le Ann Rimes

9909. "My Heart Will Go On (Love Theme
from *Titanic*)," Celine Dion

9910. "Truly Madly Deeply," Savage Garden

9911. Watch the Hawaiian surf from a
hotel balcony

9912. Share a picnic lunch in the park
during the work week

9913. "They love indeed who quake to say they love." ~ Philip Sidney

9914. Honor your partner with a "This Is Your Life" party

9915. Organize a great tailgating party for him and his sports buddies

---

9916. What does your lover need—*right now?* Connection? Comfort? Intimacy?

9917. Appreciation? Security? Enchantment?

9918. Understanding? Sex? Friendship?

9919. Passion? Food? Gifts?

9920. Time? Answers? Excitement?

9921. Affection? Adventure? Solitude?

9922. Exercise? Music? Escape?

9923. Toys? Tools? Candy?

9924. Hugs? Kisses? Compliments?

9925. Return her movies to Blockbuster

9926. For the New Year: Give a calendar with pre-marked "Mystery Dates"

9927. Go apple picking in the autumn

9928. Go beachcombing in the summer

9929. Give memories as gifts

9930. Take a classic winter sleigh ride together
9931. "The heart that loves is always young." ~ Greek proverb
9932. Attend an outdoor art festival
9933. Go tidepooling at the beach

9934–9945

12 Pairs of Gender Generalizations:

Do You Agree or Disagree?

1. Women hear "love" when you say "romance." Men hear "sex" when you say "romance"
2. Women connect many emotional issues with their sexuality. Men can easily separate their sexuality from their feelings
3. Women communicate to create relationships. Men communicate to gather information.
4. Women cooperate. Men compete
5. Women view relationships as a vast interlocking network. Men view relationships in a hierarchical manner
6. Women tend to be "right-brained"—

emotional, holistic, creative thinkers.
Men tend to be "left-brained"—logical,
linear, compartmentalized thinkers

7. Women often treat men as emotional
children. Men often treat women as
incompetents in the real world

8. Women put men in shining armor on
a white horse. Men put women on a
pedestal

9. Women are aroused through sensation.
Men are aroused visually

10. Women arouse slowly
Men arouse quickly

11. Women have been taught to hide
their angry feelings. Men have been
taught to hide their tender feelings

12. Women have been taught to suppress
their aggressive side. Men have been
taught to suppress their gentle side

9946. Give her your frequent flyer miles
9947. Frequently give him a pat on the back
9948. "Keep your eyes wide open before
marriage, and half-shut afterwards."
~ Benjamin Franklin

9949. Before getting out of bed, say: "I'm so thankful I have you in my life"

9950. Get your country western guy a new pair of cowboy boots

9951. Get your country western gal a fancy new cowgirl hat

9952. Go on a glass-bottom-boat tour

9953. List twelve sexual activities. Roll two dice to determine which activity you'll share tonight! Take turns

9954. Ride an old-fashioned carousel together

9955. Play on a co-ed softball team together

9956. Splash through rain puddles together

9957. Kiss in mid-air while skydiving

9958. "Love doesn't make the world go 'round. Love is what makes the ride worthwhile." ~ Franklin Jones

9959. Go "4-wheeling" together

9960. Create a home version of "Sexy Bingo"

9961. Join a health club together

9962. Do Tai Chi together

9963. Attend a craft fair together

9964. Eliminate from your vocabulary: "Yes, but—"

9965. Note: If you've been together ten years or more, you should be an *expert* on your partner!

9966. Build a tree fort together

9967. "Love is not love until love's vulnerable." ~ Theodore Roethke

---

9968. *Talking* is not necessarily "communicating"

9969. Sharing *feelings* is only *part* of communicating

9970. *How* you say what you say is just as important as *what* you say

9971. *Half* of communicating is simply listening

9972. There are as many communication "styles" as there are people

---

9973. A romantic weekend at the elegant Plaza Hotel in NYC: (212) 759-3000

9974. "Shared laughter is erotic, too." ~ Marge Piercy

9975. Rent every movie that stars her favorite actor

9976. Get an elegant canopy bed

9977. "The first duty of love is to listen."
~ Paul Tillich

Favorite Love Songs from 1998

9978. "I'll Be," Edwin McCain
9979. "Iris," Goo Goo Dolls
9980. "I'm Afraid This Must Be Love,"
Linda Eder
9981. "You're Still the One," Shania Twain

9982. Slip a little love note into her purse
9983. Do one of your partner's chores
9984. Grow her favorite flowers in your garden
9985. Make love in all fifty states
9986. Have a band play "your song"
9987. Buy a book on time management:
Create more time for love
9988. Believe in one another
9989. Use one of his pet names for your
ATM password
9990. Kiss at stop signs and red lights
9991. Write a love note, fold it into a paper
airplane, and sail it across the room
9992. Write "I love you" on the bathroom
mirror with soap

9993. Think about this one! "I hate to be a failure. I hate and regret the failure of my marriages. I would gladly give up my millions for just one lasting marital success." ~ J. Paul Getty

9994. When he/she calls you at work, *always* interrupt whatever you're doing to take the call

9995. Save all the "slow dances" for each other

9996. Buy her one big, humongous humdinger of a diamond

9997. Decorate the bedroom with one balloon for every year you've been together

9998. Turn to him in public and whisper, "On a scale of 1 to 10, you're a 12."

9999. Kiss the palm of her hand; close her fingers into a fist; say "Save this"

10000. Live happily ever after

About the Author

15 Facts About Gregory J.P. Godek

1. Greg has taught romance on *Oprah*.
2. He has counseled the "romantically impaired" on *Donahue*.
3. Greg has been featured in *The New York Times, Cosmopolitan, Glamour, Playboy* and *Harper's Bazaar*.
4. He has authored 12 books in 8 years.
5. More than 2 million copies of his books have sold worldwide.
6. Greg is that rare celebrity who actually practices what he preaches—he is a husband who lives his wedding vows.
7. He is one of the few relationship experts in America who has never been divorced.
8. Greg is a teacher and role model, not a therapist or theorist.
9. He is a researcher, questioner, listener.
10. He studies successful couples, happy people, and *what works*.
11. He not only believes that love *can* be taught, but that it *must* be taught.
12. Greg's is a synergistic and quirky path that combines a novelist's eye for

13. character and motivation with a teacher's passion for connecting and communicating with students.

13. Greg has been invited to teach his Romance Seminar to the U.S. Army.

14. He has consulted with the flower, chocolate, diamond, and movie industries.

15. For Greg, this was not a chosen profession, but the following of a muse, the expression of universal truths as experienced by one individual.

---

4 Curious Things Said About Gregory J.P. Godek

1. "Greg Godek should be nominated for the Nobel Peace Prize for teaching *1001 Ways To Be Romantic*."
   ~ Boston Magazine

2. "Godek is *ruining* things for us guys!"
   ~ Joe Magadatz, author of the parody *1001 Ways NOT To Be Romantic*

3. "Greg Godek is a **thirty**something Leo Buscaglia." *~ Evening Magazine*

4. "Greg teaches the truth."
    ~ Mark Victor Hansen, co-author of
    Chicken Soup for the Soul

---

7 Personal Facts About Gregory J.P. Godek

1. The "J.P." stands for John Paul.
2. Greg is a classic, romantic Pisces.
3. Yes, he really *did* have a girlfriend in kindergarten.
4. No, his father was *not* a romantic role model.
5. But Greg combined his father's passion for life with his mother's creativity.
6. His favorite TV show is *Babylon 5*.
7. "Greg really *does* practice what he preaches," says his wife, Tracey.